Cracking the
PSAT/NMSQT

Cracking the PSAT/NMSQT

By Jeff Rubenstein
and
Adam Robinson

2004 Edition

Random House, Inc.
New York

www.PrincetonReview.com

> The Independent Education Consultants Association recognizes The Princeton Review as a valuable resource for high school and college students applying to college and graduate school.

Princeton Review Publishing, L.L.C.
2315 Broadway
New York, NY 10024
E-mail: booksupport@review.com

Copyright © 2003 by Princeton Review Publishing, L.L.C.

All rights reserved under International and Pan-American Copyright Conventions. Published in the United States by Random House, Inc., New York, and simultaneously in Canada by Random House of Canada Limited, Toronto.

ISBN 0-375-76332-5

Editor: Allegra Burton
Production Editor: Maria Dente
Production Coordinator: Jennifer Arias
Illustrations by: The Production Department of The Princeton Review

Manufactured in the United States of America.

10 9 8 7 6 5 4 3 2 1

2004 Edition

ACKNOWLEDGMENTS

Thanks to Allegra Burton, Maria Dente, Jeff Soloway, Jennifer Arias, Faisel Alam, and the staff and students of The Princeton Review.

Special thanks to Adam Robinson, who conceived of and perfected the Joe Bloggs approach to standardized tests, and many other techniques in this book.

CONTENTS

PART I: ORIENTATION 1

1   **What Is the PSAT/NMSQT?** 3
2   **All About National Merit Scholarships** 11
3   **General Strategies** 17
4   **Advanced Strategies** 25

PART II: CRACKING THE PSAT/NMSQT 33

5   **Sentence Completions** 35
6   **Analogies** 47
7   **Critical Reading** 63
8   **Math Basics** 77
9   **Math Techniques** 103
10 **Advanced Math Principles** 123
11 **Writing Skills** 145
12 **Vocabulary** 179

PART III: THE PRINCETON REVIEW PRACTICE TESTS AND EXPLANATIONS 199

13 **Practice Test 1** 201
14 **Practice Test 1: Answers and Explanations** 239
15 **Practice Test 2** 267
16 **Practice Test 2: Answers and Explanations** 301

PART I

Orientation

1

What Is the PSAT/NMSQT?

WHAT IS THE PSAT/NMSQT?

The PSAT/NMSQT—from now on, we'll just call it the PSAT—is a standardized test given primarily to high school juniors to give them a "preliminary" idea of how well they'll score on the SAT I: Reasoning Test (which we'll just call the SAT from now on). The test is also used to determine which students are eligible for National Merit recognition (as well as scholarships), which is a fairly respectable addition to your college admissions profile.

Keep on Schedule
You'll take the PSAT/NMSQT in the fall of your junior year. Plan to take the SAT in either the spring of your junior year or the fall of your senior year.

HOW DO YOU PRONOUNCE PSAT/NMSQT, ANYWAY?

We're not really sure. You can pronounce it pee-sat-nim-squit if you want. But we think it's easier just to call it the PSAT.

WHEN IS THE PSAT GIVEN?

The PSAT is officially administered twice each year, on one Saturday and one Tuesday in October. Your school will announce the exact dates at the beginning of the school year, or you can find out on the Web:

The Princeton Review at www.PrincetonReview.com, or the College Board at www.collegeboard.com

HOW DO I SIGN UP FOR THE PSAT?

You don't have to do anything to sign up for the PSAT; your school will do all the work for you.

WHAT ABOUT STUDENTS WITH SPECIAL NEEDS?

If you have a diagnosed learning difference, you will probably qualify for special accommodations on the PSAT. However, it's important that you get the process started early. The first step is to speak to your school counselor who handles learning differences. Only he or she can file the appropriate paperwork. You'll also need to gather some information (documentation of your condition) from a licensed practitioner and some other information from your school. Then your school counselor will file the application for you.

Happily, you only need to apply for accommodations once; with that single application you'll qualify for accommodations on the PSAT, SAT, SAT II, and AP tests. The one exception to this rule is that if you change schools, you'll need to have a counselor at the new school refile your paperwork.

DOES THE PSAT PLAY A ROLE IN COLLEGE ADMISSIONS?

No. The PSAT plays no role in college admissions. It's really just a practice test for the SAT.

The one exception is for that very small group of students, about 4 percent of all students nationwide, whose PSAT scores qualify them for National Merit recognition. (We'll tell you more than you ever wanted to know about that in the next section.) Recognition as a commended scholar, semifinalist, or finalist for

National Merit is a fairly impressive addition to your college admissions portfolio, and is something that you should certainly pursue if you're seriously in contention for it.

What Happens to the Score Report from the PSAT?

Only you and your high school will receive copies of your score reports. They won't be sent to colleges.

And What Will Be on It?

The Math sections of the PSAT test only basic arithmetic, algebra, and geometry. But the questions are often confusingly worded and ETS has planted plenty of trap choices to seduce you into picking incorrect answers. You may get the feeling at times that ETS has rigged the game against you—and you'd be right to feel that way. We'll review the basic math that you need to know, show you easier ways to solve the problems on the PSAT, and help you to avoid ETS's traps.

The Verbal sections of the SAT are largely a test of vocabulary and of your ability to pick out facts from a reading passage. In this book, we'll help you improve your vocabulary and make the most of the vocabulary you have. Moreover, we'll show you how to find facts in a passage in an efficient way designed for the PSAT.

The Writing Skills section, oddly enough, has nothing to do with writing. At best, it tests your ability to recognize a narrow range of errors in English grammar, and certain points of style. In a way, it's more of an editing test than anything else. In this book, we'll review all the basic points of grammar you need to know (don't worry, there aren't many of them!).

UPCOMING CHANGES TO THE PSAT

Does It Apply to Me?

You may have heard that there are going to be some changes to the PSAT down the road. These changes may not affect you. The changes will affect anyone who is:

- Taking the SAT in the spring of 2005 or after (students wishing to start college in 2006)
- Taking the PSAT in the fall of 2004

And the Changes Are...

The first victim of the new-look PSAT is the Verbal section: it is now named the Critical Reading section, which is what it essentially becomes. Gone are the frustrating analogies that tortured students with the relationship between two words they had rarely seen and never used in common conversation. ETS has added more Critical Reading passages to the newly-named Critical Reading section; the added passages are now "paragraph" length. This simply means they will ask you one or, at the most, two questions per paragraph. If that gets you down, at least Sentence Completions have not been touched!

The next change made to the PSAT is the elimination of Quantitative Comparisons. This section contained two columns of numerical information and asked students to decide which is larger. Good-bye! If you have older siblings, they may remember how much "fun" they had doing this section. Instead of adding a new question format, ETS has decided to simply "beef up" the type of math covered by their multiple-choice questions. The new Math section will now include questions pertaining to skills learned in Algebra I, Geometry, and Algebra II. This, ETS hopes, will align the PSAT with standard high school curricula.

Don't Worry, Be Happy

What this all means to you is: Don't worry. Even though there will be a media blitz about the "new" and "improved" PSAT, there isn't all that much that is new or improved for you to be worried about. The bottom line is that the test is still coachable and ETS is still only testing a narrow spectrum of knowledge.

And that's why you're holding this book.

Who Writes the PSAT, Anyway?

The PSAT is written and administered by the Educational Testing Service (ETS), under contract by the College Entrance Examination Board. You might think that the people at ETS are educators, or professors of education, or teachers. Well, they're not. The people who work for ETS are average folks who just happen to make a living writing tests. In fact, they write hundreds and hundreds of tests, for all kinds of organizations. They're a group of "testers-for-hire" who will write a test for whomever asks them.

The folks at ETS aren't really paid to educate; they're paid to write and administer tests. And even though you are paying them to take the SAT, you're not their customer. The people really being served by ETS are the colleges, who get the information they want at no cost. This means that you should take everything that ETS says with a grain of salt, and realize that their testing "advice" isn't always the best advice. (Getting testing advice from ETS is a bit like getting tax advice from the IRS.)

Every test reflects the interests of the people who write it. If you know who writes the test, you will know a lot more about what kind of answers will be considered "correct" answers on that test.

Now, let's take a closer look at ETS, the people who write the PSAT. Who are they? What kind of values do they have? The people at ETS like to think of themselves as average, middle-class Americans, with views to match. How do they feel about capitalism, democracy, progress, and the American way of life? The people at ETS love these things. What do you think their feelings are toward other cultures? That they are, of course, interesting and that we should be respectful of them.

What do you think would happen if ETS wrote bad things about any particular group of people? They'd get lots of nasty letters, there would be lawsuits, and colleges might stop using the SAT. Would ETS risk this? Nope. One thing ETS will avoid at all costs is a potentially controversial answer choice. While ETS might say something negative about a particular person, they will avoid generalizing about an entire group.

When we get to the lesson on reading passages, you'll see how this knowledge can help you eliminate some wrong answer choices, and find the correct answer from among the ones that are left.

WHAT IS THE PRINCETON REVIEW?

The Princeton Review is the nation's leading test-preparation company. In just a few years, we became the nation's leader in SAT preparation, primarily because our techniques work. We offer courses and private tutoring for all of the major standardized tests, and we publish a series of books to help in your search for the right school for you. If you'd like more information about our programs or books, give us a call at 800-2-Review, or find us on the Web at www.PrincetonReview.com.

Shortcuts
The Princeton Review's techniques are the closest thing there is to a shortcut to the PSAT. However, there is no shortcut to learning these techniques.

HOW TO USE THIS BOOK

This book is divided into two parts. The first part of the book (Chapters 1–12) contains both general testing strategies and question-specific problem-solving instruction. The back of the book contains two practice PSATs. We suggest that you start by taking the first test in the back of the book. This will help give you an idea of where your strengths and weaknesses are. Then, work on the instructional chapters (Chapters 3–12). Ideally, you'll have a few weeks do to this. If you've gotten this book early, the best advice is to start working on your vocabulary right now (see Chapter 12). Once you've worked through the instructional chapters, go back to your first test, retake it, and fix your mistakes. Then try the second test to see how much you've improved.

One important note: In this book, any sample question you see will have a question number that indicates the number that question would have on a PSAT. That's why you may see a question 4 followed by a question 14—the question number indicates where in the PSAT it would appear, instead of its order in the chapter.

HOW IS THE PSAT STRUCTURED AND SCORED?

The PSAT has five sections, which are always given in the same order:

Section	Number of Questions	Time
Verbal	25	25 minutes
Math	20	25 minutes
Verbal	27	25 minutes
Math	20	25 minutes
Writing Skills	39	30 minutes

You'll receive three scores for the PSAT: A Verbal score, a Math score, and a Writing Skills score. Each of these scores will be reported on a scale of 20–80, where 20 is the lowest score and 80 is the highest score. You should receive your scores by mail about six to eight weeks after you take the test.

HOW DOES THE SAT DIFFER FROM THE PSAT?

The SAT differs significantly from the PSAT in structure, though its questions are very similar to those on the Verbal and Math sections of the PSAT.

The SAT has seven sections. The first five sections last 30 minutes each, and the last two sections last 15 minutes each, for a total of 3 hours of testing (ugh!). One of these sections won't count toward your score; its only purpose is to try out questions to see whether they can be used in later tests.

The Verbal sections of the SAT are slightly longer than their counterparts on the PSAT; there will always be a total of 78 questions on the three scored Verbal sections and a total of 60 questions on the three scored Math sections. The "experimental" section may either be Math or Verbal; since the sections on the SAT appear in a random order, you can't tell which one is the Experimental section.

Here's a breakdown of how the tests differ:

	SAT	PSAT
Structure	7 sections	5 sections
Length	3 hours	2 hours 10 minutes
Purpose	College admissions	NMSQT (See Chapter 2)
Scoring	1600	Selection index out of 240

Here's how an SAT might look, compared to the PSAT. (Remember, though, that the sections on the SAT can come in a different order.)

SAT		
Section	Number of Questions	Time
Verbal	30	30 minutes
Math	25	30 minutes
Verbal	35	30 minutes
Math	25	30 minutes
Experimental	?	30 minutes
Verbal	13	15 minutes
Math	10	15 minutes

PSAT		
Section	Number of Questions	Time
Verbal	25	25 minutes
Math	20	25 minutes
Verbal	27	25 minutes
Math	20	25 minutes
Writing Skills	39	30 minutes

You'll notice that the PSAT is shorter than the SAT, and contains the Writing Skills section, which doesn't appear on the SAT. (The questions in this section are, however, similar to the ones you'll find on the SAT II: Writing Test, so it's good practice to start learning how to do them!)

What Does the PSAT Score Mean for My SAT Score?

The PSAT has three scores, which are scored on a scale of 20–80:

> Verbal 20–80
> Math 20–80
> Writing Skills 20–80

The SAT has two scores, on a scale of 200–800:

> Verbal 200–800
> Math 200–800

The PSAT is designed to give you an approximate idea of where your SAT scores would be: If you add a zero to the end of your PSAT Math or Verbal score, you'll get an approximate SAT score. That is, a 55 Verbal on the PSAT is roughly equivalent to a 550 on the SAT. However, there's a significant margin of error (about plus or minus 30 points). So a 55 Verbal really means that you'll probably score in the range of 520–580 on the SAT.

The Writing Skills section of the PSAT is designed to be roughly equivalent to the score on the SAT II: Writing Test, in the same fashion. That is, a 60 on the PSAT Writing Skills is equivalent to about a 570–630 on the SAT II: Writing Test.

How Much Should I Prepare for the PSAT?

If you're in that very small group of students who are in contention for National Merit recognition, it may be worth your while to put in a good deal of time preparing for this test. After all, if you can raise your scores from 71 or 72 to 74 or 76 on one or more of the sections on the PSAT, this may well put you in a better position for National Merit. Otherwise, you should prepare enough so that you feel more in control of the test, and have a better testing experience. (Nothing feels quite as awful as being dragged through a testing experience, feeling like you don't know what you're being tested on or what to expect. Except perhaps dental surgery.) The other reason to prepare for the PSAT is that it will give you some testing skills that will help you begin to prepare for the tests that actually count, namely the SAT and SAT IIs.

The bottom line is: The best reason to prepare for the PSAT is because it will help you get an early start on your preparation for the SAT.

Study

If you were getting ready to take a biology test, you'd study biology. If you were preparing for a basketball game, you'd practice basketball. So, if you're preparing for the PSAT (and eventually the SAT), study the PSAT. ETS can't test everything (in fact, they test very little), so concentrate on learning what they *do* test.

2
All About National Merit Scholarships

ALL ABOUT NATIONAL MERIT SCHOLARSHIPS

The NMSQT part of the name PSAT/NMSQT stands for National Merit Scholarship Qualifying Test. That means that the PSAT also serves as the test that will establish whether or not you are eligible for National Merit recognition.

How Do I Qualify for National Merit?

To qualify for any National Merit recognition, you must:

- Be a US citizen or permanent resident who intends to become a US citizen
- Be enrolled full-time in high school
- Take the PSAT/NMSQT in the third year of high school (for four-year programs). Slightly different rules apply if you're in a three-year program or other course of study.
- Be fully endorsed and recommended for a Merit scholarship by your high school principal
- Have a record of strong academic performance throughout high school
- Complete the NMSC Scholarship Application
- Obtain high scores on the SAT, which you'll take later in the year

The Index

How does your PSAT score qualify you for National Merit? The people at National Merit use a selection index, which is the sum of your Math, Verbal, and Writing Skills scores. For instance, if your PSAT scores were 60 Math, 50 Verbal, and 60 Writing Skills, your index would be 170.

Math + Verbal + Writing Skills = National Merit Index
60 + 50 + 60 = 170

The Awards and the Process

In the fall of their senior year, about 50,000 students will receive one of two letters from NMSC: either a Letter of Commendation, or a letter stating that they have qualified as semifinalists for National Merit.

> **Letter of Commendation**
> These letters are awarded to students who score between the 95th and the mid-99th percentile.

- **Commended Students**

Roughly two-thirds of these students (about 34,000 total students each year) will receive a Letter of Commendation by virtue of their high scores on the test. This looks great on your college application, so if you have a reasonable chance of getting one, it's definitely worth your time to prepare for the PSAT. Make no mistake, though: These letters are not easy to get. They are awarded to students who score between the 95th and the mid-99th percentiles—that means to the top 4–5 percent in the country.

If you receive this honorable mention from NMSC, you should be extremely proud of yourself. Even though you won't continue in the process for National Merit scholarships, this commendation does make you eligible for special scholarships sponsored by certain companies and organizations, which vary in their amounts and eligibility requirements.

- **Semifinalists**

The other third of these students—those 16,000 students who score in the upper 99th percentile in their states—will be notified that they are National Merit semifinalists. If you qualify, you'll get a letter announcing your status as a semifinalist, along with information about the requirements for qualification as a finalist. These include maintaining high grades, performing well on your SAT, and getting an endorsement from your principal.

Becoming a National Merit semifinalist is quite impressive, and if you manage it, you should certainly mention it on your college applications.

What does "scoring in the upper 99th percentile in the state" mean? It means that you're essentially competing against the other people in your state for those semifinalist positions. Since some states have higher average scores than others, this means that if you're in states like New York, New Jersey, Maryland, Connecticut, or Massachusetts, you need a higher score to qualify than if you live in other states. However, the majority of the indices are in the range of 200–215. (This means approximate scores of 70 Verbal, 70 Math, 70 Writing Skills.)

Many students want to know exactly what score they need. Sadly, National Merit is notoriously tight-lipped about these numbers. They only release them on rare occasions, and generally don't like to announce them. The latest public release of all the indices was in 1998, at which time the indices by state were:

State	Index	State	Index
Alabama	209	Missouri	211
Alaska	212	Montana	207
Arizona	210	Nebraska	204
Arkansas	202	Nevada	207
California	216	New Hampshire	214
Colorado	213	New Jersey	221
Connecticut	220	New Mexico	206
D.C.	221	New York	218
Delaware	217	North Carolina	215
Florida	214	North Dakota	206
Georgia	215	Ohio	211
Hawaii	215	Oklahoma	207
Idaho	206	Oregon	215
Illinois	214	Pennsylvania	215
Indiana	210	Rhode Island	215
Iowa	210	South Carolina	211
Kansas	214	South Dakota	205
Kentucky	209	Tennessee	216
Lousiana	208	Texas	215
Maine	214	Utah	202
Maryland	221	Vermont	213
Massachusetts	221	Virginia	220
Michigan	210	Washington	214
Minnesota	213	West Virginia	202
Mississippi	202	Wisconsin	210
		Wyoming	200

Note, however, that while these numbers are probably roughly the same from year to year, they do change somewhat. These should only be used to give you a rough idea of the range of scores for National Merit recognition.

- **Finalists**

The majority of semifinalists (more than 90 percent) go on to qualify as finalists. Students who meet all of the eligibility requirements will be notified in February of their senior year that they have qualified as finalists. This means that they are now eligible for scholarship money; though this doesn't necessarily mean that they'll get any. In fact, only about half of National Merit finalists actually win scholarships. What determines whether a student gets money or not? There is a final screening process, based on criteria that NMSC doesn't release to the public, to determine who actually gets these scholarships. There are about 8,000 total scholarships awarded, which fall into three groups: National Merit $2,500 scholarships, scholarships sponsored by businesses, and scholarships sponsored by colleges. These scholarships are based on various criteria, and the awards are of varying amounts.

Though the amounts of money are never huge, every little bit helps, and the award itself looks great in your portfolio. So if you think you are in contention for National Merit recognition, go for it. If not, prepare for the PSAT because it is good practice for the SAT.

> **National Merit**
> If you think you are in contention for National Merit recognition, go for it.

BUT I'M NOT A JUNIOR IN HIGH SCHOOL YET...

If you are not yet a junior, and you're interested in National Merit, you will have to take the test again your junior year in order to qualify.

A certain number of schools give the PSAT to students in their sophomore year—and sometimes even earlier. These schools hope that earlier exposure to these tests will help their students perform better in later years. If you're not yet in your junior year, the PSAT won't count for National Merit scholarship purposes, so it's really just a trial run for you. It's still a good idea to go into the test prepared in order to feel and test your best. After all, there's nothing more unpleasant than an unpleasant testing experience. (Well, except maybe having your gums scraped.)

WHAT IF I'M IN A THREE-YEAR, OR OTHER NON-STANDARD COURSE OF STUDY?

If you're going to spend only three years in secondary school, you have two options for when to take the PSAT for National Merit purposes: You can take it either in your next-to-last year or in your last year of secondary school. However, our advice is this: If you're in any program other than a usual four-year high school, be sure to talk to your guidance counselor. He or she will consult with NMSC and help ensure that you take the PSAT at the right time. This is important, because not taking the PSAT at the right time can disqualify you for National Merit recognition.

WHAT IF I MISS THE PSAT ADMINISTRATION MY JUNIOR YEAR?

If you aren't concerned about National Merit scholarships, there's no reason to do anything in particular—except, perhaps, to obtain a few PSAT booklets to practice on, just to see what fun you missed.

However, if you want to be eligible for National Merit recognition, then swift action on your part is required. If an emergency arises that prevents you from taking the PSAT, you should write to the National Merit Scholarship Corporation *immediately* to request alternate testing dates. If your request is received soon enough, they should be able to accommodate you. (NMSC says that this kind of request must absolutely be received by March 1 following the missed PSAT administration.) You'll also need a signature from a school official.

FOR MORE INFORMATION

If you have any questions or problems, the best person to consult is your school guidance counselor, who can help make sure you're on the right track. If you need further help, contact your local Princeton Review office at 800-2-REVIEW, or www.PrincetonReview.com. Or, you can contact National Merit directly:

National Merit Scholarship Corporation
1560 Sherman Avenue, Suite 200
Evanston, IL 60201-4897
(847) 866-5100
www.nationalmerit.org

3
General Strategies

In this chapter, we'll discuss some strategies that apply to the PSAT as a whole. Keep these in mind throughout the entire test, and you'll improve your score.

PROCESS OF ELIMINATION

You don't have to know how to solve a problem in order to get the correct answer (or to at least be able to make a good guess). *Aggressively using Process of Elimination (which we'll call POE from now on) will get you points on the PSAT.*

    1. What is the capital of Malawi?

If you were to see this problem on the PSAT (don't worry, you won't), you'd probably be stuck—not to mention a little upset. But the majority of the problems on the PSAT don't look like the problem above. They look like the following problem:

    1. What is the capital of Malawi?
          (A) Washington
          (B) Paris
          (C) Tokyo
          (D) London
          (E) Lilongwe

Not so bad anymore, is it? By knowing which choices must be wrong, you can often figure out what the answer is—even without knowing *why* it's the correct answer.

In many cases, finding the wrong answers is easier than finding the right ones, especially as the problems get more difficult. Your best strategy is to plan to solve most of the more difficult problems by POE.

    5. Although the piranha, <u>a species of</u>
                               A

carnivorous fish, is <u>native to</u> the waters
                      B

of the Amazon, <u>they</u> can be seen in aquariums
                 C

<u>throughout</u> the world. <u>No error</u>
    D   E

Here's a sample Writing Skills question. Sometimes the correct answer on a Writing Skills question may jump out at you as you read the question; in most cases, however, it won't. This means you should use POE. Let's look at each part in turn. "A species of" is okay, so (A) can't be the answer. "Native to" is the correct idiom, so (B) can also be crossed off. We might have a question with (C): Should the word here be "they" or "it"? If we're unsure, we can leave (C) alone for the moment. How about (D)? "Throughout the world" is okay, so (D) can be eliminated. So now we're down to either (C) or (E). (The answer is (C).)

Whether or not you got the correct answer, what's most important is the technique you use. You had a 1 in 2 shot on this problem. Those are fantastic odds, and you should take a guess. In cases where you're genuinely not sure of the answer (and this may happen often), immediately think POE. Better guesses mean more points on the PSAT!

A Moral Dilemma

What if someone approached you moments before the SAT began and offered to give you the answers to the test? You'd be shocked. SHOCKED! Right? But what if we told you that the person making the offer was the proctor running the test? The fact is that every student who takes the test gets to see virtually all of the answers ahead of time: They're printed in the test booklet, right underneath each question.

Let's try POE with a question you're more likely to see on the PSAT. Try to answer this question using POE before reading the explanation below.

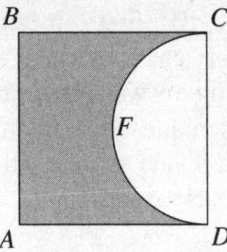

Be Test-Smart

Many students with good grades get below-average scores because they refuse to guess.

18. If ABCD is a square with side 8, and CFD is a semicircular arc, what is the area of the shaded region?
    (A) $16 - 8\pi$
    (B) $16 - 16\pi$
    (C) $64 - 8\pi$
    (D) $64 - 16\pi$
    (E) 64

Even before we try to solve this problem, let's use POE. We know that the value of π is a little more than 3. If we replace π with 3 in the answers above, what do you notice? Choices (A) and (B) are negative numbers! They can't be right. If we get no further on this problem, we can guess from among (C), (D), and (E), which is a guess that we should take. We can also eliminate (E), because a square with side 8 will have an area of 64; the area of the shaded region must be less than that. Without even trying the math, we've got a 1 in 2 shot of getting this problem right. Neat, huh? (The correct answer is (C).)

We know this isn't how you're taught to solve problems and take tests in school. In fact, your geometry teacher would probably have a fit if you were to do most of your work in class like this. That's because in school, what matters is *how* you get a problem right. But this isn't school. It's the PSAT. The only thing that matters on the PSAT is whether you have the correct bubble filled in. How you get that answer right is completely up to you. So don't treat the PSAT like a test in school. Do whatever you need to do (legally!) to get the right answer, and use strategies suited to getting the best score on this test.

Process of Elimination is a technique that can be used on every multiple-choice problem on the PSAT. By getting rid of answers that you know are wrong, you can improve your chances of guessing correctly and may be able to find the right answer to a question you don't know how to solve. Remember, it doesn't matter how you get to the right answer, as long as you get there!

GUESSING AGGRESSIVELY

Guessing *aggressively* means that if you can eliminate at least one answer choice on a problem, you should take a guess.

You may have heard, or have the impression, that the PSAT has a guessing penalty, and that you shouldn't guess on the PSAT. This is false. You should guess aggressively and often on the PSAT.

To generate your final score, ETS first computes your raw score. ETS gives you one raw score point for every correct answer and subtracts one-quarter of a raw score point for every wrong answer on your bubble sheet (one-third of a point for quantitative comparison questions). Blanks are not counted at all. This raw score is then equated to a scaled score on the 20–80 scale. (You can find sample equation tables in the back of this book.)

How the PSAT Is Scored

	Raw points
Correct answer:	+1
Blank:	0
Incorrect answer:	$-\dfrac{1}{4}$
	= Total raw score

The PSAT (or most of it, anyway) is a five-option multiple-choice test. If you guess completely randomly on five questions in a row, you should—by random chance—get one of these five correct and four of them wrong. Since you'll get one point for the one correct answer, and lose one-quarter of a point for each of the four wrong answers, your net raw score will be zero. Thus, random guessing *should not help or hurt you* on the PSAT. It simply counts for nothing.

So while it is true that you lose a fraction of a point for every incorrect answer on the test, this only has the effect of *neutralizing* completely random guessing. Guessing randomly has no effect on your score at all.

This means that you shouldn't waste your time by randomly guessing on questions that you don't even look at. However—and this is why you *should* guess aggressively and often—*if you can eliminate even one choice and guess better than randomly, then guessing will increase your score.* And on most problems that you have time to read carefully, you will be able to eliminate something. So you should get in the habit of guessing aggressively. Even if you can't get the correct answer, you should eliminate the choices you know are impossible or unreasonable, *guess* from the choices that remain, and move on to the next problem.

The better you are at POE, the more guessing will work in your favor, and the more points you'll gain on the PSAT.

Write Now
Feel free to write all over this book. You need to get in the habit of making the PSAT booklet your own.

USING YOUR BOOK

At school, you generally aren't allowed to write in your textbooks. (In some cases, they'll even charge you for the book if you do.) But on the PSAT, the booklet is yours. In fact, since you don't get any scrap paper, you have to do all of your work in your booklet. So use it! You should be doing all the math work you can on paper (which is much safer than doing it in your head) and, most importantly, crossing off the wrong answers when you find them. Take your pencil and scratch out choices as you eliminate. This will help make sure that you don't get lost when doing POE.

Don't worry about anyone looking at your booklet and seeing your messy handwriting. Though the proctor will probably collect the booklets at the end of the test for security purposes, nobody will ever look at your booklet after the test.

MAKING THE MATH WORK EASIER

BALLPARKING

On many math problems, you can save a lot of time by using common sense and *estimating* an answer before trying to solve it. Often, several of the answer choices are unreasonable (the ones "out of the ballpark") and can be eliminated right away. This will help you avoid careless mistakes and allow you to make a good guess even if you can't solve the problem.

Have a look at the following:

5. If 12 cans of food can feed 8 dogs for one week, how many cans of food would be needed to feed 6 dogs for two weeks?

   (A) 9
   (B) 12
   (C) 16
   (D) 18
   (E) 24

Before you start to calculate, estimate. If 12 cans will feed 8 dogs for one week, and we want to know how many cans we'd need for *two* weeks, the answer must be larger than 12. So eliminate (A) and (B). But we're only feeding *six* dogs for two weeks, so the answer must be less than 24. Eliminate (E). The answer must be either (C) or (D). Now, if you can calculate the answer, great. If not, you've got a 50 percent chance of a correct guess.

Here's another example of Ballparking *before* trying to solve:

2. A pair of running shoes, regularly priced at $75.00, is marked down 20% for a summer clearance sale. If sales tax of 8% is then added to the purchase price, how much will the shoes cost?

   (A) $55.20
   (B) $60.00
   (C) $64.80
   (D) $74.88
   (E) $81.00

Since the original price of the shoes is $75.00, which is then marked down by 20%, you know that the final price must be less than $75.00. So, you can immediately eliminate answers (D) and (E). Twenty percent of 75 has to be less than 20 (because 20% of 100 is 20), so answer choice (A), $55.20, is too low. That leaves you with answers (B) and (C). If you don't know how to do percentages, POE has given you a fifty-fifty chance of guessing correctly. If you know how to do percentages, you know that answer choice (C) gets you the correct answer!

Let's practice this one more time with a geometry question:

3. A rectangle has a length of 7 inches and an area of 56 inches. What is its width?
   (A) 49
   (B) 36
   (C) 21
   (D) 8
   (E) 7

The area of a rectangle is found by multiplying the length and width. In this question they give us the area and the length. We can use POE to eliminate answers (A), (B), and (C) because multiplying any of those by 7 would give us a number much larger than 56. That leaves us with answers (D) and (E). Now we can simply try choices (D) and (E) and see which one works.

Look Carefully at What the Questions Are Asking For

The test writers know that students are rushed when taking the PSAT. The writers use that to their advantage when designing questions. One of the biggest mistakes students make on the PSAT is working too quickly and making careless mistakes. A common careless mistake is answering the wrong question. You need to know what they're asking for before you can choose the correct answer. Let's look at an example:

4. If $6(3p - 2q) = 18$, what is the value of $3p - 2q$?
   (A) 2
   (B) 3
   (C) 4
   (D) 6
   (E) 18

You might be tempted to multiply out $6(3p - 2q)$ on this problem, which gives you $18p - 12q$. That seems like a logical first step, right? Unfortunately, if you do this, you'll be doing this problem the hard way. Why? Look carefully at what the problem is asking you to solve for. The question doesn't ask for the value of p or q alone, it asks for the value of $3p - 2q$. What's the easiest way to figure that out? Simply divide both sides of the equation by 6, and you get $(3p - 2q) = 3$. The moral: Always look at what the question is asking for. In math class, you're almost always asked to solve for x or y, but on the PSAT you may be asked to solve for $3x - y$, or $3p - 2q$, or some other strange expression. In these cases, there's usually an easier way to solve the problem than the way you might solve it in math class.

Taking Bite-Sized Pieces

Another common way that the question writers make life difficult for PSAT takers is throwing a lot of information at you at once to try to confuse you. When this happens, stay calm and take the information in Bite-Sized Pieces. By breaking up a wordy problem, you can transform a long, difficult problem into a few shorter, easier ones. Sound good? Let's look at one together.

16. A certain task has three steps: A, B, and C, which must be performed in order, one after the next, with no break in between. If steps A and B together take a total of 12 minutes, steps B and C take a total of 20 minutes, and the entire task takes a total of 28 minutes, then how many minutes are required to perform step B only?

    (A) 2
    (B) 4
    (C) 8
    (D) 16
    (E) 60

Read the question through where it says "12 minutes." That's the first place you'll stop. Write an equation for that information. It should look like this: $A + B = 12$. Continue reading until "20 minutes." Write another equation: $B + C = 20$. Now continue reading until "28 minutes" and write an equation for that: $A + B + C = 28$. Now you just need to solve for B.

Since we know that $A + B + C = 28$, and $A + B = 12$, we can figure out that C alone must be 16. Further, we know that $B + C = 20$. Since C is 16, we can figure out that B is equal to 4. Therefore, the answer is (B).

With some practice, you'll find that Ballparking, looking for what the question is asking you to do, and taking Bite-Sized Pieces will help you work smarter, and not harder, on the Math sections of the PSAT.

4
Advanced Strategies

In this chapter, we'll discuss an overall PSAT game plan: figuring out how many problems you should do, which problems you should do, and how to avoid the answers that ETS plants to trap the average student, who we'll call Joe Bloggs.

PACING

Most students think that you need to do every problem on the PSAT to get a great score. And most students *hurt* their score because they try to do *too many* problems.

Here's what Joe Bloggs does: Joe thinks that he has to finish every problem on the PSAT. In an attempt to do just this, he works as quickly as he can. This means that he rushes through the easy problems—the ones that he should get right—and makes some careless errors, which cost him valuable points. Then he gets to the medium problems. These take more time, are more convoluted, and have a few trap choices in them. Joe gets about half of these right. Then Joe gets to the hard questions. These are designed so Joe will get almost all of them wrong, yet Joe insists on spending more than one-third of his time on these problems—for no points at all. What kind of score does Joe get? He gets the average score of about 51.

As you can see, this probably isn't the best strategy. There are two reasons why it doesn't make sense to try every problem on the test. First, it's very hard to finish every question while maintaining a high level of accuracy. During timed tests, people naturally rush—and then they make careless errors and lose points. Almost everyone is better off *slowing down*, using the time allotted to work on *fewer* problems, and answering more of those problems correctly. You'll get a higher score if you do *only 75 percent* of the problems on this test and answer them correctly than if you do all of the problems and answer about half correctly. Likewise, you'll get a much higher score if you do *only 50 percent* of the problems on this test and answer them correctly than if you do three-quarters of them and only answer half correctly.

Second, not every question is of the same level of difficulty. In fact, most of the problems on this test are arranged in increasing order of difficulty: The earlier questions are easier, and they get gradually harder until the final questions are so difficult that only a small percentage of test takers answer them correctly. Hard questions are worth no more than easy questions, so why waste time working on them? Most testers are much better off skipping many of the hard questions and applying all their time to the easy and medium-level questions.

Even if you are scoring in a high range (and therefore need to do almost all of the problems to get the score you need), this doesn't mean that you should approach them like Joe does. As we'll see, Joe tries to solve each problem in the most straightforward way, looking for the right answer. Instead of solving these problems the way Joe does, a smarter approach is to look for an alternate way to solve these difficult problems—by using a technique such as Plugging In or by POE. (You'll see more of these techniques later in the book.)

WHICH PROBLEMS SHOULD I DO?

THE ORDER OF DIFFICULTY

You should do the problems that are easiest for *you*. In general, the questions on the PSAT are arranged in increasing order of difficulty:

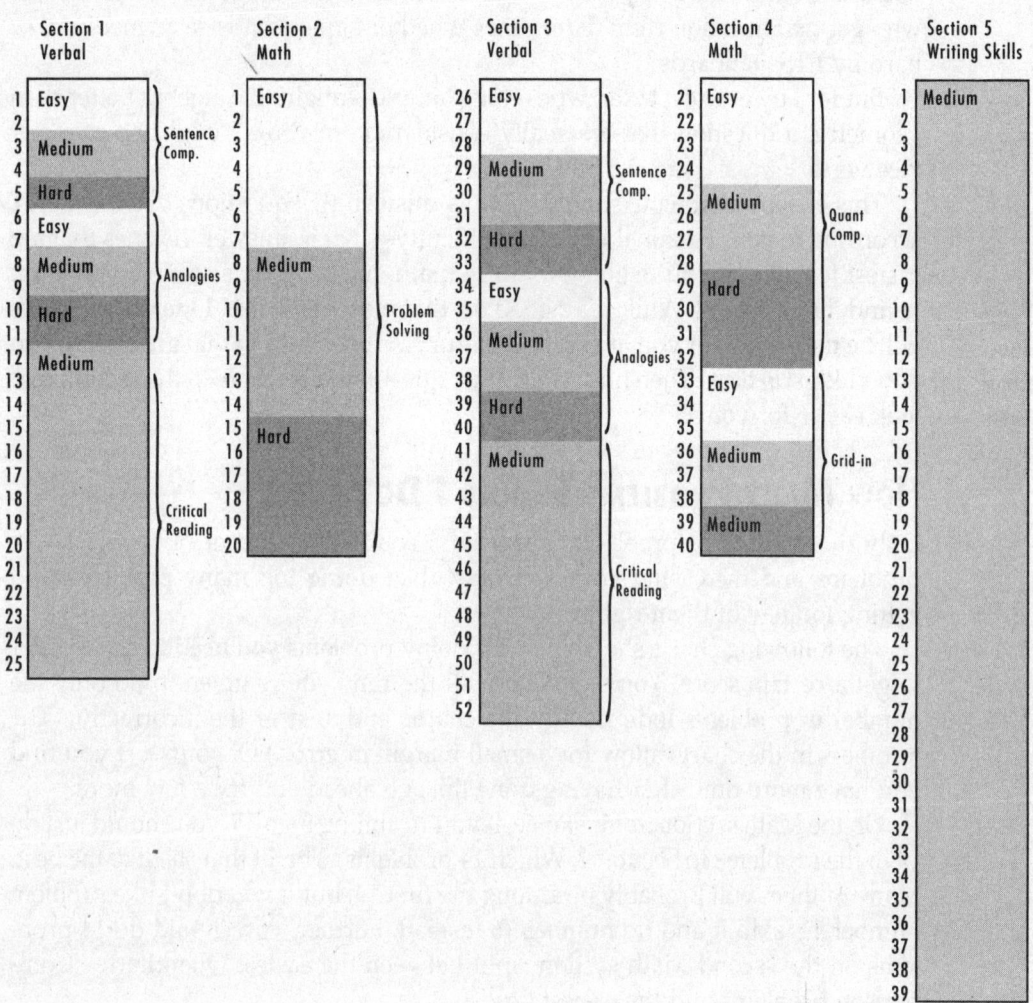

Memorize this chart now. The most important question to ask yourself whenever you come to a problem on the PSAT is How difficult is it? If it's an easy question, go ahead and answer it. If it's a medium or hard question, be careful! Try to avoid solving these problems in the usual way. Instead, use one of our techniques, or try to make a good guess using Process of Elimination (POE).

ADVANCED STRATEGIES ◆ 27

Rule #1
Answer easy questions first; save hard questions for last.

This principle of level of difficulty is *so* important that we've given all of the problems in this book the question number that they would have on the actual test. Remember to always ask yourself, Is this question easy, medium, or hard? Should I do this problem, and if so, how should I approach it?

Your Personal Order of Difficulty

The chart on the previous page shows the questions that are considered "easy," "medium," and "hard" by the average test taker. The average number of people who get that question right determines whether a question is easy, medium, or hard by ETS standards.

But for any one test taker, who—for example—might like algebra better than geometry, a question that is usually considered "medium" might be easy. Or vice versa.

This means that you should always answer the questions on the PSAT according to your Personal Order of Difficulty—that is, answer the ones that are easiest for you. If you're going to do 14 math questions on a section, you want to find the easiest 14. While it's a good bet that most of the first 14 math questions will be the easiest for you, if you find one or two questions in that group that you don't like, *skip them*. Then find a few other questions elsewhere in the section that look easier for you.

Rule #2
Easy questions tend to have easy answers; hard questions tend to have hard answers.

How Many Problems Should I Do?

Only the number of problems you need. You're *much* better off doing fewer problems and increasing your accuracy, than doing too many problems and getting too few of them right.

The following charts show you how many problems you need to do in order to get a certain score. You should use all the time you're given to do only the number of problems indicated by the charts, and answer them correctly. (The numbers in the charts allow for a small margin of error.) Of course, if you find you have more time after having done this, go ahead and try a few more.

On the Math section, for instance, if you're aiming for a 55, you should just do 14 of the problems in Section 2. Which 14 problems? The 14 that *you* like the best. Many of them will probably be among the first 14; but if you don't like problem number 11, skip it and do number 16 instead. Further, you should do 14 problems on the second Math section, split between the easiest Quantitative Comparison problems and the easiest Grid-Ins.

Math Target Score	Raw Points	Questions to Do on Section 2	Questions to Do on Section 4
35	5	5	5
40	10	8	8
45	14	10	10
50	19	13	12
55	23	14	14
60	28	17	17
65	32	18	19
70	36	all	all
75	38	all	all
80	40	all	all

Here's the chart for Verbal. If you're aiming for a 55, you want to do 18 questions on each section (for a total of 36 problems). Which 18? The ones that you like best. If you're strong in Critical Reading, maybe you'll try for 10 Critical Reading points, 4 Analogies, and 4 Sentence Corrections. If you're weak in Critical Reading, you might aim for 5 Analogies, 7 Sentence Corrections, and 6 Critical Reading questions. It's up to you. It's a good idea, though, to have a game plan in advance; stick with one that plays to your strengths.

Verbal Target Score	Raw Points	Questions to Do on Section 1	Questions to Do on Section 3
35	9	6	6
40	13	9	9
45	19	12	12
50	24	15	15
55	30	18	18
60	35	20	20
65	40	23	23
70	44	all	all
75	48	all	all
80	51	all	all

Finally, here's the pacing chart for the Writing Skills section:

Writing Skills Target Score	Raw Points	Questions to Do on Section 5
35	3	6
40	6	9
45	10	15
50	15	20
55	19	25
60	23	29
65	28	34
70	31	all
75	34	all
80	38	all

SET REASONABLE GOALS

If you're currently scoring 50, trying to score a 65 right away will only hurt you. Try to work your way up in reasonable stages. Pick a score range approximately 5 points higher than the range in which you're currently scoring. If you're currently scoring 50, aim for a 55; when you have reached 55, then you can aim for 60.

If you have not yet taken a practice PSAT, start by doing the first test in the back of this book. That will tell you where you currently stand, and will help you set a goal for your preparation.

JOE BLOGGS

Let's suppose for a moment that you could look at the page of the tester next to you (you can't). Let's also suppose that you know for a fact that every one of your neighbor's answers on the test is wrong. If on problem 20, he marked (C) as his answer, what would you do? Eliminate choice (C), right?

Even though you can't look at your neighbor's page, you can use this principle to get points on the test. We've created an imaginary tester to accompany you during the exam: Joe Bloggs.

Joe isn't stupid, he's just average. And when ETS writes the PSAT, they write it in a very particular way. They write it so that Joe will get most of the easy problems correct, some of the medium problems correct, and none of the hard ones correct.

How do they do this? The test writers are very good at knowing what kinds of answer choices are attractive to the average person. (They've been doing it for more than 40 years, so they're quite good at it.)

Joe Bloggs, the average tester, always picks the answer that first attracts him. Choices that first attract him on math problems have nice round numbers that can be easily derived from other numbers in the problem. Choices that attract him on verbal problems have familiar words that remind him of words in the question.

Question Type	Joe Bloggs Selects	How Joe Does
Easy	What seems right	Mostly right
Medium	What seems right	So-so
Hard	What seems right	All wrong!

What does this mean for you? When you're working on easy problems, pick the choice that seems right to you. When you're working on medium problems, be careful. If you got the answer too quickly, check your work. Medium problems should take more work than easy problems. If you're working on a hard problem, eliminate the choices that first seem attractive; they are almost always traps.

Remember, Joe Bloggs gets the easy problems right. *Only cross off Joe Bloggs answers on the hard problems.* How do you know how hard a question is? By its *question number*.

Take a look at the following example:

10. NEOLOGISM : LANGUAGE
    (A) rhetoric : speech
    (B) syllogism : grammar
    (C) innovation : technology
    (D) iconography : art
    (E) epistemology : philosophy

First, notice the question number. This is an Analogy number 10, which means it's a hard analogy. You may not know what the word *neologism* means, but you (and Joe) know what *language* is. Since Joe likes to pick words that seem familiar and remind him of words used in the problem, which choices do you think he will pick? *Grammar* and *speech* remind Joe of *language*, so he will tend to pick (A) or (B). If you can't get any further, guess from among (C), (D), and (E). (The answer is (C).)

Joe's Hunches

Should you always just eliminate any answer that seems to be correct? No! Remember what we said about Joe Bloggs:

1. His hunches are correct on easy questions.
2. His hunches are sometimes correct and sometimes incorrect on medium questions.
3. His hunches are always wrong on difficult questions.

On easy multiple-choice questions, pick the choice that Joe Bloggs would. On hard questions, be sure to eliminate the choices that Joe Bloggs would pick.

Take a look at this math problem:

20. Michelle rode her bicycle from her house to school at an average speed of 8 miles per hour. Later that day, she rode from school back home along the same route at an average speed of 12 miles per hour. If the round trip took her 1 hour, how many miles long is the round trip?

   (A) 8
   (B) $9\frac{3}{5}$
   (C) 10
   (D) $11\frac{1}{5}$
   (E) 12

Which choice do you think seems attractive at first to Joe? Since he sees the numbers 8 and 12 and the word "average," he will probably average 8 and 12 to get 10. Therefore, Joe will pick (C).

But now you know better. This problem is number 20, the hardest problem on the section. You know that Joe will get it wrong. So cross off choice (C).

If Joe doesn't pick (C), what else might he pick? He'll pick either (A) 8, or (E) 12, since those are the numbers that appear in the problem. Cross them off as well. Then guess from either (B) or (D). (The answer is (B). But we're not going to spend time on why right now.) If you can quickly cross off a few choices on a hard problem and make a good guess, you'll be in great shape.

Figuring out the right number of problems to do, how to pace yourself, and how to avoid the Joe Bloggs traps are keys to a good PSAT strategy. You're probably eager to get to the rest of the book, but make sure you've taken the time to understand this chapter before moving on. A solid overall approach is crucial to getting your best score on this test.

PART II

Cracking the PSAT/NMSQT

5

Sentence Completions

WHAT IS A SENTENCE COMPLETION QUESTION?

A Sentence Completion question will consist of a sample sentence in which one or two words have been replaced by blanks. Below the sentence, you'll find five answer choices, each of which consists of a word or words. Your job is to pick the choice with the word or words that best fill the blank(s) in the sentence.

Solving these questions relies on two things: first, your ability to figure out what kind of word should go in the blank, and second, your vocabulary. (This means it's really important to start working on your vocabulary right away!)

THE INSTRUCTIONS

Of course, you don't want to take up valuable time during the test to read the directions, so let's learn them now. Here are the instructions for Sentence Completions as you will see them on the PSAT and SAT:

> Each sentence below has one or two blanks, each blank indicating that something has been omitted. Beneath the sentence are five words or sets of words labeled A through E. Choose the word or set of words that, when inserted in the sentence, best fits the meaning of the sentence as a whole.
>
> Example:
>
> Medieval kingdoms did not become constitutional republics overnight; on the contrary, the change was -------.
>
> (A) unpopular (B) unexpected (C) advantageous (D) sufficient (E) gradual   Ⓐ Ⓑ Ⓒ Ⓓ ●

ETS's answer to this sample question is (E).

ORDER OF DIFFICULTY

Sentence Completion questions will appear on both Verbal sections of the PSAT. They will be questions 1–5 on Section 1 and questions 26–33 on Section 3. Their order of difficulty looks like this:

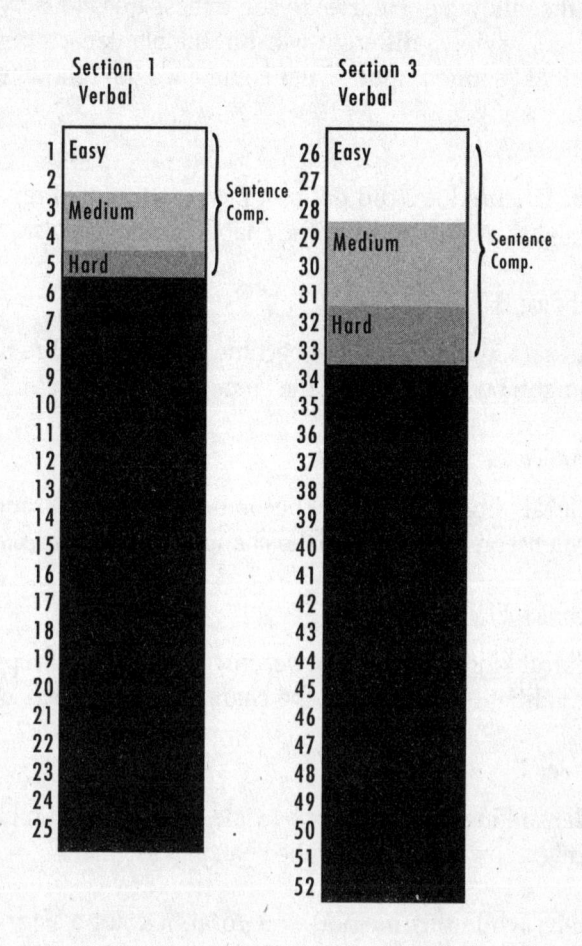

Section 1:
Questions 1–2: easy
Questions 3–4: medium
Question 5: hard

Section 3:
Questions 26–28 : easy
Questions 29–31: medium
Questions 32–33: hard

[A POINT OF] METHOD

Before we talk about the best way to solve Sentence Completions, we should first discuss how *not* to solve them. How does Joe Bloggs, the average student, approach Sentence Completions? The natural way, which seems most intuitive to Joe, is to do the following: He tries to solve these questions by rereading the sentence five times, trying a different word in the blank each time, and hoping to find the one that "sounds right." That is, he does the following:

Joe tries choice A:

> Medieval kingdoms did not become constitutional republics overnight; on the contrary, the change was *unpopular*.

Joe tries choice B:

> Medieval kingdoms did not become constitutional republics overnight; on the contrary, the change was *unexpected*.

Joe tries choice C:

> Medieval kingdoms did not become constitutional republics overnight; on the contrary, the change was *advantageous*.

Joe tries choice D:

> Medieval kingdoms did not become constitutional republics overnight; on the contrary, the change was *sufficient*.

Joe tries choice E:

> Medieval kingdoms did not become constitutional republics overnight; on the contrary, the change was *gradual*.

A Reminder
On easy questions, the answers that seem right to Joe really are right; on hard questions, the answers that seem right to Joe are wrong.

Unfortunately, while this method is natural, it's not a very good strategy. Not only is it a waste of time (why would you want to read the sentence *five times*?) but it's also unhelpful, since many of the choices will probably sound equally good or equally bad.

What Joe doesn't know is that the correct answer on a Sentence Completion question is not correct because of how it *sounds*, but because of what it *means*. So the best way to solve Sentence Completions is to figure out what the word in the blank should mean. The question is, How?

You're smarter than you think

Try the following exercise: In the following sentence, what word do you think should go in the blank?

1. Susan was ------- when the formula, which had worked just yesterday, failed to produce the expected result.

What word did you put in the blank? "Perplexed" or "confused"? Something of this sort has to be the word in the blank.

How about this one:

2. Although she was never considered pretty as a child, Margaret grew up to be a ------- adult.

What word did you put in the blank? "Beautiful" or "pretty" or "lovely"? You can figure out what the word in the blank has to mean without looking at the answer choices.

Try it once more:

3. Once a cheerful person, the years of fruitless struggle against government waste made him a very ------- man.

Even if you couldn't figure out the exact word that went in the blank, you probably figured out that it had to be a word fairly close in meaning to "unhappy" or "bitter." That will be good enough to get the right answer, or at least to make a very good guess at the right answer.

You see, you're smarter than you think. This is why you should always approach Sentence Completion questions by *speaking for yourself*. Don't look down at the answer choices; if you do, you'll be tempted to use the Joe Bloggs method of trying each word, one at a time, and hoping that one of them sounds right. In fact, you should always approach Sentence Completions the same way we just did: Read the sentence, and put *your own word* into the blank.

THE METHOD

As you've seen, speaking for yourself not only works, it's much faster than trying every answer choice. To make sure that you speak for yourself, you should actually place your hand over the answer choices so you're not tempted to read them until you've picked your own word for the blank.

So here's our method so far for solving Sentence Completions:

1. Cover the answer choices with your hand. This will ensure that you don't do what Joe does, which is to read the sentence five times, trying one of the answer choices each time.

2. Speak for yourself: Read the sentence, and put your own word in the blank.

3. Only after you've put your own word in the blank should you look down at the answer choices and pick the word that comes closest to the word that you came up with.

Sentence Completion Rule #1

Cover the answer choices until you know what the answer should be.

But how do you know what word to put in the blank? You never have to guess randomly; in fact, ETS always puts clues into the sentences to tell you what sort of word goes in the blank. By learning how to look for these clues, you can reliably figure out what sort of word has to go in the blank, every time.

SPEAK FOR YOURSELF, PART I: THE CLUE AND TRIGGER WORDS

To help you speak for yourself, learn to look for the *clue* and *trigger words*.

The clue

We saw above that you could figure out the meaning of the word in the blank without looking at the answer choices. How did you think you were able to know what word went in the blank? Without realizing it, you were using clues in the sentence. There are *always* clues in the sentence that tell you what the word in the blank is supposed to mean.

Let's look back at the first sample problem, and see what kind of clues we can find in it.

1. Susan was ------- when the formula, which had worked just yesterday, failed to produce the expected result.

How did you know that the word had to be something like "perplexed"? Because this sentence contains a clue: *the formula, which had worked just yesterday, failed to produce the expected result*. This clue tells us how Susan must feel: namely, that she felt "perplexed" or "puzzled."

How about in this sentence?

2. The park was so ------- that children could play in it for hours without getting bored.

What kind of word would you put in this blank, and why? You probably chose a word like "interesting" or "varied." You probably knew this because the park is described as a place where *children could play for hours without getting bored*. This is the clue that tells us that the park must be a terribly interesting place to be.

The meaning of the word that goes in the blank isn't random—rather, there is always evidence somewhere else in the sentence that tells you what the word in the blank should mean. This evidence is called the clue. *Every sentence has some clue in it. Look for the clue, and it will help you determine the word that goes in the blank.*

Hold an Audition

If you were directing *Romeo and Juliet*, you'd have to hold auditions in order to find actors. You wouldn't look at all the actors in the world before reading the play, would you? For the role of Juliet, you'd be looking for someone suited to the part. Everybody else would be sent packing.

Sentence Completions are the same. You have to read the sentence first to decide what kind of word would fit best *before* you look at the answer choices available. Then, like the director, you would pick the answer choice that is most like what you want and eliminate the ones that are different.

Why every sentence needs a clue

Every sentence on the PSAT must have some sort of clue in it, or else the question wouldn't have just one correct answer. In that case, the question wouldn't be a good one anymore, and ETS couldn't use it on the PSAT. Let's see why. Take a look at this problem:

1. John made some ------- comments about Marcus's artwork.
   - (A) intelligent
   - (B) critical
   - (C) interesting
   - (D) dry
   - (E) appreciative

Can you see why this problem would never appear on the PSAT? Because any of the answers might work. There's not enough information in the sentence to make one choice better than any other. Without a clue, the question just won't work. Look at this example:

1. John made some ------- comments about Marcus's artwork, which John thought was fantastic.
   - (A) intelligent
   - (B) critical
   - (C) interesting
   - (D) dry
   - (E) appreciative

In this case, the word that would best fit would be (E), because of the clue *which John thought was fantastic*. Note that if the clue changes, so does the meaning of the word in the blank.

1. John made some ------- comments about Marcus's artwork, which John thought was the worst he had ever seen.
   - (A) intelligent
   - (B) critical
   - (C) interesting
   - (D) dry
   - (E) appreciative

In this case, the answer would be (B). By changing the clue, we changed the meaning of the word that should go in the blank.

Trigger words

One more important tool for figuring out the meaning of the word in the blank is *trigger words*. These are words in the sentence that tell you how the word in the blank relates to the clue.

Trigger words are words we use every day. For instance, look at the following sentences:

I really like you, *and* _____

I really like you, *but* _____

You already know more or less how these sentences would end, don't you? The first sentence would continue with something positive that goes along with liking someone, such as

I really like you, *and I'd like to get to know you better.*

In contrast, the second sentence would change direction and end with something not quite so nice, such as

I really like you, *but you're really not my type.*

Now let's see how trigger words work in a sample sentence. Recall the second example you tried above

    2. Although she was never considered pretty as a child, Margaret grew up to be a -------- adult.

How did you know that the word in the blank had to be a word like "beautiful"? Because the word *although* told you that there was a change in direction or contrast in the sentence: She was *not pretty as a child*, but she *was* a pretty *adult*.

There are also trigger words that indicate that the word in the blank has the same meaning as the clue. For instance:

    4. Because Susan could not stand Jim's boorish manners, she -------- to be near him at parties.

In this case, what sort of word goes in the blank? The trigger word *because* tells you that the word in the blank will have a similar meaning to the clue *could not stand Jim's boorish manners*. The word in the blank must therefore be something like "hated" or "despised."

The most common same-direction trigger words are *and, because, so, therefore, since,* and *in fact*.

The most common opposite-direction trigger words are *but, however, yet, although, though, in contrast, rather,* and *despite*. When you see these words, the word in the blank will usually mean the opposite of the clue.

Same-Direction Triggers	Opposite-Direction Triggers
and	but
since	however
so	yet
therefore	although/though
because	in contrast
in fact	rather

Punctuation triggers

In addition to the words above, there are a number of punctuation triggers. Both colons (:) and semicolons (;) act as same-direction triggers and show us that what follows the colon or semicolon will be an explanation or further description of something that came before. Take a look at this sentence:

   2. John's friend was rather -------: he never spoke unless he was forced to.

In this case, we know that the word in the blank should be a word that means "unwilling to speak"—a word like "quiet" or "taciturn" would do nicely.

Time triggers

One other kind of trigger, which acts as an opposite-direction trigger, is the time trigger. A time trigger draws a contrast between what used to be true and what is true today. Here's an example:

A Reminder
Circle the triggers!

   3. Once a cheerful person, the years of fruitless struggle against government waste made him a very ------- man.

In this case, we know that the word in the blank needs to be a word opposite to "cheerful"—perhaps a word like "gloomy" or "cynical." Why? We know that at one point in the past, this person was cheerful; however, since that time, something has changed. Therefore the word in the blank should be something that contrasts with "cheerful."

When trying to find the right word for the blank, always look for the clue and trigger words. They will tell you what sort of word you need.

SENTENCE COMPLETIONS ◆ 43

Speak for Yourself — Part II

So far we've seen that the best way to solve a Sentence Completion question is to use the clue and trigger words to help you come up with your own word for the blank. If you can't think of the *exact* word, think of what *kind* of word should go in the blank. Is it a positive word? A negative word? An active or passive word? Only *after you've done this* should you look down at the answer choices and pick the word that's closest to the word that you chose.

Here are a few Sentence Completion problems from which we've removed the answer choices. (You can find the complete problem with answer choices on the next page.) Read the sentence, and put your own word in the blank. Then turn the page and see which word comes closest to the word you picked.

1. Many feature films are criticized for their ------- content, even though television news is more often the medium that depicts violent events in excessive detail.

4. In a vitriolic message to his troops, General Patton insisted that he would ------- no further insubordination, no matter how barbarous the ensuing engagements might become.

5. Chang realized that she had been ------- in her duties; had she been more -------, the disaster may well have been avoided.

1. Many feature films are criticized for their ------- content, even though television news is more often the medium that depicts violent events in excessive detail.

    (A) discretionary
    (B) graphic
    (C) dramatic
    (D) artistic
    (E) honest

Here's how to crack it
The clue in this sentence is *even though television news is more often the medium that depicts violent events*. The word in the blank should mean something like "violent." The closest answer choice is (B).

4. In a vitriolic message to his troops, General Patton insisted that he would ------- no further insubordination, no matter how barbarous the ensuing engagements might become.

    (A) impede
    (B) brief
    (C) denote
    (D) brook
    (E) expose

Here's how to crack it
The clue here is *no further insubordination, no matter how....* Did you pick a word like "tolerate" or "stand for" in this case? That's exactly the meaning of the word in the blank. The words in the answer choices are hard, but eliminate what you can, and take a good guess. The answer is (D).

5. Chang realized that she had been ------- in her duties; had she been more -------, the disaster may well have been avoided.

    (A) unparalleled . . careful
    (B) irreproachable . . aware
    (C) derelict . . vigilant
    (D) arbitrary . . interested
    (E) neglectful . . insensible

Here's how to crack it
The clue for the second blank is that the *disaster may well have been avoided*, so the second blank must be a word like "careful." This will allow us to eliminate (D) and (E). The word in the first blank must be a word like "neglectful," since Chang failed to do her duty. The only remaining choice that works for the first blank is (C).

Two blanks: Twice as easy
Some of the Sentence Completion questions will have two blanks rather than just one. To solve these questions, do them one blank at a time. Pick one blank or the

other, whichever seems easier to you, and figure out what word should go in the blank. (Hint: Often, but not always, the second blank is easier to figure out.) Then cross off all of the choices that don't work for that blank.

If more than one choice remains, then pick a word for the other blank, and see which of the remaining answer choices works best.

Have a look at this example:

2. The scientific community was ------- when a living specimen of the coelacanth, which they had feared was -------, was discovered by deep-sea fishermen.

(A) perplexed.. common
(B) overjoyed.. dangerous
(C) unconcerned.. exterminated
(D) astounded..extinct
(E) dismayed..alive

Here's how to crack it

The clue for the second blank is that a *living specimen* was found, which the scientists *feared* was... . So the second blank must mean something like "destroyed." Only choices (C) and (D) are possible, so we can eliminate the others. Now look at the first blank. How did the scientists feel about the discovery? They were probably happy about it. Of (C) and (D), which choice works with the first blank? Choice (D).

FINAL WORDS

As the questions get harder, you'll probably find harder words in the answer choices. In some cases, you'll be able to speak for yourself and put your own word in the blank, but you won't be sure which of the answer choices means what you think the blank should mean.

Now is the time to remember POE. Cross off all the words you know won't work, and if you have to take a guess from the remaining choices, you should do so—the odds are in your favor.

SENTENCE COMPLETION SUMMARY

1. Cover the answer choices with your hand.

2. Speak for yourself: Read the sentence, and put your own word in the blank.

3. Only after you've come up with your own word for the blank should you look down at the answer choices and pick the word that comes closest to the word that you chose.

4. To help you figure out the meaning of the word that goes in the blank, find the clues in the sentence. Also pay close attention to trigger words.

5. If you can't think of a precise word for the blank, at least think of what *kind* of word should go there. Is it a positive word? A negative word? An active or passive word?

6. On two-blank questions, do one blank at a time.

Shoe Store

If you were shopping for shoes and found a pair you liked, you'd ask the clerk to bring you a pair in your size to try on. Say you tried the right shoe first. If it felt horrible, would you even bother to try the left shoe on? No, because even if the left shoe was comfy, you'd have to wear it with the right shoe, which you already know causes you unspeakable pain. You would look for another pair of shoes. Two-blank Sentence Completions are like shoes. If one doesn't fit, there's no point trying the other one. Half bad is all bad.

A Gentle Reminder

Your aim is to eliminate wrong answers. Get rid of as many incorrect choices as you can, guess from among the remaining choices, and then move on.

6 Analogies

WHAT IS AN ANALOGY?

An Analogy question presents you with two capitalized words that are called the "stem words." These words have some relationship to one another. Your job is to find which of the answer choice pairs has the same relationship as the stem words.

Even more than Sentence Completion questions, Analogies rely heavily on your knowledge of words. So be sure to keep working on your vocabulary.

THE INSTRUCTIONS

Here are the directions as you will see them on the PSAT:

> Each question below consists of a related pair of words or phrases, followed by five pairs of words or phrases labeled A through E. Select the pair that best expresses a relationship similar to that expressed in the original pair.
>
> Example:
>
>   CRUMB : BREAD ::
>
> (A) ounce : unit
> (B) splinter : wood
> (C) water : bucket
> (D) twine : rope
> (E) cream : butter   Ⓐ ● Ⓒ Ⓓ Ⓔ

ETS's answer to this question is (B). A crumb is a piece of bread, and a splinter is a piece of wood.

ORDER OF DIFFICULTY

Analogies will appear on both Verbal sections of the PSAT. They will be questions 6–11 on Section 1 and questions 34–40 on Section 3. Their order of difficulty looks like this:

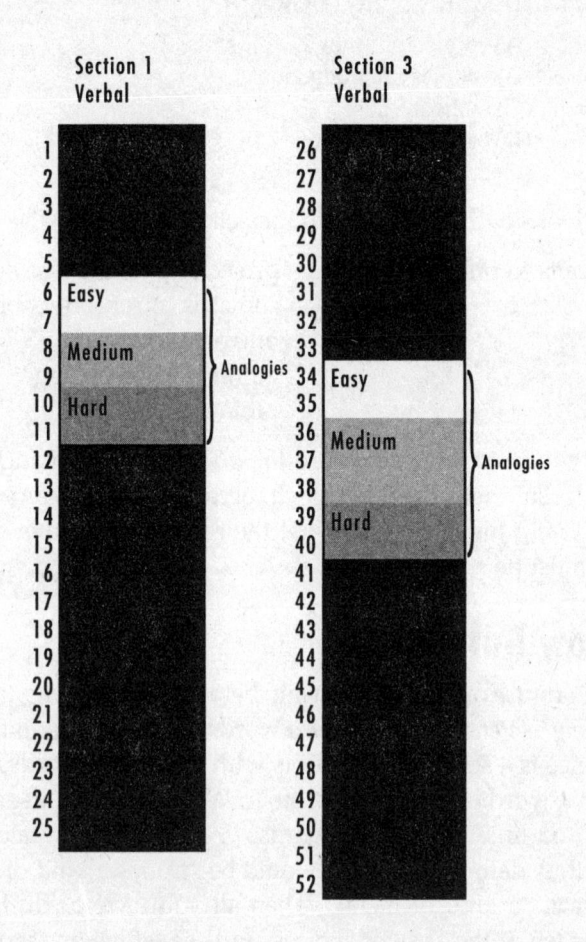

Section 1:
Questions 6–7: easy
Questions 8–9: medium
Questions 10–11: hard

Section 3:
Questions 34–35: easy
Questions 36–38: medium
Questions 39–40: hard

DON'T BE LIKE JOE

What does the typical student do when faced with an Analogy? Take a look at the problem below.

10. CAMERA : PHOTOGRAPH ::
    (A) projector : movie
    (B) copier : reproduction
    (C) mirror : pose
    (D) guitar : recording
    (E) cabinet : file

Joe Bloggs looks at this and says to himself:

Camera is to photograph as…   projector is to movie?
                              copier is to reproduction?
                              mirror is to pose?
                              guitar is to recording?
                              cabinet is to file?

Of course, you probably see where Joe goes wrong. Saying "camera is to photograph" doesn't help Joe very much, because saying "camera is to photograph" doesn't help Joe figure out what the relationship is between these two words. There must be a better way.

IF YOU KNOW BOTH WORDS

The best way to figure out the relationship between the two capitalized words is to *make a defining sentence* using the two words. What is a defining sentence? A defining sentence is a sentence that starts with one of the words, and then goes on to define that word in terms of the other. When possible, use the words "is" or "means" to link the two words. For instance, take the words IRON : METAL. A defining sentence would be "iron is a kind of metal" or "the word 'iron' means a kind of metal." Then all you have to do is try the same sentence with each of the answer choices, and see which one works best.

Here's the complete problem:

10. IRON : METAL ::
    (A) coach : team
    (B) doctor : hospital
    (C) leaf : tree
    (D) fly : insect
    (E) army : soldier

Now let's read the choices using our sentence.

(A) Is a *coach* a type of *team*? No.
(B) Is a *doctor* a type of *hospital*? Definitely not.
(C) Is a *leaf* a type of *tree*? No.
(D) Is a *fly* a type of *insect*? Yes, this is a possible answer.
(E) Is an *army* a type of *soldier*? Nope.

The Dictionary, Please

Your sentence should read like a dictionary definition, defining one word in terms of the other. For example, "KENNEL : DOG." If you were to look up *kennel* in the dictionary, you would find something like, "A *kennel* is a place to keep *dogs*."

Therefore the best answer is (D). It is the only choice that works with the sentence we made to define iron and metal.

Now let's go back to the Analogy question from the start of this chapter.

10. CAMERA : PHOTOGRAPH ::
    - (A) projector : movie
    - (B) copier : reproduction
    - (C) mirror : pose
    - (D) guitar : recording
    - (E) cabinet : file

You will probably make a sentence like the following for the stem words: "A camera is used to make a photograph." Now let's read the choices using the same sentence:

- (A) Is a *projector* used to make a *movie*? No, it's used to show a movie.
- (B) Is a *copier* used to make a *reproduction*? Yes, this is a possible answer.
- (C) Is a *mirror* used to make a *pose*? No.
- (D) Is a *guitar* used to make a *recording*? Well, it *might* be… so let's leave it in.
- (E) Is a *cabinet* used to make a *file*? Nope.

Which of these choices seems the best? (D) might sound tempting, but it's not as good as we'd like. A guitar *might* be used to make a recording, but that doesn't really define what the word guitar means—guitars are often used in ways that don't involve recording, and lots of other things might be used to make a recording. However, the right word for the instrument that makes a reproduction is a copier. Therefore (B) has the strongest relationship, and is the best answer.

TIPS FOR MAKING GOOD SENTENCES

Making a sentence is the best way to solve Analogies. To make your job easier, here are a few guidelines:

1. Make your sentence as brief and straightforward as possible. Keep it simple!

2. Begin your sentence with one of the capitalized words, followed by the word "is" or "means," and end the sentence with the other capitalized word.

3. Try to maintain the words exactly as they are written. For instance, don't change "FIGHT" into "FIGHTING." You may find that it takes some practice to learn to make good sentences this way, but it's well worth the effort.

Make It Clear

Your sentence should be short, sweet, and to the point. If you are using words like "could," "might," or "sometimes," you are not identifying the defining relationship between the words.

Make a more precise sentence

Sometimes the first sentence you make for an Analogy isn't sufficient to get the right answer. Have a look at the following example:

HELMET : CYCLIST ::

(A) baseball : catcher
(B) badge : sheriff
(C) goggles : welder
(D) brush : painter
(E) shoe : runner

Let's say that the first sentence that we made was "a helmet is worn by a cyclist." Check all five answer choices.

(A) Is a *baseball* worn by a *catcher*? No. Eliminate this choice.
(B) Is a *badge* worn by a *sheriff*? Yes.
(C) Are *goggles* worn by a *welder*? Yes.
(D) Is a *brush* worn by a *painter*? No. Eliminate this choice.
(E) Is a *shoe* worn by a *runner*? Yes.

We only eliminated two choices using our original sentence. Now what? Make a slightly more precise sentence. Keep the original sentence, but add one more detail to it. In this case, why does a cyclist wear a helmet? For protection. So our new sentence will be: "A helmet is worn by a cyclist *for protection*." Now check the three choices that are left.

(A) [already eliminated]
(B) Is a *badge* worn by a *sheriff* for protection? No. Eliminate.
(C) Are *goggles* worn by a *welder* for protection? Yes.
(D) [already eliminated]
(E) Is a *shoe* worn by a *runner* for protection? No. Eliminate.

Therefore the best answer is (C). Neat, huh?

RECYCLED RELATIONSHIPS

A few relationships appear over and over on the SAT. Learn them!

Part of/Kind of/Member of

PETAL : FLOWER

BAT : MAMMAL

ACTOR : CAST

A *petal* is part of a *flower*. A *bat* is a kind of *mammal*. An *actor* is a member of a *cast*.

Degree (larger/smaller degree of)

BREEZE : GALE

FAMISHED : HUNGRY

ARID : DRY

A *gale* is a strong *breeze*. *Famished* means very *hungry*. *Arid* means very *dry*.

Function (used to/serves to)

ORNAMENT : ADORN

SCISSORS : CUT

BUTTRESS : SUPPORT

An *ornament* is something used to *adorn*. *Scissors* are used to *cut*. A *buttress* is used to *support*.

Without/Lack of

AMORPHOUS : FORM

NAIVE : SOPHISTICATION

JUVENILE : MATURITY

Amorphous means without *form*. *Naive* is the lack of *sophistication*. Something or someone *juvenile* is lacking in *maturity*.

Now practice making sentences from the following word pairs:

a. GIGANTIC : LARGE :: _____

b. FADE : BRILLIANCE :: _____

c. DICTIONARY : WORDS :: _____

d. ADHESIVE : BIND :: _____

e. LETTERS : ALPHABET :: _____

f. ETERNAL : END :: _____

g. COTTAGE : HOUSE :: _____

h. VERSE : POEM :: _____

i. SYLLABUS : COURSE :: _____

j. ANTISEPTIC : SANITIZE :: _____

k. ZOOLOGIST : ANIMALS :: _____

a. *Gigantic* means very *large*.
b. *Fade* means to lose *brilliance*.
c. A *dictionary* contains *words*.
d. An *adhesive* is used to *bind*.
e. The *alphabet* is made up of *letters*.
f. *Eternal* means without *end*.
g. A *cottage* is a type of *house*.
h. A *verse* is a part of a *poem*.
i. A *syllabus* is the plan for a *course*.
j. An *antiseptic* is used to *sanitize*.
k. A *zoologist* studies *animals*.

Now try the following analogies:

6. MANSION : HOUSE ::
   (A) novelist : writer
   (B) leaf : tree
   (C) boulder : pebble
   (D) desert : sand
   (E) engine : automobile

7. HAMMER : CARPENTER ::
   (A) bread : baker
   (B) brush : painter
   (C) gun : farmer
   (D) courtroom : juror
   (E) secret : criminal

10. METEOROLOGY : WEATHER ::
    (A) philology : love
    (B) epistemology : disease
    (C) physiology : mind
    (D) demography : population
    (E) astrology : planets

Here's how to crack them

6. (C) A *mansion* is a large *house*, and a *boulder* is a large *pebble*.

7. (B) A *hammer* is a tool used by a *carpenter*, and a *brush* is a tool used by a *painter*.

10. (D) *Meteorology* is the study of *weather*, and *demography* is the study of *population*.

WHAT IF YOU DON'T KNOW BOTH WORDS?

Of course, what you've learned so far works only if you know both stem words. However, this will only be the case with some of the Analogies. After a while you'll probably come across some hard words that you don't know. But all is not lost! If you don't know the capitalized words, or don't know them well enough to make a sentence, you can *still* get the correct answer (or at least take a very good guess) by using Process of Elimination. There are two important ways to use POE on Analogies: Working Backward and Side of the Fence.

Working Backward: Step 1

The first step to Working Backward is to look at the five answer choices, one at a time. Ask yourself of each choice: Do these words have a clear relationship to one another? Many of the wrong answer choices will contain unrelated words. *If the words in an answer choice have no clear relationship, then they cannot possibly be the correct answer on an Analogy question.*

How do you determine if a pair of words has a relationship? Try to make a defining sentence with them. If you know the words but can't make a good sentence with them, then it's likely that they have no relationship to one another.

Some of the pairs may sound like they go well together, like "salt : pepper" or "push : fight." But can you really make a good sentence that defines one of these words in terms of the other? Is salt a *kind* of pepper? A very *big* pepper? No. These words have no direct relationship.

The same goes for "push : fight." You certainly *might* push someone in a fight, but is "fight" really part of the *meaning* of the word "push"? Does a "push" mean an action that starts a fight? Does a fight always involve a push? It might seem like these words go together well, but they have no clear relationship to each other.

If a pair of words is unrelated, cross it off. It can't be the answer to an Analogy. If you have to really stretch to make a good sentence, then it's likely that the pair of words is only weakly related, and you should strongly avoid that choice.

An exercise

Decide which of the following pairs have a clear relationship by making sentences with them. If you think a pair of words has no relationship, put an "X" next to that pair. If you don't know the words well enough to tell whether the words are related, leave it blank.

a. tadpole : frog _____

b. soporific : sleep _____

c. predicted : disaster _____

d. solitary : conviction _____

e. bias : prejudiced _____

f. enlarge : picture _____

Take Five (Seconds)

If you can't find the relationship between two words after looking at them for five seconds (assuming you know the meanings of both words), then you should probably assume that there is no relationship. ETS isn't interested in how imaginative you are. You won't score any points for coming up with a brilliant justification for an incorrect answer. ETS thinks that the Analogy section is fairly straightforward.

g. resolute : determined _____
h. verifiable : debate _____
i. vague : clarity _____
j. harden : shape _____
k. integrity : motion _____
l. stubborn : injury _____

a. A *tadpole* is a young *frog*.
b. *Soporific* means causing *sleep*.
c. No relationship.
d. No relationship.
e. *Prejudiced* means having a *bias*.
f. No relationship.
g. *Resolute* means very *determined*.
h. No relationship.
i. *Vague* means lacking in *clarity*.
j. No relationship.
k. No relationship.
l. No relationship.

Working Backward: Step 2

Sometimes you'll find that an answer-choice pair has a relationship, but not a relationship that could work with even one of the stem words. For instance, what if you saw the following Analogy:

9. [Some word you don't know] : MOTION ::

    (A) stubborn : injury
    (B) mansion : dwelling
    (C) kitten : cat
    (D) splinter : wood
    (E) [some words you don't know]

First, we know we can eliminate (A), because these words have no relationship. We can't make a defining sentence with these words.

But now let's look at choices (B), (C), and (D). These pairs have perfectly good defining sentences: A *mansion* is a type of *dwelling*, a *kitten* is a baby *cat*, and a *splinter* is a small bit of *wood*. However, these sentences can't work with the word "motion" since nothing is a type of motion in the way that a mansion is a type of dwelling, nothing is a baby motion like a kitten is a baby cat, and nothing is a small bit of motion like a splinter is a small bit of wood.

This means we can eliminate these choices, and the answer has to be (E), even if we don't know the meaning of the words in choice (E)!

The complete Working Backward chart

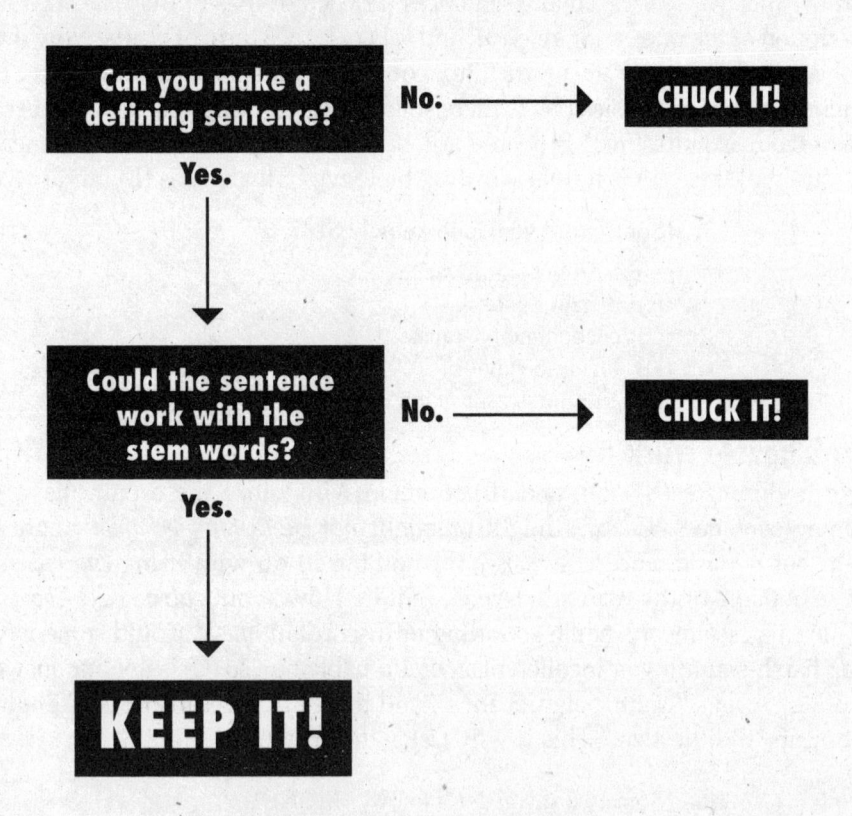

```
Can you make a defining sentence? --No.--> CHUCK IT!
         |
        Yes.
         ↓
Could the sentence work with the stem words? --No.--> CHUCK IT!
         |
        Yes.
         ↓
      KEEP IT!
```

So here are the two ways we can eliminate choices by Working Backward:

1. Check to see if each stem pair has a defining sentence. If it doesn't, we can cross it off.

2. Check to see if each stem pair has a sentence that could work with the stem words. If it doesn't, we can cross it off.

Then take your best guess from among the choices that are left.

Now let's see how this works in practice. Here are a few Analogies in which we've left out one of the words. (This is how we'll pretend you don't know one of the words.)

10. [Some word you don't know] : LIFE ::
    (A) zoology : oceans
    (B) explanation : event
    (C) meteorology : mind
    (D) philosophy : physics
    (E) botany : plants

Here's how to crack it

Let's first see which choices we can cross off for having no relationship at all. There's no defining sentence for choices (A), (C), or (D), so we can cross them off. *Zoology* has nothing to do with *oceans*; *meterology* deals with the weather, not with *mind*; and *philosophy* is about the meaning of life, not *physics*. So we're left with (B) and (E). We can make sentences for each of these: An *explanation* is a description of the reason for an *event*, and *botany* is the study of *plants*. Now if we try these sentences with the word "life," could they both still work? Let's try the sentence we had for choice (B). Is there some word that might mean "a description of the reason for life?" Probably not. But there might be a word that means the "study of life." (In fact, that word is "biology.") This makes (E) our answer.

9. [Some word you don't know] : SIZE ::

    (A) trifling : significance
    (B) distant : galaxy
    (C) cacophonous : music
    (D) lucid : behavior
    (E) enormous : sensation

Here's how to crack it

We can eliminate (B), (D), and (E) to begin with, since these pairs have no defining sentences. *Galaxies* might or might not be *distant*; *behavior* might or might not be *lucid*, and *sensations* have nothing to do with being *enormous*. If you're not sure of the words in (A), leave it in. How about choice (C)? *Cacophonous* in this case means harsh-sounding or discordant *music*. Could some word mean harsh-sounding or incoherent size? Probably not, so (C) is not our answer. "Trifling" means "of little significance," and there are several words in English that mean "of little size." This is why (A) is the answer.

10. [Some word you don't know] : MONEY ::

    (A) genius : ovation
    (B) altruism : selfishness
    (C) permission : impudence
    (D) surplus : theory
    (E) irritation : abrasive

Here's how to crack it

Genius has nothing to do with an *ovation*, so we can eliminate (A). Likewise, *surplus* has nothing to do with *theory*, so (D) can also be eliminated. If you're not sure of the words in (B) and (C), leave them in. A sentence for (E) might be "irritation is caused by an abrasive" but we can't say that something is "caused by money" so (E) probably isn't the answer. If that's as far as we get, we're down to two, and can make an intelligent guess between (B) and (C). The answer is (B), since the missing word was "destitution," which means the lack of money, and altruism is a lack of selfishness.

The point of this exercise is to show that you can often make a very intelligent guess, even if you don't know all the words in an Analogy. Don't forget, you'll probably never know every word on the PSAT. But good technique will help you make the most of the vocabulary you do have. Intelligent guessing leads to more points!

SIDE OF THE FENCE

If you don't know the capitalized words well enough to make a sentence with them, but you have some sense of their relationship, try to figure out if the two words are on the "same side of the fence" or on "opposite sides of the fence." If the words are similar in meaning, then the correct answer choice must also contain words similar in meaning. If the words are opposites, then the correct answer choice will be a pair of opposites as well. Take, for instance, the following problem:

37. THERMAL : HEAT ::

    (A) pure : polluted
    (B) parched : moisture
    (C) fictional : character
    (D) terrestrial : land
    (E) loyal : traitor

Here's how to crack it

You may have trouble making a sentence with the words *thermal* and *heat*. But you probably know that they are very close in meaning. The correct answer choice must also have a pair of words that are close in meaning. So we can cross off any words that have no relationship or that are opposites. How about (A)? *Pure* and *polluted* are opposites. So are *loyal* and *traitor*. The words in (C) don't really have a clear relationship. If you don't know the words in (B) or (D), leave them both in, and take a guess. In fact, the answer is (D).

Try one more:

38. ENLIGHTEN : IGNORANT ::

    (A) insist : successful
    (B) abridge : concise
    (C) free : constrained
    (D) insult : complimentary
    (E) cure : healthy

Here's how to crack it

This is a tough analogy. If you find it difficult to make a sentence between the words *enlighten* and *ignorant*, try Side of the Fence. Are these words similar or opposite in meaning? Opposite. So check the answer choices. The correct answer must also be a pair of opposites. The only real opposites here are choices (C) and (D). If you can't get any farther, you've still got a 50 percent chance of answering this question correctly. (By the way, the answer was (C). To *enlighten* means to make someone less *ignorant*. To *free* someone means to make that person less *constrained*.)

Side of the Fence exercise
Are the following words similar or opposite?

a. astonish : surprise _____

b. outcast : popularity _____

c. evil : malefactor _____

d. caricature : portrait _____

e. experienced : naïve _____

f. funny : hilarious _____

g. anarchist : authority _____

h. esoteric : comprehend _____

i. humid : moisture _____

j. extemporaneous : preparation _____

k. deliberate : forethought _____

a. Similar (*astonish* means to *surprise* a great deal)

b. Opposite (an *outcast* lacks *popularity*)

c. Similar (a *malefactor* intends/does *evil*)

d. Similar (a *caricature* is an exaggerated *portrait*)

e. Opposite (an *experienced* person is not *naïve*)

f. Similar (*hilarious* means very *funny*)

g. Opposite (an *anarchist* rejects all forms of *authority*)

h. Opposite (something *esoteric* is difficult to *comprehend*)

i. Similar (*humid* means the presence of a great deal of *moisture*)

j. Opposite (*extemporaneous* means without *preparation*)

k. Similar (something *deliberate* is performed with *forethought*)

SUMMARY ANALOGY DRILL

Now try the following Analogies. They range from medium to difficult, so if you can't make a good sentence, use Working Backward and Side of the Fence to make a good guess.

36. ENRAGED : ANGRY ::
    (A) ecstatic : happy
    (B) juvenile : nonchalant
    (C) dangerous : enticing
    (D) taciturn : verbose
    (E) jealous : greedy

Here's how to crack it

Enraged means very *angry*. If you aren't sure of the meaning of the words, you probably know that they are similar in meaning. The words in choices (B) and (C) have no clear relationship and can be eliminated. The words in choice (D) are opposite in meaning. The best choice is (A), since *ecstatic* means very *happy*.

37. HOT : INFERNAL ::
    (A) proud : sophisticated
    (B) modest : tactful
    (C) surprising : shocking
    (D) strange : habitual
    (E) trivial : important

Here's how to crack it

Infernal means very *hot*. Again, even if you can't make a sentence between the two words, they are very similar in meaning. Choices (A) and (D) have no clear relationship, and the words in choice (E) are opposite in meaning. Since *shocking* means very *surprising*, the best choice is (C).

38. CHASTISE : CRITICIZE ::
    (A) exculpate : accuse
    (B) intensify : placate
    (C) alert : liberate
    (D) rebuke : rebuff
    (E) doubt : gainsay

Here's how to crack it

To *chastise* means to *criticize* very severely. These words are similar in meaning, so we can eliminate choices (A) and (B), which are opposites. Choices (C) and (E) have no clear relationship, so the best choice is (D).

ANALOGIES SUMMARY

1. **If you know both of the capitalized words, make a defining sentence.**
   See which of the choices fits the same sentence. Start with the most simple, straightforward sentence possible. If necessary, make the sentence more precise until you find which choice is the best match.

2. **If you don't know one of the capitalized words, Work Backward.**

   a. See which of the choices have good relationships by making defining sentences for the words in the answer choices. If you are sure that the words in a given answer choice have no relationship, eliminate that choice.

b. For each answer choice for which you can make a sentence, Work Backward to see if that sentence could work with the capitalized words. If not, eliminate that choice.

c. If you don't know whether the words in a choice are related, leave it in. It *could* be right.

3. **If you can't make a sentence, but you think that the two words are related, use Side of the Fence.** If the capitalized words are similar, the correct answer will contain similar words. If the capitalized words are opposite, the correct answer must be a pair of opposites.

4. **If you don't know either of the capitalized words, eliminate unrelated answer choice pairs and guess.**

7
Critical Reading

WHAT IS CRITICAL READING?

Critical Reading (which is commonly called "Reading Comprehension") consists of a passage or two, followed by a number of multiple-choice questions. These questions are supposed to measure how well you understood what you read. In reality, they really measure how quickly you can find information in the passage and paraphrase that information.

THE INSTRUCTIONS

Here are the directions as you will see them on the test:

> The passage below is followed by questions based on its content. Answer the questions on the basis of what is <u>stated</u> or <u>implied</u> in the passage and in any introductory material that may be provided.

ORDER OF DIFFICULTY

Critical Reading questions will appear on both Verbal sections of the PSAT. They will be questions 12–25 on Section 1 and questions 41–52 on Section 3. On any given section, you might see one long passage, two shorter passages, or a "dual passage." If you have two shorter passages, and you feel short on time, pick the one you feel more comfortable with.

Unlike the other Verbal questions, the questions on Critical Reading are *not* arranged in order of difficulty. Instead, as we'll see, certain types of questions (the Line Reference, Lead Word, and Vocab-in-Context questions) are easier than others, and you should do those easier questions first.

APPROACHING CRITICAL READING

The problem with Critical Reading is, of course, that these passages are boring, dense, brutish, and long. How can you get the most points in the least amount of time, and in the most reliable way? It's not by reading the whole passage carefully. It's by knowing *where to find the answers quickly*, and then finding *the choice that restates what is said in the passage.*

You might think that this means that you need to read the passage carefully, understand it thoroughly, or make complex inferences from the information contained in the passage. You don't.

Think of Critical Reading as a treasure hunt: All the answers to the questions *are buried somewhere in the passage.* All you've got to do is *find* them.

The Fact Book

Somebody once asked notorious thief Willie Sutton why he robbed banks. "Because that's where the money is," he replied. While cracking Critical Reading is safer and slightly more productive than larceny, the same principle applies: Concentrate on the questions and answer choices, because that's where the points are. The passage is just a place for ETS to stash facts and details. You'll find them when you need to. What's the point of memorizing all 67 pesky details about plankton if ETS only asks you about 12?

THINK OF THE PASSAGE AS AN ENCYCLOPEDIA

If someone were to give you a ten-volume encyclopedia and ask you the year of Pasteur's death, would you begin reading at the As and work all the way through to the Ps until you found Pasteur? Of course not. You'd go right to the entry on Pasteur and read only the five or six lines that you needed to. That's how to approach Critical Reading questions.

YOUR TREASURE HUNT

Here are the steps to finding your answers in the most efficient way:

1. Read the "blurb" (the introductory material).
2. Go to the questions. Do the Specific questions first and the General questions later.
3. Put the question in your own words so you know exactly what you're being asked.
4. Find the answer to the question in the passage and put your finger on it.
5. Pick the answer choice that comes closest to the answer that you found in the passage. Use POE!
6. Always use common sense and avoid extremes.

STEP 1: READ THE BLURB

Every passage begins with a short 3–4-line introduction, in italics, which will give you a little background about the passage. Read it! You'll find a lot of information about the main idea of the passage. (Often, the blurb will be enough to answer any main point questions you find.)

But after reading the blurb, don't bother reading the passage. Instead, go right to the questions.

STEP 2: GO TO THE QUESTIONS

Let's face it. There's more information in the passage than you could possibly memorize, and you actually only need to read the parts of it that you're asked about. So it's much smarter to go right to the questions, and then go back to the passage and simply read what you need.

Remember that we said that the questions were not arranged in any order of difficulty? Well, instead, they are a mix of questions, some of which are harder and some of which are easier. We group these questions into three kinds:

Specific Questions (the easiest)

General Questions (usually a little harder)

Weird Questions (the hardest—or at least the longest)

Passage Types

Critical Reading passages come from four broad subject areas:

1. Science: discoveries, controversies, or other topics in physics, chemistry, astronomy, biology, medicine, botany, zoology, and the other sciences.

2. Humanities: excerpts from essays about art, literature, music, philosophy, or folklore; discussions of artists, novelists, or historical figures.

3. Social sciences: topics in politics, economics, sociology, or history.

4. Narrative: usually excerpts from novels, short stories, or humorous essays. (We have yet to see a poem on the PSAT.)

ETS usually includes a passage involving a historically overlooked community or social group. This "ethnic" passage, as we call it, is usually either a social science or humanities passage.

Your best plan is to do the Specific questions first, then the general questions, and save the Weird ones for last.

Specific questions

Almost every question on Critical Reading will be a Specific question. That is, it will ask you for a fact from a particular part of the passage. Some questions give you a specific line number, some give you a key concept (what we call Lead Words), and some ask you for the definition of a word.

To answer any Specific question, the method is the same: Hunt for the answer in the passage using the clues in the question, read that area of the passage to find the answer to the question, and then pick the answer choice that is the *best paraphrase of what the passage says*.

The most common kinds of Specific questions are **Line Number**, **Lead Word**, and **Vocabulary-in-Context** questions.

Line Number questions are just like they sound—they're questions that contain references to certain lines in the passage. Here are some examples of Line Number questions:

> According to lines 8–10, why are malamutes stronger than huskies?

> The author mentions Milton in the second paragraph (lines 15–20) in order to

> The author quotes Dr. Silas saying 'The findings were surprising' (lines 18–22) to show

Lead Word questions contain a word or phrase that can be located easily and quickly in the passage. Examples of Lead Word questions include:

> The author introduces the Iroquois in order to show

> The Brooklyn Bridge is cited by the author to support the claim that

> According to the passage, Type II diabetes is characterized by

Vocab-in-Context questions ask you for the meaning of a word in the passage. Here's what a Vocab-in-Context question looks like:

> The word 'domestic' (line 43) most nearly means

One thing to watch out for in Vocab-in-Context questions is that ETS often picks words that have more than one meaning, and the words are usually not used in their ordinary sense.

Vocabulary in Context: The Student's Friend

Since VIC questions are little more than Sentence Completions, you really don't have to find the main idea of the passage or anything else in order to answer them. Even if you don't plan to answer every Critical Reading question, you should still try every VIC question. They're short, predictable, and don't require you to read very much. And they earn you the same points you'd earn answering longer, more complicated questions.

General questions
General questions ask about the main idea of the passage. There will usually be one, or perhaps two, General questions per passage. Here are some examples of General questions:

> Which of the following best expresses the main idea of the passage?
>
> Which of the following titles would be most appropriate for this passage?
>
> The author's primary purpose in writing this passage is to

Weird questions
The "Weird" questions are the hardest questions, and they should be saved for last.
Examples of Weird questions are:

> According to the passage, all of the following statements about Shakespeare are true EXCEPT
>
> Which of the following is NOT mentioned as a cause of the Great Depression?

In the Form of a Question
One way ETS confuses test-takers is by replacing questions with incomplete sentences: "The primary purpose of the passage is…" instead of "What is the primary purpose of the passage?" Many students find it easier to understand what ETS is driving at if they rephrase those incomplete sentences as questions beginning with "What" or "Why." "What" questions ask for things (facts, ideas). "Why" questions ask for reasons.

STEPS 3 AND 4: PUT THE QUESTION INTO YOUR OWN WORDS, THEN FIND THE ANSWER IN THE PASSAGE AND PUT YOUR FINGER TO IT

Finding the answers to Specific questions
The rule to remember for Specific questions is: The answer to every Specific question is somewhere in the passage. It's there, in black and white. You never have to guess, extrapolate, or try to imagine what the answer might be. You've just got to locate it among all the other facts in the passage. The difficulty is finding the answer as quickly as possible.

For **Line Number questions:** If the question gives you a line reference, go back to the passage and read those lines in context. This means reading the area in which those lines are found, often from about 5 lines before the line reference, to 5 lines following the line reference. The answer to the question will almost always be in this part of the passage. Find the answer, and put your finger on it.

Here's an example:

> We are told that the trouble with Modern Man is that he has been trying to detach himself from nature. He sits in the topmost tiers of polymer, glass,
> *Line* and steel, dangling his pulsing legs, surveying at a
> 5 distance the writhing life of the planet. In this scenario, Man comes on as a stupendous lethal force, and the Earth is pictured as something delicate, like rising bubbles at the surface of a country pond, or flights of fragile birds.
> 10 But it is illusion to think that there is anything fragile about the life of the Earth; surely this is the toughest membrane imaginable in the universe, opaque to probability, impermeable to death.

21. The author mentions the "flights of fragile birds" (line 9) in order to

(A) stress the interconnectedness of all species
(B) contrast the natural world with the world of human intervention
(C) suggest that human beings are not inherently more important than any other life form
(D) provide an example of a way in which the Earth is often represented
(E) prove that nature is in little danger from human activities

They Don't Care What You Know

More than one million students take the PSAT every year. They can't all have studied the same subjects, so ETS can't expect you to know anything it hasn't told you. This is important to remember on Specific questions. All you have to do is find something the passage already states.

Here's how to crack it

This question gives us a line reference (line 9), so let's go to that part of the passage and read that line in context. The line says that the "flights of fragile birds" is one of the ways that "the Earth is pictured." This has to be our answer. So now we just need to find a paraphrase of this idea: that this is one way the Earth is pictured. Choice (A), the interconnectedness of species, is definitely not a paraphrase of this idea. While the passage does mention a contrast between humans and nature, this is not a paraphrase of the idea that "flights of fragile birds" is one way that "the Earth is pictured." This means we can eliminate (B). Choice (C) brings in ideas that are not mentioned at all in the passage, so we can cross it off as well. But choice (D) does restate the idea that the flight of birds is a way that the Earth is pictured. That makes (D) our answer.

Likewise, for **Lead Word** questions, you'll almost always be able to quickly spot where in the passage that lead word or phrase is discussed. If you're not certain where that lead word is mentioned, skim through the passage until you find it. Reread these lines in context to find the answer to your question.

Have a look at this example:

> Isolated at Versailles at an early stage by his own pride, the machinations of a woman and a few priests and courtiers, Louis neither knew nor cared that his age was becoming the Age of Enlightenment: of Reason, of Science, and of Liberty. From first to last, he refused to recognize the power of Holland, the nature of England, or the birth of an embryo German nation.
>
> And yet he and his colleagues left behind them a France that was territorially larger, militarily better defended, with a more effective administration, and to a large extent pacified. And although he neglected it and often fought against it, there was a time when he built up and maintained what was to be, for a long time to come, the real greatness of France.

19. It can be inferred that Louis XIV's attitude toward the Age of Enlightenment was

  (A) enthusiastic
  (B) curious
  (C) skeptical
  (D) respected
  (E) uninterested

> **Cross It Off**
>
> On CR questions, it is very likely that you may need to read a few of the answer choices more than once. To avoid confusion, be sure you cross off each answer entirely when you eliminate something. That way, if you have two or three choices you are considering, you can easily tell which choices are left in the running and which you have eliminated.

Here's how to crack it

The lead word "Age of Enlightenment" should be pretty easy to find in the passage. Once we've found it, let's read what it says. In the portion of the passage above, we find that Louis "neither knew nor cared that his age was becoming the Age of Enlightenment." That is, he was not at all interested in the Enlightenment. Now we need to look for a paraphrase, and choice (E) seems to be the closest.

For **Vocab-in-Context** questions: Treat these questions like Sentence Completion questions. Go back to the sentence in the passage where the word occurs, and put your finger over it. Then read the sentence, and pick your own word to put in its place. This will give you an idea of what the word should mean. (Be careful, since the word in question may not be used according to its ordinary meaning!)

Try this one:

> 35 While the revolution in art came from the artist's desire for freedom, the source of the separation of man and art lies in the credo which electrified all artists shortly after the turn of the 19th century as is summed up in the "Art for art's sake" slogan coined
> 40 by Theophile Gautier and Charles Baudelaire.

18. The word "coined" in line 39 most nearly means

  (A) stamped
  (B) invented
  (C) financed
  (D) minted
  (E) shaped

Here's how to crack it

Put your finger over the word "coined" in the paragraph above. Now let's pretend we're solving a Sentence Completion question. What word would we put into this sentence? Probably a word like "made up" or "created." What choice comes closest to this idea? (B) does.

Finding the answers to General questions

For General questions: If you save these for last, the process of answering the Specific questions will probably have given you all the information you need to answer any General questions. In addition, don't forget to read the blurb, which can prove extremely useful in answering General questions.

The following passage is an analysis of the rule of Louis XIV, who was the king of France during the Age of Enlightenment from 1643–1715.

20. The author's primary purpose is to
    (A) criticize a ruler who has been excessively praised by historians
    (B) reveal facts about Louis XIV's personal life that eventually led to his downfall
    (C) celebrate and praise the reign of a famous French monarch, a reign that inevitably ended in civil war
    (D) discuss the accomplishments and shortcomings of a French king in the context of his time
    (E) explain the historical origins of the Age of Enlightenment

Here's how to crack it

If we use our heads, we can get this one right by reading the blurb alone. The blurb makes it clear that this passage is about the accomplishments of the king of France and his relationship to his era. Choice (E) doesn't mention the king, so it's not on the topic, and we can eliminate it. The blurb doesn't sound like the passage is critical, nor does it mention the king's personal life, so choices (A) and (B) don't sound very plausible. Choice (C) is tempting, but the word "inevitably" is much too strong to be correct. Choice (D) is a nice choice, which could easily be describing the same passage that the blurb describes. That makes (D) our answer.

Finding the answers to Weird questions

For most of the Weird questions (the EXCEPT/LEAST/NOT or I/II/III questions) you'll actually have to look at four or five places in the passage to find the answers. Approach these questions the same way you would approach Specific questions, but for EXCEPT/LEAST/NOT questions you'll have to find the four details in the answer choices that *are* mentioned in the passage and eliminate them. The answer choice that is NOT mentioned in the passage will be the answer.

> **EXCEPT...NOT!**
> ETS's EXCEPT/LEAST/NOT questions are big time-wasters. Think about it: You're really answering four questions for the price of one. Most of these questions expect you to find four pieces of information in the passage, but only reward you with one measly point. Do them last, if at all.

Step 5: Pick the Answer Choice that Comes Closest to the Answer that You Found in the Passage. Use POE!

Once you've found the answer in the passage, it's time to figure out which answer choice is the best one. On Critical Reading, assume that you'll answer the questions by POE. Why? Often, none of the choices are very good. In fact, they may all stink. But your job is to find the one that stinks the least. The most reliable way to do this is to eliminate the ones that stink the most.

How do you find the best answer for **Specific questions**? *Paraphrase, paraphrase, paraphrase.* Look for a choice that paraphrases (restates) what the passage actually says. The test writers at ETS aren't very clever: Every correct answer is simply a restatement of something that is stated in the passage. If you can honestly say that an answer choice says the same thing as the answer you found in the passage, then you should feel confident picking that answer. If you have to work hard to justify an answer, it probably isn't correct.

For **General questions**, look for a choice that best restates the idea of the passage as a whole. The two biggest reasons why incorrect choices are incorrect are:

- Too specific
- Impossible to accomplish

Choices that are only discussed in one part of the passage are too specific to be the main point. The main point of a passage is something that relates to the passage as a whole. Also, use common sense: Any choice that is impossible to accomplish in a couple of paragraphs (such as "prove that comets killed the dinosaurs") can't be the answer to a General question.

Step 6: Use Common Sense and Avoid Extremes

ETS does not pick extreme or offensive passages to put on its tests. If you see an answer choice that's very extreme (extreme choices sometimes use words such as *must*, *always*, *only*, *every*) or potentially very offensive to a certain class of people, eliminate it.

Here are some examples of choices that you can eliminate:

- Judges deliberately undermine the constitution
- Doctors are the only people who can cure malaria
- It was entirely misleading
- Disparage the narrow-mindedness of modern research
- All his beliefs about his parents were wrong

Buzzwords

Avoid answer choices that contain the following words:

must
always
impossible
never
cannot
each
every
totally
all
solely
only

Likewise, for questions that ask you about the author's attitude or tone, eliminate extremes, such as:

- sarcasm
- ridicule
- repugnance
- condemnation

Why is avoiding extremes so important on Critical Reading?

On Critical Reading questions, it's almost always easier to find the correct answer by eliminating the four wrong ones—the ones that *weren't* stated in the passage. In fact, once you get good at POE on Reading Comprehension questions, you'll find that you can eliminate a lot of choices even without reading the passage. How?

Remember what we said about the test writers back at the beginning of the book? The folks at ETS are ordinary people, with a generally positive outlook on things. While they might be critical of an individual or viewpoint, they will never be insulting or offensive, especially to large groups of people. For this reason, they won't write correct answers that are generally offensive to anyone.

Moreover, the test writers want to have correct answers that can be justified based on what is stated in a passage, so they need to stick to answers that could reasonably be defended on the basis of what a passage says. For this reason, they will always avoid answers that are too extreme or that express strong emotions. Does *everyone* think that Shakespeare was the *greatest* English writer? No, and no reasonable person would make such a claim. At least nobody whose books would be used as reading passages on the PSAT.

Here are some examples of extreme answer choices:

(A) Everyone believes that Shakespeare was the greatest writer ever.
(B) Nineteenth-century scientists were foolish and ignorant to believe in the existence of Ether.

These choices won't be the correct answer on the PSAT because it's too easy to dispute them—it would only take one person who didn't like Shakespeare to prove this answer wrong. Were *all* scientists of the nineteenth century *ignorant*? No. You could eliminate this answer choice because it's extreme and potentially offensive.

If you see answer choices such as these, you can cross them off. They won't be the right answer. Now you can choose more intelligently from the answer choices that are left. If nothing else, you've got a better guess.

Try the following two questions. Even without reading the passage, what could you eliminate?

Choose Vague

The vague choice is usually correct. And the specific choice is usually incorrect. So when you are trying to decide between two choices, both of which seem good, the more specific choice will be much easier to poke holes in. And a choice that is easier to poke holes in will most likely be the wrong choice.

24. It can be inferred that contemporary English poetry is similar to Japanese poetry because

(A) both employ devices like pillow and pivot words
(B) both favor the use of imagery over direct statement
(C) both view the traditionalist as overly concerned with aestheticism
(D) neither uses any form of rhetoric
(E) neither is related to contemporary life or literature

25. The passage suggests that Japanese poetry

(A) is used to make a point more than to create a mood
(B) uses imagery more than puns or other types of word play
(C) is expressed in abstract symbols that make it impossible for students to understand
(D) tends to be shorter and more dense than other types of poetry
(E) is preferable to English poetry because it requires more interpretation on the part of the reader

For question 24, choices (D) and (E) are not the sorts of answers that would be correct. Do you really think that English poetry doesn't use *any* rhetorical devices? That seems unlikely, so we can eliminate (D). Would any poetry be entirely unrelated to everyday life? That's also pretty extreme. So (E) can be crossed off as well.

For question 25, we can safely cross off choices (C) and (E). (C) is extreme, and (E) borders on saying that one culture is better than another—something that the test writers just won't do. The other answers are nice, boring, harmless choices that might be correct.

DUAL PASSAGE

One section of your PSAT will probably contain a "dual passage," that is, two passages that have differing viewpoints on a common theme. Following the passage will be some questions that are relevant to only one passage or the other, and some questions that ask you to compare the two passages. These comparison questions are usually more difficult; therefore the best strategy is:

1. Read the blurb on Passage 1
2. Answer the questions on Passage 1
3. Read the blurb for Passage 2
4. Answer the questions for Passage 2
5. Answer any questions that ask you to compare the two passages

This way, you'll save the hardest problems for last—and if you run out of time, you can *skip them entirely*.

Try your hand at the following passage:

John Dewey was an American educator and thinker. In the following excerpt from <u>Democracy and Education</u>, he explains why education is necessary for human beings.

The most notable distinction between living and inanimate things is that the former maintain themselves by renewal. A stone when struck resists. If its resistance is greater than the force of the blow struck, it remains outwardly unchanged. Otherwise, it is shattered into smaller bits. Never does the stone attempt to react in such a way that it may maintain itself against the blow, much less so as to render the blow a contributing factor to its own continued action. While the living thing may easily be crushed by superior force, it nonetheless tries to turn the energies which act upon it into means of its own further existence. If it cannot do so, it does not just split into smaller pieces (at least in the higher forms of life), but loses its identity as a living thing. As long as it endures, the living thing struggles to use surrounding energies in its own behalf. It uses light, air, moisture, and the material of soil. Life is a self-renewing process through action upon the environment.

With the renewal of physical existence goes, in the case of human beings, the recreation of beliefs, ideals, hopes, happiness, misery, and practices. The continuity of any experience, through renewing of the social group, is a literal fact. Education, in its broadest sense, is the means of this social continuity of life. Every one of the constituent elements of a social group, in a modern city as in a savage tribe, is born immature, helpless, without language, beliefs, ideas, or social standards. Each individual, each unit who is the carrier of the life-experience of his group, in time passes away. Yet the life of the group goes on.

The primary ineluctable facts of the birth and death of each one of the constituent members in a social group determine the necessity of education. Even in a savage tribe, the achievements of adults are far beyond what the immature members would be capable of if left to themselves. With the growth of civilization, the gap between the original capacities of the immature and the standards and customs of the elders increases. Mere physical growing up, mere mastery of the bare necessities of subsistence will not suffice to reproduce the life of the group. Deliberate effort and the taking of thoughtful pains are required. Beings who are born not only unaware of, but quite indifferent to, the aims and habits of their social group have to be rendered cognizant of them and actively interested. Education, and education alone, spans the gap.

Society exists through a process of transmission quite as much as biological life. Without this communication of ideals, hopes, expectations, standards, opinions, from those members of society who are passing out of the group life to those who are coming into it, social life could not survive. If the members who compose a society lived on continuously, they might educate the newborn members, but it would be a task directed by personal interest rather than social need. Now it is a work of necessity. If a plague carried off the members of a society all at once, it is obvious that the group would be permanently done for. Yet the death of each of its constituent members is as certain as if an epidemic took them all at once. But the graded difference in age, the fact that some are born as some die, makes possible through transmission of ideas and practices the constant reweaving of the social fabric. Yet this renewal is not automatic. Unless pains are taken to see that genuine and thorough transmission takes place, the most civilized group will relapse into barbarism and then into savagery.

13. The author discusses a stone (lines 3–11) in order to explain
    (A) the forces necessary to destroy rock
    (B) the difference between living and nonliving beings
    (C) why living things cannot be split into pieces
    (D) why living things are easier to crush than stones
    (E) the nutritional requirements for life

Here's how to crack it

This is a Line Number question, so we know where we should look to find the answer. The stone is mentioned here to illustrate something. What is it here to illustrate? Read about five lines above (in this case, from the beginning of the passage) to about five lines below the example, and look for an idea that the case of the stone is supporting. The answer is in the first line: The "distinction between living and inanimate things is that the former maintain themselves by renewal." Which choice paraphrases this line? (B) does.

14. The primary purpose of the passage is to
    (A) argue that we should spend more money on public schools
    (B) explain why the author wants to be a teacher
    (C) prove that humans would die without education
    (D) recount the author's own experience as a student
    (E) support the claim that good education is essential for human beings

Here's how to crack it

Since this is a General Question, save it for last. Not only is the blurb a good clue to the main point, but notice that many of the answer choices revolve around the question of education. Choice (A) might be something that the author believes, but *public schools* are never mentioned in the passage. (C) is simply too big a task to be accomplished in a short passage. Choices (B) and (D) are too personal; the author never discusses his own memories or wishes. Therefore the best choice is (E).

15. The word "ineluctable" as used in line 37 most nearly means
    (A) unhappy
    (B) absurd
    (C) unchangeable
    (D) indifferent
    (E) proven

Here's how to crack it

This is a Vocab-in-Context question. Cross off the word "ineluctable" in line 37, reread the line, and pick your own word to go in the blank. The word that fills the blank must be something like "unavoidable" or "certain." Which choice comes closest in meaning? Choice (C) does.

16. According to the passage, the "necessity of education" (lines 39–40) is based on the fact that humans

    (A) have mothers and fathers
    (B) have larger brains than any other animal
    (C) are more advanced than other animals
    (D) are mortal
    (E) are born unable to feed themselves

Here's how to crack it
Reread lines 39–40 in context, and see what the passage says. It states, "the primary ineluctable facts of the birth and death of each one of the constituent members in a social group determine the necessity of education." This says that education is required because humans are born and die. Now we need to look for a paraphrase of this line. The fact that humans are born and die—that is, because they are mortal—explains the necessity of education. So the answer is (D).

17. The author implies in the last paragraph that without a concerted effort to educate the young, humans

    (A) will become extinct
    (B) may return to a more savage lifestyle
    (C) would not be as happy as those with education
    (D) will become more like stones
    (E) may have poorly behaved children

Here's how to crack it
In the very last line of the passage, the author claims, "unless pains are taken to see that genuine and thorough transmission takes place, the most civilized group will relapse into barbarism and then into savagery." That is to say that without education, people will become barbarians again. What choice paraphrases this line? (B) does.

CRITICAL READING SUMMARY

1. Read the "blurb" (the introductory material).

2. Go to the questions. Do the Specific questions first and the General questions later.

3. Put the question into your own words, so you know exactly what you're being asked.

4. Find the answer to the question in the passage, and put your finger on it.

5. Pick the answer choice that comes closest to the answer that you found in the passage. Use POE!

6. Always use common sense and avoid extremes.

8

Math Basics

HOW TO THINK ABOUT PSAT MATH

One of the more humiliating aspects of the PSAT (and the same applies to its big brother, the SAT) is that ETS claims that the Math section only tests sixth- to ninth-grade math. While this may be technically true—you'll see no trigonometry or calculus, only concepts that you'll have learned in algebra and geometry—what they don't tell you is that they will use these concepts in very sneaky ways. Often you'll see very basic concepts that are used in ways you've never seen or been taught before, and that makes PSAT math much trickier than the math you're probably used to.

So what do you need to do? There are three important steps:

1. **Know the basic content.** Obviously you do need to know the basics of arithmetic, algebra, and geometry, and know this stuff cold. We'll cover what you need to know in this chapter.

2. **Learn some PSAT-specific problem-solving skills.** Since these basic concepts appear in ways you're probably not used to from math class, you need to prepare yourself with a set of test-specific problem-solving skills designed to help you solve PSAT math problems. We'll cover the most important ones in the next chapter.

3. **Have a sound overall testing strategy.** This means knowing the order of difficulty of questions, and having a plan to pace yourself to get the maximum number of points in the time allotted. Be sure to read carefully the material in Chapter 4, to make sure you're using the strategy that will get you the greatest number of points in the time you have.

ORDER OF DIFFICULTY

The Math sections on the PSAT are Sections 2 and 4. Section 2 contains 20 multiple-choice Problem Solving questions. Section 4 is divided into Quantitative Comparison and Grid-In problem types. Note that the order of difficulty goes from easy to hard within each of these types—don't forget that questions 33–35 are easy, and questions 36–38 are medium. This means that if you're going to skip some problems, it's likely that you'll want to skip some of the questions numbered 29–32 and 39–40.

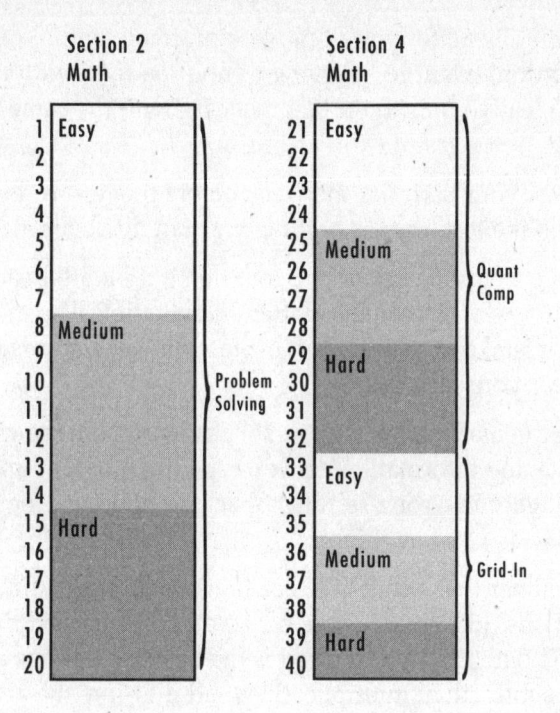

Section 2:
Questions 1–7: Easy Problem Solving
Questions 8–14: Medium Problem Solving
Questions 15–20: Hard Problem Solving

Section 4:
Questions 21–24: Easy Quant Comp
Questions 25–28: Medium Quant Comp
Questions 29–32: Hard Quant Comp
Questions 33–35: Easy Grid-Ins
Questions 36–38: Medium Grid-Ins
Questions 39–40: Hard Grid-Ins

USING YOUR CALCULATOR

You are allowed to use a calculator on the PSAT, and you should definitely do so. You can use any graphing, scientific, or plain old four-function calculator, provided that it doesn't have a keyboard, a tape printout, or make any funny bleeping noises during the test. (This tends to annoy proctors, as well as your fellow testers.)

There are a few simple rules to remember when dealing with your calculator:

1. Use the calculator you're most comfortable with. You definitely don't want to be trying to find the right button on test day. Ideally you should be practicing with the same calculator you'll use on test day.

2. Change your batteries the week before the test. If they run out during the test, there's nothing you can do about it.

3. Be sure to hit the "clear" or "on/off" button after each calculation to reset the calculator after an operation. The most common mistake to make when using your calculator is to forget to clear your last result.

4. Your calculator is very good at calculating, but watch out for mis-keying information. (If you type the wrong numbers in, you'll get the wrong result.) Check each number on the display as you key it in.

5. Remember that, while it's nice to have all those funky scientific functions (like sine, cosine, etc.), you'll never need them on the PSAT. The most you'll need is the basic operations of addition, subtraction, multiplication, and division; the ability to convert fractions to decimals and vice versa; and the ability to do square roots and exponents.

6. Then, there's one really big, important rule whenever you think about using your calculator:

    A calculator can't think, it can only calculate.

What does this mean? It means that a calculator can't think through a problem for you. You have to do the work of understanding and setting up the problem correctly to make sure you know what the right calculation will be to get the answer. Only then can you use the calculator to calculate the answer. A calculator can't replace good problem-solving skills. It can only help make sure that you do basic calculations correctly.

Also, your calculator can't help you set up a problem in the way pencil and paper can. You should always be sure to set up your problem in your test booklet; writing it down is still the best method—this will help you catch any errors you might make and allow you to pick up where you left off if you lose focus.

In fact, ETS will often create a problem that will tempt you into using your calculator when using your calculator may be a waste of time. There is often a shortcut or a simple manipulation that will get you the answer without needing to calculate at all. So be sure you have worked the problem through, and really need to do a calculation, before you break out your calculator.

DEFINITIONS

One of the reasons that good math students often don't get the credit they deserve on the PSAT is that they've forgotten one or more of these definitions. Be sure you know these cold!

Integers are numbers that have no fractional or decimal parts. Examples of integers are –10, –3, –2, –1, 0, 1, 2, 3, 10, 23, and 50. Zero is an integer. What kinds of numbers are *not* integers? 2.3, $\frac{1}{2}$, .6666, and so on.

Positive numbers are numbers larger than zero. Zero itself is *not* positive. Examples of positive numbers are $\frac{1}{2}$, 1, 2.33, and 5.

Negative numbers are numbers less than zero. Zero itself is *not* negative. Examples of negative numbers are $-\frac{1}{2}$, –1, –2.33, and –5.

Even numbers are integers that can be divided by 2 with no remainder. Examples of even numbers are –4, –2, 0, 2, 4, and 6. Note that zero *is* even (even though it is neither positive nor negative!).

Odd numbers are integers that cannot be divided by 2 evenly. Examples of odd numbers are –3, –1, 1, 3, 5, and 7.

Factors of 12 are the numbers that 12 can be divided by. The easiest way to find them is in pairs. 12 can be written as 1×12, 2×6, or 3×4. Therefore 12 can be divided by 1, 2, 3, 4, 6, and 12. These are the factors of 12.

Multiples of 12 are the numbers that can be divided by 12. The easiest way to find these numbers is to count up by 12. $12 \times 1 = 12$; $12 \times 2 = 24$; $12 \times 3 = 36$.... So the first three positive multiples of 12 are 12, 24, and 36. However, we can keep counting up by 12 forever: 12, 24, 36, 48, 60, 72, 84... *all* of these numbers are multiples of 12.

[Hint: if you tend to confuse factors and multiples, remember this tip: Factors are Few, Multiples are Many. There are only a few factors for any given number. But there is always an infinite number of multiples!]

Prime numbers are numbers that can be divided only by 1 and themselves. The first six prime numbers are 2, 3, 5, 7, 11, and 13. Note that 0 and 1 are *not* prime, and that 2 is the only even prime number.

Distinct numbers are different numbers. For example, how many distinct numbers are there in the set {2, 5, 2, 6, 5, 7}? There are only four distinct numbers in this set: 2, 5, 6, and 7.

A **digit** is a figure from 0 through 9 that holds a place. For instance, the number 345.862 is composed of six digits. The digit 3 is in the *hundreds* place, the digit 4 is in the *tens* place, and the digit 5 is in the *units* place. The digit 8 is in the *tenths* place, the digit 6 is in the *hundredths* place, and the digit 2 is in the *thousandths* place.

Consecutive numbers are numbers that are "in a row." 4, 5, and 6 are consecutive integers; 6, 8, and 10 are consecutive *even* integers.

Divisible means can be divided with no remainder. 6 is divisible by 3, but 6 is not divisible by 5.

Negative Land

Think of integers as steps on a staircase leading up from the cellar (the negatives), through a doorway (zero), and above the ground (the positives). Five steps down (–5) is farther below ground than four steps down (–4) because you're one step farther away from the cellar door (0). Integers are like stairs because when climbing stairs, you can't use a fraction of a step.

Zero Is:
- an integer
- not positive
- not negative
- even
- not prime

The **remainder** is what is left over after you divide. For example, when you divide 18 by 8, there is a remainder of 2.

A **sum** is the result of addition.

A **difference** is the result of subtraction.

A **product** is the result of multiplication.

A **quotient** is the result of division.

FINDING FACTORS

The easiest way to find the complete list of the factors of a number is to begin trying all the integers beginning with 1, and see which of the integers go into that number. For instance, let's find the factors of 36.

Factor List:
Does 1 go into 36? Yes, 1 times 36.
Does 2 go into 36? Yes, 2 times 18.
Does 3 go into 36? Yes, 3 times 12.
Does 4 go into 36? Yes, 4 times 9.
Does 5 go into 36? No.
Does 6 go into 36? Yes, 6 times 6.

Once you get to an integer that you've already seen in the factor list (in this case, 6) you know you're finished. So the factors of 36 are 1, 2, 3, 4, 6, 9, 12, 18, and 36.

Let's try this once more. What are all the factors of 40?

Does 1 go into 40? Yes, 1 times 40.
Does 2 go into 40? Yes, 2 times 20.
Does 3 go into 40? No.
Does 4 go into 40? Yes, 4 times 10.
Does 5 go into 40? Yes, 5 times 8.
Does 6 go into 40? No.
Does 7 go into 40? No.

We don't have to try 8, since the number 8 has already appeared in our list of factors. So the factors of 40 are 1, 2, 4, 5, 8, 10, 20, and 40.

MANAGING MULTIPLES

One type of question you'll see frequently on the PSAT involves finding common multiples. The easiest way to find a common multiple is to start listing out the multiples of the numbers you're given until you find which ones they have in common.

Here are some examples:

4. If a number p is a positive multiple of both 3 and 8, p must also be a multiple of

   (A) 5
   (B) 11
   (C) 12
   (D) 14
   (E) 18

Here's how to crack it

Let's start by listing the multiples of 3: 3, 6, 9, 12, 15, 18, 21, 24, 27.... Now let's list the multiples of 8: 8, 16, 24, 32, 40....

Which numbers belong to both groups? 24 does. So the numbers that are multiples of both 3 and 8 must be multiples of 24. Of course, 24 itself isn't listed as an answer (that would be too easy.) But 24 (and every multiple of 24) will have a factor of 12 in it, so the answer is (C).

5. How many integers between 1 and 100 are multiples of both 4 and 6?

   (A) 8
   (B) 12
   (C) 18
   (D) 22
   (E) 24

Here's how to crack it

Let's start by listing the multiples of 4: 4, 8, 12, 16, 20, 24, 28.... Now the multiples of 6: 6, 12, 18, 24, 30....

After just a few multiples, you should be able to see the pattern. The numbers 12 and 24 (and likewise, every multiple of 12: the numbers 36, 48, etc., will also work) are the common multiples of both 4 and 6. So the real question is, How many multiples of 12 are there between 1 and 100? That's not too difficult to figure out. We can list them out with the help of a calculator: 12, 24, 36, 48, 60, 72, 84, 96. So there are a total of 8, and that's (A).

Now try a few yourself

Answers can be found on page 85.

a. What are 3 consecutive odd integers whose sum is 15? _____

b. What are the factors of 10? _____

c. What are the prime factors of 10? _____

d. What are the factors of 48? _____

e. What are the prime factors of 48? _____

f. What are the first 7 positive multiples of 6? _____

g. What are the first 7 positive multiples of 4? _____

h. Numbers that are multiples of both 6 and 7 are also multiples of _____.

i. The product of two positive integers x and y is 30 and their sum is 11. What are x and y? _____

j. The product of two positive integers x and y is 30 and their difference is 13. What are x and y? _____

MATH BASICS ◆ 83

1. Which of the following does NOT have a remainder of 1?

   (A) $\dfrac{15}{7}$

   (B) $\dfrac{17}{8}$

   (C) $\dfrac{51}{3}$

   (D) $\dfrac{61}{4}$

   (E) $\dfrac{81}{10}$

2. Which of the following numbers has the digit 4 in the thousandths place?

   (A) 4000.0
   (B) 40.0
   (C) 0.4
   (D) 0.04
   (E) 0.004

3. Which of the following numbers is NOT prime?

   (A) 11
   (B) 23
   (C) 27
   (D) 29
   (E) 31

4. What is the least of 3 consecutive integers whose sum is 21?

   (A) 4
   (B) 5
   (C) 6
   (D) 7
   (E) 8

5. If a, b, c, d, and e are consecutive even integers, and $a < b < c < d < e$, then $d + e$ is how much greater than $a + b$?

   (A) 10
   (B) 12
   (C) 14
   (D) 16
   (E) 18

6. All numbers divisible by both 3 and 14 are also divisible by which of the following?
   - (A) 6
   - (B) 9
   - (C) 16
   - (D) 28
   - (E) 32

Answers

a. 3, 5, 7

b. 1, 2, 5, 10

c. 2, 5

d. 1, 2, 3, 4, 6, 8, 12, 16, 24, 48

e. 2, 3

f. 6, 12, 18, 24, 30, 36, 42

g. 4, 8, 12, 16, 20, 24, 28

h. 42

i. 5 and 6

j. 15 and 2

1. (C) 51 can be divided evenly by 3 with no remainder.

2. (E) The thousandths place is the third to the right of the decimal.

3. (C) 27 can be divided by 3 and 9.

4. (C) The three consecutive integers must be 6, 7, and 8. The least of them is 6.

5. (B) If the numbers are 2, 4, 6, 8, and 10 then 8 + 10 = 18 and 2 + 4 = 6. The last two numbers are 12 greater than the first two. (Don't forget that the numbers have to be consecutive and even!)

6. (A) Look at the numbers that can be divided by 3 and 14. The numbers that 3 goes into are:

   3, 6, 9, 12, 15, 18, 21, 24, 27, 30, 33, 36, 39, 42, 45, 48…
   The numbers that 14 goes into are 14, 28, 42, 56. What is the first number that both 3 and 14 go into? 42. Since the only number in the answer choices that goes into 42 is 6, the answer must be (A).

EXPONENTS AND SQUARE ROOTS

Exponents are easy to deal with, if you write them out. $3^3 = 3 \times 3 \times 3$.

- You can multiply and divide exponents with the same base.
- When you multiply, add the exponents:
$3^4 \times 3^3 = 3 \times 3 \times 3 \times 3 \times 3 \times 3 \times 3 = 3^7$
- When you divide them, subtract the exponents:
$$\frac{3^4}{3^3} = \frac{3 \times 3 \times 3 \times 3}{3 \times 3 \times 3} = 3^1$$
- If you raise an exponent to a power, multiply the exponents: $(3^2)^3 = 3 \times 3 \times 3 \times 3 \times 3 \times 3 = 3^6$.
- Two special rules:

  Anything to the zero power is equal to 1: $3^0 = 1$

  Anything to the first power equals itself: $3^1 = 3$

Square root is just the opposite of raising a number to the second power:

$$\sqrt{4} = 2, \text{ since } 2^2 = 4$$

Square roots work just like exponents: You can *always* multiply and divide roots, but you can only add and subtract with the *same* root.

Multiplication and Division:

$\sqrt{8} \times \sqrt{2} = \sqrt{16} = 4$

$\sqrt{\frac{1}{4}} = \frac{\sqrt{1}}{\sqrt{4}} = \frac{1}{2}$

$\sqrt{400} = \sqrt{4 \times 100} = \sqrt{4} \times \sqrt{100} = 2 \times 10 = 20$

Addition and Subtraction:

$2\sqrt{2} + 3\sqrt{2} = 5\sqrt{2}$

$4\sqrt{3} - \sqrt{3} = 3\sqrt{3}$

$2\sqrt{3} + 3\sqrt{2}$ *Cannot be added, since the terms do not have the same root.*

Your turn:

a. $3^3 \times 3^2 =$ _____

b. $\dfrac{3^3}{3^2} =$ _____

c. $(3^3)^2 =$ _____

d. $x^6 \times x^2 =$ _____

> **Warning**
> The rules for multiplying and dividing exponents do not apply to addition or subtraction:
> $2^2 + 2^3 = 12$
> $(2 \times 2) + (2 \times 2 \times 2) = 12$
> It does not equal 2^5 or 32.

e. $\dfrac{x^6}{x^2} = $ _____

f. $\left(x^6\right)^2 = $ _____

3. If $3^4 = 9^x$, then $x=$
   - (A) 2
   - (B) 3
   - (C) 4
   - (D) 5
   - (E) 6

5. If $\left(3^x\right)^3 = 3^{15}$, what is the value of x?
   - (A) 3
   - (B) 5
   - (C) 7
   - (D) 9
   - (E) 12

10. If $x^y \times x^6 = x^{54}$ and $(x^3)^z = x^9$, then $y + z =$
    - (A) 10
    - (B) 11
    - (C) 48
    - (D) 50
    - (E) 51

Answers

a. 3^5

b. 3^1

c. 3^6

d. x^8

e. x^4

f. x^{12}

3. (A) If $3^4 = 9^x$, then $81 = 9^x$. Therefore $x = 2$. You could also rewrite 3^4 as $3 \times 3 \times 3 \times 3 = 9 \times 9$.

5. (B) If $\left(3^x\right)^3 = 3^{15}$, then $3^x \times 3^x \times 3^x = 15$, so $x = 5$.

10. (E) Since $x^y \times x^6 = x^{54}$, y must be 48. Likewise, since $(x^3)^z = x^9$, z must be 3. Therefore $y + z = 51$.

EQUATIONS AND INEQUALITIES

Learn Them, Love Them

Don't get bogged down looking for a direct solution. Always ask yourself if there is a simple way to find the answer. If you train yourself to think in terms of shortcuts, you won't waste a lot of time. However, if you don't see a quick solution, get to work. Something may come to you as you labor away.

An *equation* is a statement that contains an equals sign, such as $3x + 5 = 17$.

To solve an equation, you want to get the variable x alone on one side of the equals sign, and everything else on the other side.

The first step is to put all of the variables on one side of the equation and all of the numbers on the other side, using addition and subtraction. As long as you perform the same operation on both sides of the equals sign, you aren't changing the value of the variable.

Then you can divide both sides of the equation by the *coefficient*, which is the number in front of the variable. If that number is a fraction, you can multiply everything by its reciprocal.

For example: $3x + 5 = 17$

$$\begin{array}{rl} 3x + 5 &= 17 \\ -5 & -5 \end{array}$$ Subtract 5 from each side

$$\begin{array}{rl} 3x &= 12 \\ \div 3 & \div 3 \end{array}$$ Divide 3 from each side

$$x = 4$$

Always remember the rule of equations:

Whatever you do to one side of the equation, you must also do to the other side.

An *inequality* is any statement with one of these signs:

- < (less than)
- > (greater than)
- ≤ (less than or equal to)
- ≥ (greater than or equal to)

You can solve inequalities in the same way you solve equations, with one exception: Whenever you multiply or divide an inequality by a negative value, you must change the direction of the sign. This means that when you multiply or divide by a negative value, a < becomes a >, and a ≤ becomes ≥.

For example: $3x + 5 > 17$

$$\begin{array}{rl} 3x + 5 &> 17 \\ -5 & -5 \end{array}$$ Subtract 5 from each side

Warning!

When you multiply or divide an inequality by a negative number, you must reverse the inequality sign.

$$\begin{array}{rl} 3x &> 12 \\ \div 3 & \div 3 \end{array}$$ Divide 3 from each side

$$x > 4$$

In this case, we subtracted 5 but we didn't multiply or divide by a negative value, so the direction of the sign should not change. However, if we were to divide by a negative value, we would need to change the direction of the sign:

$$\begin{array}{rl} -3x+5 & > 17 \\ -5 & -5 \end{array}$$ Subtract 5 from each side

$$\begin{array}{rl} -3x & > 12 \\ \div -3 & \div -3 \end{array}$$ Divide –3 from each side

$$x < -4$$

GEOMETRY DEFINITIONS

LINES AND ANGLES

Whenever you have angles on a line, remember the *rule of 180*: The angles on any line must add up to 180. In the figure below, what is the value of x? We know that $2x + x$ must add up to 180, so we know that $3x = 180$. This makes $x = 60$.

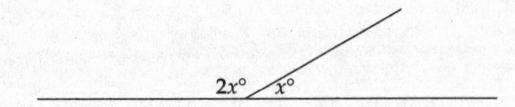

If two lines cross each other, they make *vertical angles*. These angles will always have the same measure. In the figure below, we know that z must equal 60, since $130 + z$ must equal 180. We know that y is 130 since it is across from the angle 130. We also know that x is 60, since it is across from z.

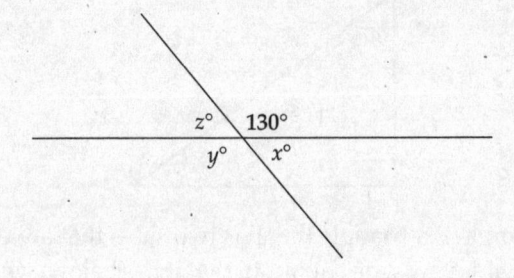

Anytime you have two parallel lines and a line that crosses them, you'll have two kinds of angles: big angles and small angles. All of the big angles will have the same measure, and all of the small angles will have the same measure. In the figure below, angles a, d, e, and h all have the same measure; angles b, c, f, and g also all have the same measure.

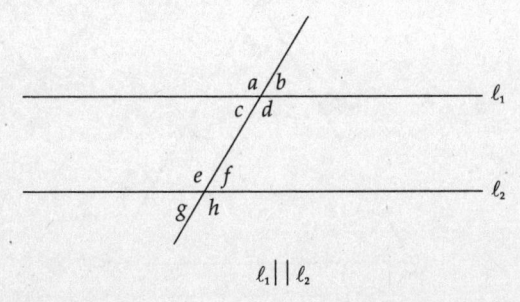

$\ell_1 \| \ell_2$

Four-Sided Figures

Little Boxes

Here's a progression of quadrilaterals from least specific to most specific:

quadrilateral = 4-sided figure
↓
parallelogram = a quadrilateral in which opposite sides are parallel
↓
rectangle = a parallelogram in which all angles = 90°
↓
square = a rectangle in which all sides are equal

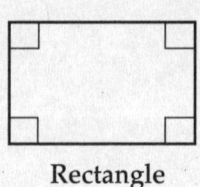

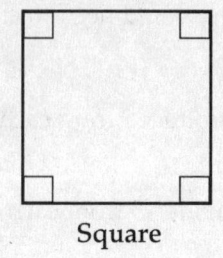

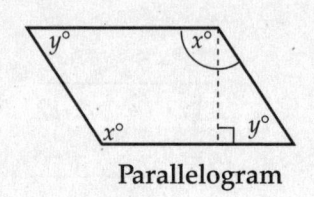

Rectangle   Square   Parallelogram

A figure with two sets of parallel sides is a *parallelogram*. In a parallelogram, the opposite angles are equal, and any adjacent angles add up to 180. (In the figure above, $x + y = 180$.) Opposite sides are also equal.

If all of the angles are also right angles, then the figure is a rectangle. And if all of the sides are the same length, then the figure is a *square*.

The *area* of a square, rectangle, or parallelogram is *length* × *width*. (In the parallelogram above, the length is shown by the dotted line.)

The *perimeter* of any figure is the sum of the lengths of its sides. A triangle with sides 3, 4, and 5 has a perimeter of 12.

Triangles

The rule of 180 not only holds for lines but it also holds for triangles: The sum of the angles inside a triangle must equal 180. This means that if you know two of the angles in a triangle, you can always solve for the third. Since we know that two of the angles in the figure below are 90 and 60, we can solve for the third angle, which must be 30.

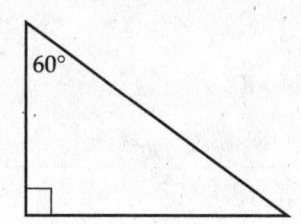

An *isosceles* triangle is a triangle that has two sides that are equal. Angles that are opposite equal sides must be equal. In the figure below, we have an isosceles triangle. Since $AB = BC$, we know that angles x and y are equal. And since their sum must be 150 (to make a total of 180 when we add the last angle), they each must be 75.

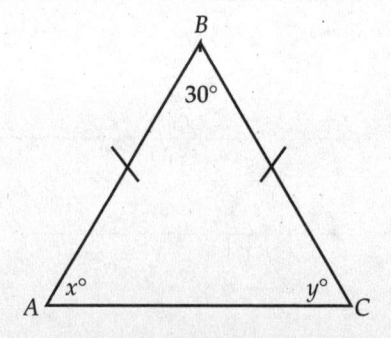

The *area* of a triangle is $\frac{1}{2}$ *base* × *height*. Note that the height is always perpendicular to the base.

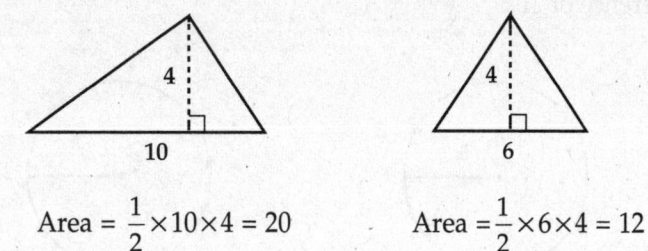

Area = $\frac{1}{2} \times 10 \times 4 = 20$ Area = $\frac{1}{2} \times 6 \times 4 = 12$

An *equilateral* triangle has all three sides equal and all of its angles equal to 60 degrees.

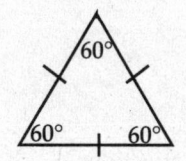

CIRCLES

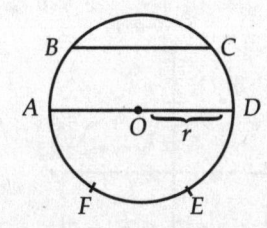

The *radius* of a circle is the distance from the center to the edge of the circle. In the figure above, *OD* is a radius. So is *OA*.

The *diameter* is the distance from one edge, through the center, to the other edge of the circle. The diameter will always be twice the measure of the radius, and will always be the longest line you can draw through a circle. In the figure above, *AD* is the diameter.

A *chord* is any line drawn from one edge of the circle to the other that does not pass through the center. It will always be shorter than the diameter. In the figure above, *BC* is a chord.

An *arc* is any section of the circumference (the rim) of the circle. *EF* is an arc in the figure above.

The *area* of a circle with radius r is πr^2. A circle with a radius of 5 has an area of 25π.

The *circumference* of a circle with radius r is $2\pi r$. A circle with radius of 5 has a circumference of 10π.

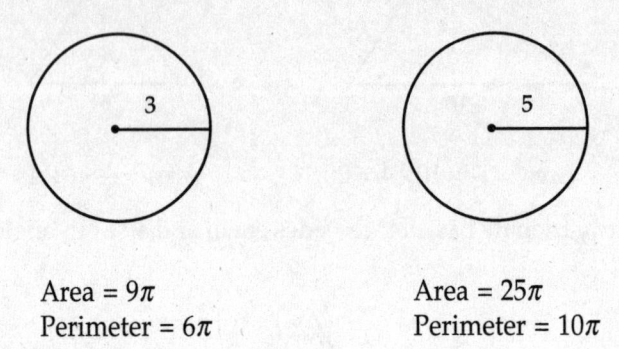

Area = 9π
Perimeter = 6π

Area = 25π
Perimeter = 10π

THE COORDINATE PLANE

You'll probably see one or two questions on the PSAT that involve the coordinate plane. The biggest mistake that people make on these questions is getting the *x*- and *y*-axes reversed. So let's just review:

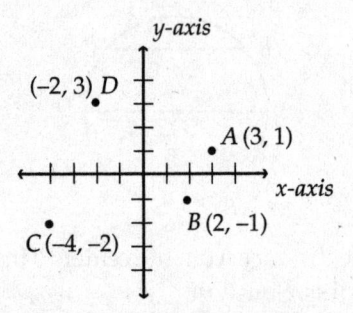

The *x*-axis is the horizontal axis, and the *y*-axis is the vertical axis. Points are given on the coordinate plane with the *x*-coordinate first. Positive *x*-values go to the right, and negative to the left; positive *y*-values go up the axis and negative ones go down. So point *A* (3, 1) is 3 points to the right on the *x*-axis, and 1 point up the *y*-axis. Point *B* (2, –1) is two points to the right on the *x*-axis and 1 point down on the *y*-axis.

Slope is a measure of the steepness of a line on the coordinate plane. On most slope problems you only need to recognize whether the slope is positive, negative, or zero. A line that goes up and to the right has positive slope; a line that goes down and to the right has negative slope, and a flat line has zero slope. In the figure on the next page, line 1 has positive slope, line 2 has zero slope, and line 3 has negative slope:

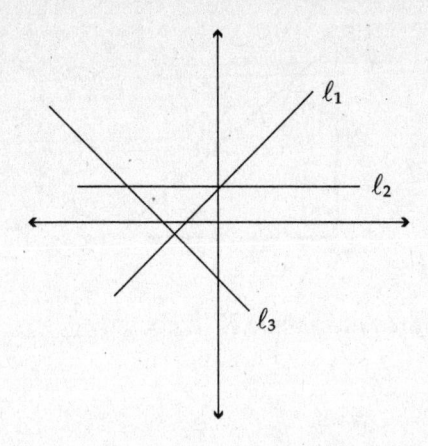

If you do need to calculate the slope, here's how: The *slope* of a line is equal to $\frac{rise}{run}$. To find the slope, take any two points on the line and count off the distance you need to get from one of these points to the other as follows:

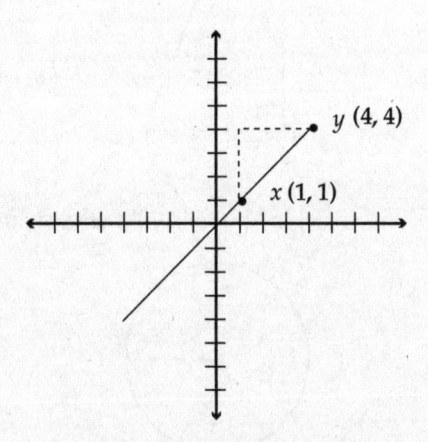

$$\text{slope} = \frac{\Delta y}{\Delta x}$$

In the graph above, to get from point *x* to point *y* we count up (rise) 3 points, and count over (run) 3 points. Therefore the slope is $\frac{rise}{run} = \frac{3}{3} = 1$.

Now try a few

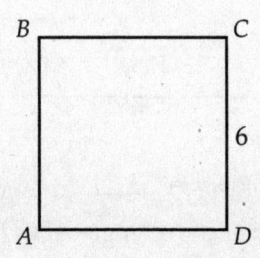

a. What is the area of square *ABCD* above? _____

MATH BASICS ◆ 93

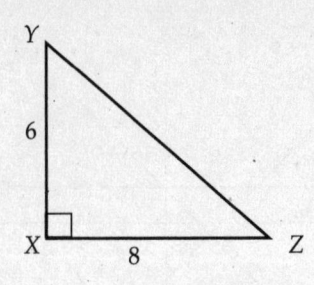

b. What is the area of triangle XYZ above? _____

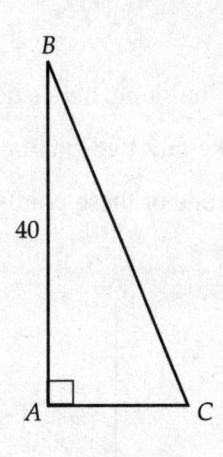

c. If the area of the triangle above is 400, what is its base?

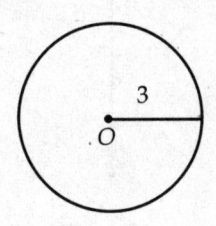

d. What is the area of the circle above with center O? _____
e. What is its circumference? _____

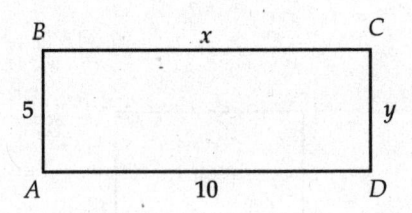

f. If ABCD is a rectangle, x = _____   y = _____
g. What is the perimeter of rectangle ABCD? _____

94 ◆ CRACKING THE PSAT/NMSQT

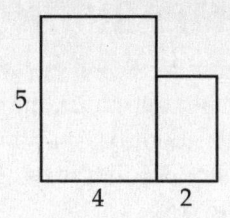

h. If the above figure is composed of two rectangles, what is the perimeter of the figure above? _____

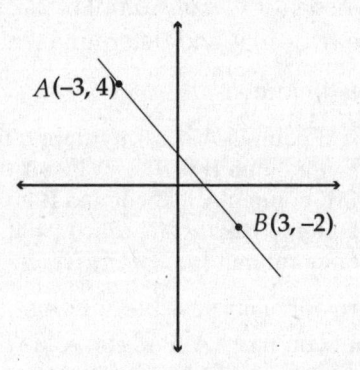

i. How many points do you count up (rise) to get from point A to point B? _____

j. How many points must you count over (run) to get from point A to point B? _____

k. What is the slope of the line above? _____

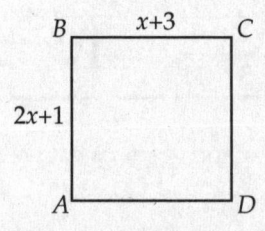

5. If ABCD is a square, what is the area of the square?

(A) 4
(B) 9
(C) 16
(D) 25
(E) 36

Answers

a. 36
b. 24
c. 20
d. 9π
e. 6π
f. 10, 5
g. 30
h. 22
i. –6
j. 6
k. –1

5. (D) Since this is a square, the two sides are equal. Therefore $2x + 1 = x + 3$. Solve for x, and you get that x must be 2. Therefore a side equals $x + 3$ or $2x + 1 = 5$ so the area equals 25.

MATH BASICS ◆ 95

QUANTITATIVE COMPARISON AND GRID-INS

There are two question types on the PSAT that you have probably never seen before. Just like the standard math questions, the Quantitative Comparison and Grid-In problems ask questions about basic arithmetic, algebra, and geometry. But they ask the questions in very peculiar ways. Let's take a moment to look at what these problems ask you to do.

QUANTITATIVE COMPARISON: THE BASICS

Quantitative Comparison (or Quant Comp) is exactly what it sounds like: Your job is to compare the two sides and determine which is larger.

Here are the rules to know:

Choose A if column A is *always* larger than column B
Choose B if column B is *always* larger than column A
Choose C if column A and column B are *always* equal
Choose D if you *cannot tell* which is larger—column A *might* be larger or column B *might* be larger.

> **D Is for Different**
>
> Mark D when you come up with two answers to the same Quant Comp question. Remember that D stands for "different" or "depends on what number you use."

Note that there are only *four* possible answers. *There is no choice (E) on Quant Comp.* We suggest that you write A B C D on some paper, so that you know there are only four choices. Cross off these letters as you eliminate; this will make it easy to tell which choices are still possible.

The most important rule for solving Quant Comp is: You don't always have to solve; you only have to compare.

Take a look at this problem:

	Column A	Column B
21.	$\frac{1}{2}+\frac{1}{3}+\frac{1}{11}$	$\frac{1}{2}+\frac{1}{4}+\frac{1}{11}$

In this case, each side has $\frac{1}{2}$ and $\frac{1}{11}$, so what we're really comparing is $\frac{1}{3}$ and $\frac{1}{4}$. Since $\frac{1}{3}$ is larger, the answer is (A).

Let's try one more:

	Column A	Column B
22.	The number of distinct prime factors of 36	The number of distinct prime factors of 28

How many distinct prime factors of 36 are there? Two of them (2 and 3). How many distinct prime factors of 28 are there? Two (2 and 7). So the answer is (C).

Your turn:

	Column A	Column B
21.	$3 + \frac{2}{3}$	$\frac{11}{3}$

23. The total cost of three hamburgers and two milkshakes is $2.40.

	Column A	Column B
	The cost of one hamburger	The cost of one milkshake

24. Square $ABCD$ is inscribed in a circle.

	Column A	Column B
	The length of arc ABC	The length of arc BCD

25. $n + 4 = -4$

	Column A	Column B
	n	0

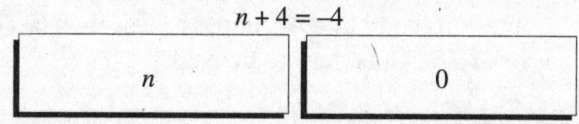

27. Two of the sides of an isosceles triangle have lengths 3 and 8.

	Column A	Column B
	The length of the third side	8

28.

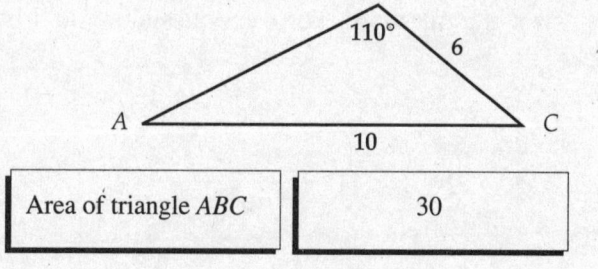

	Column A	Column B
	Area of triangle ABC	30

Write It Down

As you read through a Quant Comp question, jot down "A B C D" next to the problem. ETS doesn't supply you with answer choices to cross out, so do it yourself.

Answers

21. (C) $3 + \frac{2}{3}$ is the same number as $\frac{11}{3}$.

23. (D) Knowing the total of all five items does not allow us to solve for the individual price of any one of them. (You can think of this problem as an equation with two unknowns: $3h + 2m = \$2.40$.)

24. (C) If a square is inscribed in a circle, all of its points are equally spaced on the circle. Therefore the arcs have the same measure.

MATH BASICS ◆ 97

25. (B) This question only requires that we solve for the variable n. If we subtract 4 from each side of the equation, we get $n = -8$. This makes n less than zero, therefore the answer must be (B).

27. (C) Because an isosceles triangle needs to have two equal sides, the two possibilities are a triangle with sides 3, 8, and 8, or a triangle with sides 3, 8, and 3. But a triangle cannot have sides 3, 8, and 3. Try to draw one, accurately, and you'll see why it doesn't work. (The rule you may remember from school is: The sum of two sides of a triangle must be larger than the third side.) Therefore the triangle must have sides 3, 8, and 8. The third side must be 8, and so the two columns are equal.

28. (B) Since the base of ABC is 10, if the height were equal to 6 then the area would be 30. But side BC is 6, so we know that the height of the triangle (which you can draw from point B down to line AC) must be less than 6. Therefore the area of ABC must be less than 30.

GRID-INS: THE BASICS

You will see eight questions on the PSAT that ask you to bubble in a numerical answer on a grid, rather than answer a multiple-choice question. These questions are arranged in order of difficulty, and can be solved according to the methods outlined for the multiple-choice problems on the test.

The only difficulty with Grid-Ins is getting used to the way in which you are asked to answer the question. For each question, you'll have a grid like the following:

We recommend that you write the answer on top of the grid to help you bubble, but it's important to know that the scoring machine only reads the bubbles. *If you bubble incorrectly, the computer will consider the answer to be incorrect.*

Here are the basic rules of gridding:

1. If your answer uses fewer than four boxes, you can grid it anywhere you like.

    You can grid an answer of three boxes in any of the four boxes.

    To avoid confusion, we suggest that you start at the leftmost box.

Keep Left
No matter how many digits in your answer, always start gridding in the left-most column. That way, you'll avoid omitting digits and losing points.

2. You can grid your answer as either a fraction or a decimal, *if* the fraction will fit.

    You can grid an answer of .5 as either .5 or $\frac{1}{2}$.

MATH BASICS ◆ 99

3. You do not need to reduce your fractions, *if* the fraction will fit.

   If your answer is $\frac{2}{4}$, you can grid it as $\frac{2}{4}$, $\frac{1}{2}$, or .5.

Relax

If your answer is a fraction and it fits in the grid (fraction bar included), don't reduce it. Why bother? ETS won't give you an extra point. However, if your fraction doesn't fit, reduce it or turn it into a decimal on your calculator.

4. If you have a decimal that will not fit in the spaces provided, you *must grid as many places as will fit*.

   If your answer is $\frac{1}{3}$, you can grid it as $\frac{1}{3}$, .333, or .334 but .33 is *not* acceptable.

   You do *not* need to round your numbers, so we suggest that you don't.

5. You cannot grid mixed numbers. Convert all mixed numbers to ordinary fractions.

If your answer is $2\frac{1}{2}$, you must convert it to $\frac{5}{2}$ or 2.5.
Try gridding the following:

a. 125 b. $\frac{2}{12}$ c. $3\frac{1}{4}$ d. .8958

Here's how to grid them:

Don't Mix

Never grid in a mixed number. Change it into a top-heavy fraction or decimal.

a. 125 b. 2/12 c. 3.25 d. .895

Let's try a few

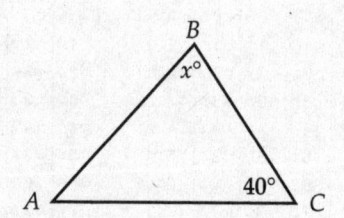

33. In triangle ABC above, if AB = BC then x =

34. The sum of five consecutive integers, arranged in order from least to greatest, is 100. What is the sum of the next four consecutive integers?

35. If $5x^2 = 125$, what is the value of $5x^3$?

36. If 40 percent of 200 is equal to 300 percent of n, then n is equal to what number?

Answers

33. Since the triangle is isosceles with $AB = BC$, we know that angles A and C must have the same measure. So angle A must also be 40 degrees. Angles A and C have a combined measure of 80 degrees, and we need 180 total degrees in the triangle. Therefore x must measure 100.

34. If five consecutive integers have a sum of 100, they must be 18, 19, 20, 21, and 22. The next four consecutive integers are 23, 24, 25, and 26. Their sum is 98.

35. Since $5x^2 = 125$, we know that $x^2 = 25$ and $x = 5$. Therefore $5x^3 = 5 \times 125 = 625$.

36. 40 percent of 200 is equal to $\frac{40}{100} \times 200 = 80$. So 80 is 300 percent of n. We can solve for n by translating this as $80 = \frac{300}{100} \times n$. So n must be $\frac{80}{3}$ or 26.667 (which you can grid either as 26.6 or 26.7).

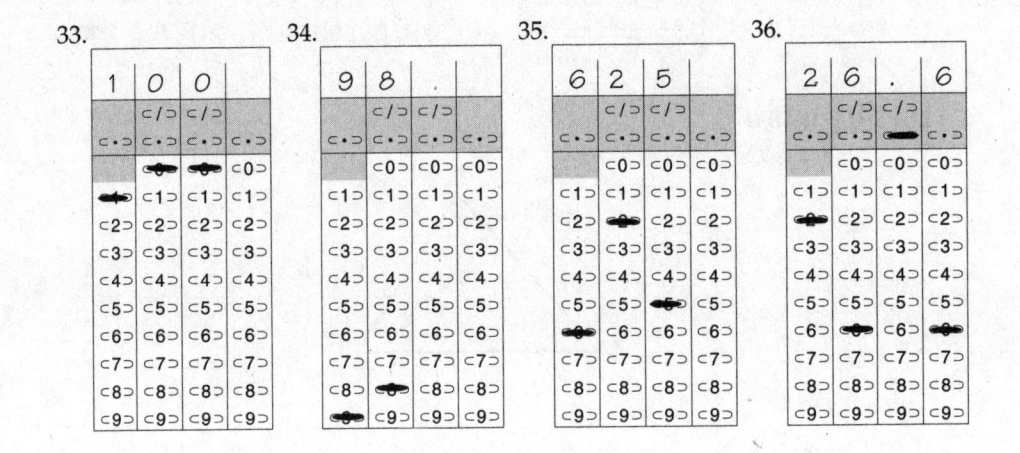

33. 100
34. 98
35. 625
36. 26.6

9
Math Techniques

MATH TECHNIQUES

In the previous chapter, we mentioned that one of the keys to doing well on the PSAT is to have a set of test-specific problem-solving skills. This chapter discusses some powerful strategies, which—though you may not use them in school—are specifically designed to get you points on the PSAT. Learn them well!

PLUGGING IN

One of the most powerful problem-solving skills on the PSAT is a technique we call Plugging In. Plugging In will turn nasty algebra problems into simple arithmetic, and help you through the particularly twisted problems that you'll often see on the PSAT. There are several varieties of Plugging In, each suited to a different kind of question.

PLUGGING IN YOUR OWN NUMBERS

When to Plug In
- Phrases like "in terms of k" in the question
- Variable in the answers
- Unspecified values and fractions

The problem with doing algebra is that it's just too easy to make a mistake. Whenever you see a problem with variables in the answer choices, PLUG IN. Start by picking a number for the variable in the problem (or for more than one variable, if necessary), solve the problem using that real number, and then see which answer choice gives you the correct answer.

Take a look at the following problem:

2. If x is a positive integer, then 20 percent of $5x$ equals

   (A) x
   (B) $2x$
   (C) $5x$
   (D) $15x$
   (E) $20x$

Here's how to crack it

Let's start by picking a number for x. Let's plug in a nice round number such as 10. When we plug in 10 for x, we change every x in the whole problem into a 10. Now the problem reads:

2. If 10 is a positive integer, then 20 percent of 5(10) equals

   (A) 10
   (B) 2(10)
   (C) 5(10)
   (D) 15(10)
   (E) 20(10)

Look how easy the problem becomes! Now we can solve: 20 percent of 50 is 10. Which answer says 10? (A) does.

Let's try it again:

8. If $-1 < x < 0$, then which of the following has the greatest value?

   (A) x
   (B) x^2
   (C) x^3
   (D) $\dfrac{1}{x}$
   (E) $2x$

Here's how to crack it

This time when we pick a number for x, we have to make sure that it is between -1 and 0, because that's what the problem states. So let's try $-\dfrac{1}{2}$. If we make every x in the problem into $-\dfrac{1}{2}$, the problem now reads:

8. If $-1 < -\dfrac{1}{2} < 0$, then which of the following has the greatest value?

   (A) $-\dfrac{1}{2}$
   (B) $\left(-\dfrac{1}{2}\right)^2$
   (C) $\left(-\dfrac{1}{2}\right)^3$
   (D) $\dfrac{1}{-\dfrac{1}{2}}$
   (E) $2\left(-\dfrac{1}{2}\right)$

Now we can solve the problem. Which has the greatest value? Choice (A) is $-\dfrac{1}{2}$, choice (B) equals $\dfrac{1}{4}$, choice (C) equals $-\dfrac{1}{8}$, choice (D) equals -2, and choice (E) equals -1. So choice (B) is the greatest.

Plugging In is *such* a great technique, that it makes even the hardest algebra problems easy. *Anytime you can, plug in!*

MATH TECHNIQUES ◆ 105

WHAT IF THERE'S NO VARIABLE?

Sometimes you'll see a problem that doesn't contain an *x*, *y*, or *z*, but which contains a hidden variable. If your answers are percents or fractional parts of some unknown quantity (total number of marbles in a jar, total miles to travel in a trip) try plugging in a number.

Take a look at this problem:

8. In a certain high school, the number of seniors is twice the number of juniors. If 60% of the senior class and 40% of the junior class attends the last football game of the season, what fraction of the combined junior and senior class attends the game?

   (A) 60%
   (B) 53%
   (C) 50%
   (D) 47%
   (E) 40%

Here's how to crack it

What number, if we knew it, would make the math work on this problem incredibly easy? The number of students. So let's plug in a number, and work the problem. Let's suppose that the number of seniors is 200 and the number of juniors 100.

If 60% of the 200 seniors and 40% of the 100 juniors go to the game, that makes 120 seniors and 40 juniors, or 160 students. What fraction of the combined class went to the game? $\frac{160}{300}$, or 53%. So the answer is (B).

PLUGGING IN ON QUANT COMP

Whenever you have variables on Quant Comp problems, plug in! The only difference is that on Quant Comp, you must plug in *more than once*.

First, try an ordinary number and see what answer you get. If you find that column A is larger, this doesn't prove that column A is *always* larger. But it does show us that (B) and (C) can't be right, and we can cross them off. Then you have a fifty-fifty chance: the answer is either (A) or (D).

Then, to see whether column A is always larger, try plugging in different numbers and see whether you can get a different answer to the problem. (It's especially helpful to try a few "weird" numbers such as 0, 1, negatives, and fractions.) If you can find a number for which column A is *not* always biggest, then the actual answer to the problem is (D). If, however, you find that column A *is* always larger, then the answer is (A).

Likewise, if on your first plug-in you find that column B is larger, you can eliminate (A) and (C), and the only possible choices are (B) and (D). If trying other numbers shows you that column B is always larger, then the answer is (B). If column B is not always larger, then the answer is (D).

What Are the Weird Numbers?
- fractions
- negatives
- big numbers
- 1 and 0

If on your first plug-in you find that the two columns are equal, you can eliminate (A) and (B) and the answer must be (C) or (D). Try a different number and see whether they are always equal. If they are, the answer is (C). If not, the answer is (D).

Take a look at the following problems:

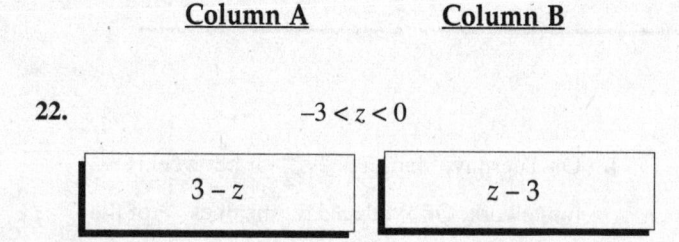

Column A	Column B

22. $-3 < z < 0$

$3 - z$	$z - 3$

Here's how to crack it
Let's start by plugging in an easy number for z. Let's plug in -2, since z must be between -3 and 0. If z is -2, which column is larger? Column A is. So we can cross off (B) and (C). Now let's plug in again. We can't use 0 or 1 for z, so let's try a fraction. Suppose z is $-\frac{1}{2}$. Now which column is larger? Column A is still larger. So the answer is (A).

Now take a look at the following:

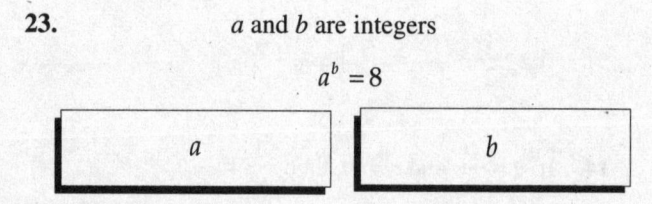

23. a and b are integers

$a^b = 8$

a	b

Here's how to crack it
Let's start by plugging in the obvious numbers for a and b. If $a = 2$ and $b = 3$, then $a^b = 8$. Which column is larger? Column B. However, could we plug in different numbers and get a different answer? Yes. If $a = 8$ and $b = 1$, then $a^b = 8$. Now which column is larger? Column A. So the answer to this problem is (D).

Try a few:

	Column A	Column B
	\multicolumn{2}{c}{$ab = 0$}
21.	a	0

4. On Tuesday, Martha does $\frac{1}{2}$ of her weekly homework. On Wednesday, she does $\frac{1}{3}$ of the remaining homework. After Wednesday, what fractional part of her homework remains to be done?

   (A) $\frac{1}{6}$
   (B) $\frac{1}{5}$
   (C) $\frac{1}{4}$
   (D) $\frac{1}{3}$
   (E) $\frac{1}{2}$

14. If $a = \frac{b}{c^2}$ and $c \neq 0$, then $\frac{1}{b^2} =$

   (A) ac^2
   (B) $a^2 c^4$
   (C) $\frac{1}{ac^2}$
   (D) $\frac{1}{a^2 c^4}$
   (E) $\frac{a^2}{c^4}$

17. If $p \neq 0$, then $\dfrac{\frac{1}{8}}{2p} =$

   (A) $\dfrac{1}{4p}$

   (B) $\dfrac{p}{4}$

   (C) $\dfrac{4}{p}$

   (D) $\dfrac{4p}{3}$

   (E) $4p$

Here's how to crack them

2. **(D)** For our first plug-in, let's plug in 0 for a and 5 for b. This makes it true that $ab = 0$. Which column is bigger? They're equal. So we can cross off (A) and (B). Now can we plug in different numbers that will give us different answers? Let's plug in 5 for a and 0 for b. This still makes it true that $ab = 0$, but this time, column A is larger than column B. So the answer is (D).

4. **(D)** Let's plug in a number for the amount of homework Martha has. Let's say she has 12 pages of work to do. If she does half of this on Tuesday, she does 6 pages, and there are 6 pages left. If, on Wednesday, she does one-third of the remaining 6 pages, that means she does 2 more pages. So she has 4 pages left over from the original 12. What fractional part is left over? $\dfrac{4}{12}$ or $\dfrac{1}{3}$.

14. **(D)** Let's pick numbers for a, b, and c such that $a = \dfrac{b}{c^2}$. We can pick $4 = \dfrac{16}{2^2}$. Now the question becomes what is $\dfrac{1}{b^2}$ or $\dfrac{1}{16^2}$. The answer is $\dfrac{1}{256}$. Which choice says this? (D) does.

17. **(B)** Let's pick a number for p. How about 2? Now the problem reads $\dfrac{\frac{1}{8}}{2(2)} =$ and the answer is $\dfrac{1}{2}$. Which choice says $\dfrac{1}{2}$? (B) does.

PLUGGING IN THE ANSWER CHOICES

You can also plug in when the answers to a problem are actual values, such as 2, 4, 10, or 20. Why would you want to do a lot of complicated algebra to solve a problem, when the answer is *right there on the page*? All you have to do is figure out *which* choice it is.

MATH TECHNIQUES ◆ 109

How can you tell which is the correct answer? Try every choice *until you find the one that works*. Even if this means you have to try all five choices, Plugging In is still a fast and reliable means of getting the right answer.

But if you use your head, you almost never have to try all five choices. When you plug in the answer choices, begin with choice (C), the middle number. If choice (C) works, you're done. If choice (C) doesn't work because it's too small, try one of the larger numbers. If choice (C) doesn't work because it's too big, try one of the smaller numbers. You can almost always find the answer in two or three tries.

Let's try the following problem:

4. If the average (arithmetic mean) of 8 and x is equal to the average of 5, 9, and x, what is the value of x?

   (A) 1
   (B) 2
   (C) 4
   (D) 8
   (E) 10

Here's how to crack it

Let's start with choice (C) and plug in 4 for x. The problem now reads:

4. If the average (arithmetic mean) of 8 and 4 is equal to the average of 5, 9, and 4...

Does this work? Does the average of 8 and 4 equal the average of 5, 9, and 4? Yes. Therefore (C) is the answer. Neat, huh?

Let's try one more:

10. If $(x-2)^2 = 2x - 1$, which of the following is a possible value of x?

    (A) 1
    (B) 2
    (C) 3
    (D) 6
    (E) 7

Here's how to crack it

If we try plugging in (C) 3 for x, the equation becomes $1 = 5$, which is false. So (C) can't be right. If you're not sure which way to go next, just pick a direction. It won't take very long to figure out the correct answer. If we try plugging in (B) 2 for x, the equation becomes $0 = 3$, which is false. If we try plugging in (A) 1 for x, the equation becomes $1 = 1$, which is true. So the answer is (A).

Plugging In Works

Don't try to solve problems like this by writing equations and "solving for *x*" or "solving for *y*." Plugging In is faster, easier, and less likely to produce errors.

PLUGGING IN ON GEOMETRY

You can also plug in on geometry questions, just as you can for algebra. Any time that you have variables in the answer choices, or hidden variables, plug in! As long as you follow all the rules of geometry while you solve, you'll get the answer.

Take a look at this problem:

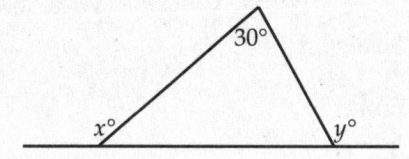

8. In the figure above, what is the value of $x + y$?
   (A) 120
   (B) 140
   (C) 180
   (D) 190
   (E) 210

Here's how to crack it

We could solve this problem using algebra, but why? We can plug in whatever numbers we want for the other angles inside the triangle—as long as we obey the rule of 180, and make sure that all the angles in the triangle add up to 180 degrees. So let's plug in 60 and 90 for the other angles inside that triangle. Now we can solve for x and y: If the angle next to x is 60 degrees, then x will be equal to 120. If the angle next to y is equal to 90 degrees, then y will be equal to 90. This makes the sum $x + y$ equal to $120 + 90$, or 210. No matter what numbers we pick for the angles inside the triangle, we'll always get the same answer, (E).

Now try these problems:

8. If $3^{x+2} = 243$, what is the value of x?
   (A) 1
   (B) 2
   (C) 3
   (D) 4
   (E) 5

14. If $\dfrac{24x}{4} + \dfrac{1}{x} = 5$, then $x =$
    (A) $-\dfrac{1}{6}$
    (B) $\dfrac{1}{6}$
    (C) $\dfrac{1}{4}$
    (D) $\dfrac{1}{2}$
    (E) 2

MATH TECHNIQUES ◆ 111

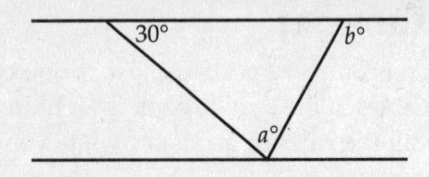

15. In the figure above, what is the value of *b* in terms of *a*?

    (A) $30 - a$
    (B) $30 + a$
    (C) $60 + a$
    (D) $80 - a$
    (E) $90 + a$

Here's how to crack them

8. (C) Let's begin by plugging in the middle number, 3, for *x*. Is $3^5 = 243$? Yes. So the answer is (C).

14. (D) If we try plugging in (C) $\frac{1}{4}$ for *x*, the equation becomes $\frac{6}{4} + 4 = 5$, which is false. If we try plugging in (D) $\frac{1}{2}$ for *x*, the equation becomes $\frac{12}{4} + 2 = 5$, which is true.

15. (B) This is another great example of Plugging In. Let's plug in a number for *a*. How about 90, just to make the math easy? If $a = 90$, then the other angle inside the triangle must be equal to 60. Therefore *b* must be equal to 120. What choice says 120, remembering that $a = 90$? (B) does.

THE AVERAGE PIE

You probably remember the average formula from high school, which says: *Average* (arithmetic mean) $= \frac{\text{total}}{\text{\# of things}}$. However, it's rare that on the PSAT you'll be asked to take a simple average. Of the three parts of an average problem—the average, the total, and the number of things—you'll always be given two of these parts, but often in tricky combinations.

Therefore the most reliable way to solve average problems is always to use the average pie:

112 ◆ CRACKING THE PSAT/NMSQT

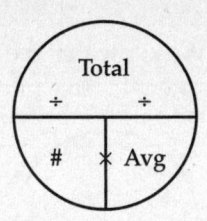

What the pie shows you is that if you know any two of these parts, you can always solve for the third. Once you fill in two of the elements, the pie shows you how to solve for the third part. If you know the total and the number, you can solve the average (total divided by number); if you know the total and the average, you can solve for the number (total divided by average); if you know the number and average, you can solve for the total (number times average).

Let's try this example:

4. The average of 3 numbers is 22 and the smallest of these numbers is 2. If the other two numbers are equal, each of them is

   (A) 22
   (B) 32
   (C) 40
   (D) 64
   (E) 66

Here's how to crack it

Let's start by filling in our average pie. We know that 3 numbers have an average of 22. So we can fill in our pie, and the pie shows us that the sum total of these numbers must be 22 times 3, or 66.

> **Total**
> When calculating averages, always find the total. It's the one piece of information that ETS loves to withhold.

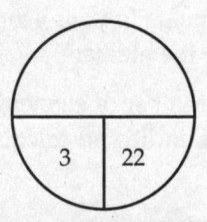

Now we also know that one of these numbers is 2. This means that the other two numbers must have a sum of 64. Since these numbers are equal, they must each be 32. This means the answer is (B).

Try one more:

8. Caroline scored 85, 88, and 89 on three of her four history tests. If her average score for all tests was 90, what did she score on her fourth test?

   (A) 90
   (B) 93
   (C) 96
   (D) 98
   (E) 99

MATH TECHNIQUES ◆ 113

Here's how to crack it

Let's start with what we know: We know that the average of all 4 of her tests was 90. So we can fill in an average pie with this information:

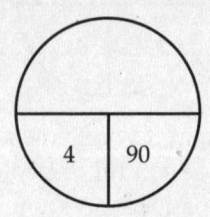

Now the pie tells us that the sum total of the scores on these 4 tests will be 4 times 90, or 360. Since 3 of these tests have a sum of 85 + 88 + 89, or 262, we know that the score on the fourth test must be equal to 360 – 262, or 98. This makes the answer (D).

TWO MORE KINDS OF AVERAGE: MEDIAN AND MODE

There are two more terms you should know: median and mode. You'll see at most one question on the PSAT that tests these ideas, but you might as well get it right.

The *median* of a group of numbers is the number in the middle. (Just as the "median" is the large divider in the middle of a road.) To find the median, here's what you do:

- First, line up the elements in the group in numerical order from lowest to highest.

- If the number of elements in your group is *odd*, find the number in the middle. That's the median.

- If you have an *even* number of elements in the group, find the two numbers in the middle and calculate their average (arithmetic mean).

Try this on the following two problems:

11. If the 5 students in Ms. Jaffray's math class scored 91, 83, 84, 90, and 85 on their final exams, what is the median score for her class on the final exam?

    (A) 84
    (B) 85
    (C) 86
    (D) 86.6
    (E) 90

Here's how to crack it
First, let's place these numbers in order from lowest to highest: 83, 84, 85, 90, 91. The number in the middle is 85, so the median of this group is 85 and the answer is (B).

12. If the 6 students in Mr. Elliott's math class scored 91, 83, 84, 90, 93, and 85 on their final exams, what is the median score for his class on the final exam?
    - (A) 83.3
    - (B) 85
    - (C) 86
    - (D) 87.5
    - (E) 87.67

Here's how to crack it
When we place these numbers in order, we get 83, 84, 85, 90, 91, 93. Since the numbers in the middle are 85 and 90, we take their mean, which is 87.5. Our answer is (D).

The *mode* of a group of numbers is the number that appears the most. (Remember: *mode* sounds like *most*.) To find the mode of a group of numbers, line up the elements in numerical order, and see which element appears the greatest number of times.

Try this one:

33. If the 7 students in Ms. Holoway's math class scored 91, 83, 92, 83, 91, 85, and 91 on their final exams, what is the mode of her student's scores?

Median Median
To find the median of a set containing an even number of items, take the average of the two middle numbers.

Here's how to crack it

If we place these numbers in order, we get: 83, 83, 85, 91, 91, 91, 92. Since the number 91 is the one that appears most often in the list, the mode of these numbers is 91.

PERCENTS

Percent just means "divided by 100." So 20% = $\frac{20}{100} = \frac{1}{5}$ or .2.

Likewise, 8% = $\frac{8}{100} = \frac{2}{25}$ or .08.

Any percent question can be translated into algebra—just use the following rules:

Percent	÷ 100
Of	x
What	x (or any variable)
Is, Are, Equals	=
8 percent of 10	becomes	$.08 \times 10 = .8$
10 percent of 80	becomes	$.1 \times 80 = 8$
5 is what percent of 80?	becomes	$5 = \frac{x}{100} \times 80$
5 is 80 percent of what number?	becomes	$5 = \frac{80}{100} x$
What percent of 5 is 80?	becomes	$\frac{x}{100} \times 5 = 80$

PERCENT INCREASE OR DECREASE

Percent Increase or *Percent Decrease* is always $\dfrac{change}{original\ amount}$.

For example: If an $80 item is reduced to $60 during a sale, the percent decrease is the change in price ($20) over the original amount ($80), or 25%.

PROPORTIONS AND RATIOS

You will probably encounter one or two questions on the PSAT that give you information about a sample of items in a group and ask you to draw conclusions about the whole group. The way to solve these is by setting up a ratio or a proportion.

For instance, let's say we know that for every 10 students in a school, 3 are boys. We can write this as the fraction $\dfrac{3}{10}$. Of course, if we say that out of every 10 students 3 are boys, this doesn't tell us exactly how many students we have. We might have 10 students and 3 boys, or 20 students and 6 boys, or 100 students and 30 boys. What will happen on the PSAT is you will be given one relationship of part to whole (3 boys for every 10) and one other number (the actual number of boys or the actual whole number). This is your sign that it's time to set up a proportion:

$$\dfrac{A}{B} = \dfrac{C}{D}$$

Whenever you set up two equal fractions, you know that $A \times D$ is equal to $C \times B$. The only thing you have to make sure to do is keep the same thing on top and bottom of each fraction.

In this case, if we know that 3 of every 10 students is a boy, and that there are 200 students, we can figure out the number of boys by setting up these fractions:

$$\dfrac{boys}{total}\ \dfrac{3}{10} = \dfrac{x}{200}$$

Now we can cross-multiply: $10x = 3 \times 200$. This means that $x = 60$, and that there will be 60 boys in a group of 200.

Let's try the following problem:

2. John receives $2.50 for every 4 pounds of berries he picks. How much money will he receive if he picks 90 pounds of berries?

(A) $27
(B) $36
(C) $42.25
(D) $48.50
(E) $56.25

Ratios vs. Fractions
Keep in mind that a ratio compares part of something to another part. A fraction compares part of something to the whole thing.

Here's how to crack it
To solve this, set up a proportion:

$$\frac{dollars}{pounds} \quad \frac{\$2.50}{4} = \frac{x}{90}$$

Now we can cross-multiply. $2.50 \times 90 = 4x$, so $x = 56.25$, and the answer is (E).

Sometimes, instead of a part and a whole, you'll be given the relationship of two parts (which is known as a ratio). For instance, you might be told that the ratio of boys to girls in a class is 3 to 7, and there is a total of 40 students in the class.

Whenever you see a problem like this, one of the keys to the problem will be the total number of students (which will always be the sum of the parts). To help you remember this, whenever you're given a ratio, set up a ratio box:

	Boys	Girls	Whole
Ratio	3 +	7 =	10
Multiply by	×	×	×
	=	=	=
Actual #			

The ratio box tells us that we need to add the number of boys and girls to get the total number of students: $3 + 7 = 10$ total students. This is the "whole" of our ratio.

Once you've got a ratio box, all you have to do is remember this rule: Whatever factor you use as the multiplier in one column, you have to use in every column. Since we know that the total number of the students in the group is 40, we put that number into the "actual" row of the ratio box, and the box tells us that we need to multiply the "whole" by a factor of 4. So we can now fill in the rest of our ratio box:

Boys	Girls	Whole
3 +	7 =	10
×	×	×
4	4	4
=	=	=
12	28	40

Since we need to multiply 10 by 4 to get 40, we need to multiply every column by 4. This tells us that if the number of students is 40, they must be 12 boys and 28 girls.

Try this one:

3. If a certain kind of lemonade is made by mixing water and lemon juice in a ratio of $3\frac{1}{2}$ cups of water for every $\frac{1}{2}$ cup of lemon juice, how many cups of lemon juice will there be in 24 cups of lemonade?

   (A) 3
   (B) 8
   (C) 16
   (D) $16\frac{1}{2}$
   (E) 21

Here's how to crack it

Water	Lemon	Whole
$3\frac{1}{2}$ +	$\frac{1}{2}$	4
× 6 =	× 6 =	× 6
21	3	24

Let's set up our ratio box. We have $3\frac{1}{2}$ cups of water and $\frac{1}{2}$ cup of lemon juice, which makes a total of 4 cups of lemonade; that's our "whole." Now we need to figure out how much lemon juice is in 24 cups of lemonade, so if we put 24 into the box, we can see that we need to multiply each column by 6. This means that there will be a total of 3 cups of lemon juice in 24 cups of lemonade. This makes (A) the answer.

Now try these:

a. If a student scores 70, 90, 95, and 105, what is the average for these tests? _____

b. If a student has an average score of 80 on 4 tests, what is the total of the scores received on those tests? _____

c. If a student has an average of 60 on tests whose totals add up to 360, how many tests has the student taken? _____

d. If the average of 4 and x is equal to the average of 2, 8, and x, what is the value of x? _____

e. What percent of 5 is 6? _____

f. 60 percent of 90 is the same as 50 percent of what number? _____

g. Jenny's salary increased from $30,000 to $33,000. By what percent did her salary increase? _____

h. In 1980, factory X produced 18,600 pieces. In 1981, factory X only produced 16,000 pieces. By approximately what percent did production decrease from 1980 to 1981? _____

i. In a certain bag of marbles, the ratio of red marbles to green marbles is 7:5. If the bag contains 96 marbles, how many green marbles are in the bag? _____

4. The average (arithmetic mean) of 4 numbers is 80. If two of the numbers are 50 and 60, what is the sum of the other two numbers?

11. 60% of 80 is the same as 40% of what number?
    (A) 100
    (B) 105
    (C) 110
    (D) 120
    (E) 140

14. A group of 30 adults and 20 children went to the beach. If 50 percent of the adults and 80 percent of the children went swimming, what percent of the group went swimming?
    (A) 30%
    (B) 46%
    (C) 50%
    (D) 62%
    (E) 65%

Answers

a. 90

b. 320

c. 6

d. $x = 8$

e. 120

f. 108

g. 10%

h. $\dfrac{2,600}{18,600}$ = approximately 14%

i. 40

4. 210

11. 60% of 80 translates as $\frac{60}{100} \times 80$, which is the same as 48. So the problem now reads: 48 is the same as 40% of what number? We can translate this question as $48 = \frac{40}{100} x$. Then we solve for x, which equals 120, which is choice (D).

14. (D) 50% of the adults = 15 and 80% of the children = 16, so 31 total people went swimming. 31 out of 50 is 62%.

10
Advanced Math Principles

So far we've covered the basic knowledge and some PSAT-specific problem-solving skills. Now we'll look at some of the more advanced skills tested on the PSAT.

EXPANDING, FACTORING, AND SOLVING QUADRATIC EQUATIONS

Ah, factoring. You're likely to see at least one problem on the PSAT that asks you to do this sort of complex algebraic manipulation. Since it may have been a little while since you've done this, let's review.

EXPANDING

Most often you'll be asked to expand an expression simply by multiplying it out. When working with an expression of the form $(x + 3)(x + 4)$, multiply out using the following rule:

$$\text{FOIL} = \text{First Outer Inner Last}$$

Start with the first figure in each set of parentheses: $x \times x = x^2$
Now do the two outermost figures: $4 \times x = 4x$
Next, the two inner figures: $3 \times x = 3x$
Finally, the last figure in each set of parentheses: $3 \times 4 = 12$
Add them all together, and we get $x^2 + 4x + 3x + 12$, or $x^2 + 7x + 12$

FACTORING

If you ever see an expression of the form $x^2 + 7x + 12$ on the PSAT, there is a very good chance that you will be required to factor it.

Here are the steps:

Step 1: Find the factors of the constant (in this case, 12).

Step 2: See which pair of factors you can either add or subtract to get the coefficient of x (in this case, 7).

Step 3: Put those factors into parentheses along with the appropriate signs.

How does this work for the expression $x^2 + 7x + 12$?

Step 1: We can factor 12 either as 1×12, 2×6, or 3×4.

Step 2: We can get 7 by taking +3 and adding +4, so put 3 and 4 into parentheses.

Step 3: Add the plus signs, since +3 and +4 together make 7.

$$x^2 + 7x + 12$$
$$(x \quad)(x \quad)$$
$$(x \quad 3)(x \quad 4)$$
$$(x + 3)(x + 4)$$

If you want to double-check your work, try expanding out $(x + 3)(x + 4)$ and you'll get the original expression.

Now try the following problem:

13. If $\dfrac{x^2+7x+12}{(x+4)}=5$, then what is the value of x?

    (A) 1
    (B) 2
    (C) 3
    (D) 5
    (E) 6

Here's how to crack it

Since we know we can factor $x^2+7x+12$, we should do so. When we factor it, we get $\dfrac{(x+3)(x+4)}{(x+4)}=5$. Now we can cancel the $(x + 4)$ and we're left with $x + 3 = 5$. If we solve for x we find $x = 2$ and our answer is (B).

Solving Quadratic Equations

Sometimes you'll see an expression that you can factor contained within an equation. In this case, there will be two possible values for x, sometimes called the roots of the equation. To solve for x, use the following steps:

Step 1: Make sure that the equation is set equal to zero.

Step 2: Factor the equation.

Step 3: See which values for x will make either part of the equation equal to zero. For $(x + 3)$, if $x = -3$ then the value in parentheses will be equal to zero. For $(x - 3)$, if $x = 3$ then the value in parentheses will be equal to zero.

Try the following problem:

14. If $x^2+2x-15=0$, then the possible values of x are

    (A) 2 and 4
    (B) −13 and −4
    (C) 5 and −4
    (D) −5 and 3
    (E) 6 and 3

Here's how to crack it
Let's try the steps:

Step 1: The equation is already set equal to 0.

Step 2: We can now factor the left side of the equation, to get

$(x + 5)(x - 3) = 0$.

Step 3: The two values for x that would fit this equation are −5 and 3. Therefore the answer is (D).

Usually you'll be given a problem where the expression is already equal to zero; if it's not, you'll have to manipulate the equation so that it does equal zero:

15. If $x^2 + 7x + 15 = 3$, then the possible values of x are
    (A) 3 and 4
    (B) −3 and −4
    (C) 3 and −4
    (D) −3 and 6
    (E) −3 and −6

Here's how to crack it
In this case, we'll need to subtract 3 from each side, in order to make sure that the expression is equal to zero. When we subtract 3 from each side, we get:

$$x^2 + 7x + 12 = 0$$

We can now factor the left side, to get:

$$(x + 3)(x + 4) = 0$$

And the two values for x that would fit this equation are −3 and −4. Therefore the answer is (B).

BEING AGGRESSIVE ON GEOMETRY PROBLEMS

Once you've learned the basic geometry definitions from Chapter 8, you're ready to tackle some more complex geometry problems.

Geometry problems on the PSAT are not hard because the rules of geometry are difficult. There are actually only a few rules to learn, and most of them are printed on your test booklet. (The formulas for area of a circle, square, and triangle can always be found on the first page of every Math section.)

So what makes geometry difficult on the PSAT? What makes it difficult is that ETS doesn't simply ask you to use a formula. You almost always have to use *more* than one rule to solve a problem. And often it's difficult to know which rule to use first.

The most important problem-solving technique for tackling PSAT geometry is to learn to *be aggressive*. This means, *whenever you have a diagram, ask yourself: What else do I know? Write everything you can think of on your booklet.* You may not see right away why it's important. But write it down anyway. Chances are good that you will be making progress toward the answer, without even knowing it.

Let's try this with the following problem:

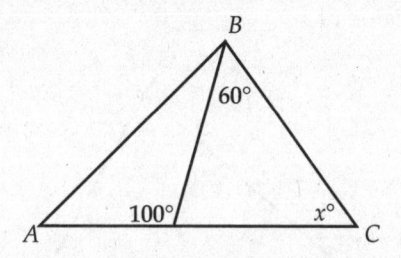

13. In triangle *ABC* above, $x =$
    (A) 30
    (B) 40
    (C) 50
    (D) 60
    (E) 70

Here's how to crack it
We know that the angle adjacent to the 100 degree angle must equal 80 degrees since we know that a straight line is 180 degrees. And since we know that the sum of the angles contained in a triangle must equal 180 degrees, we know that $80 + 60 + x = 180$, so $x = 40$. That's (B).

BE AGGRESSIVE!
Try the following:

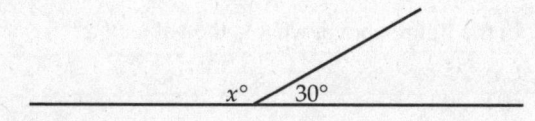

a. What is the sum of 30 and *x*? _____
b. What is the value of *x*? _____

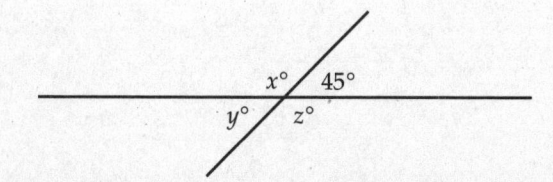

c. What is the value of *x*? _____ *y*? _____ *z*? _____

ADVANCED MATH PRINCIPLES ◆ 127

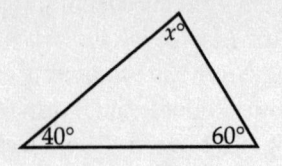

d. What is the sum of 60, 40, and x? _____

e. What is the value of x? _____

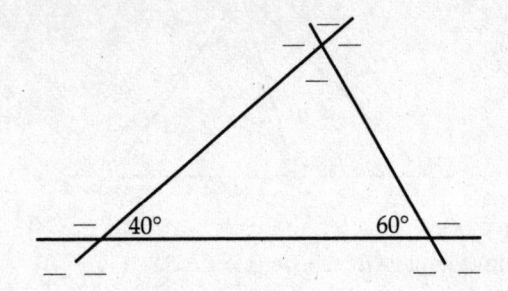

f. What are all of the angles on the above diagram?

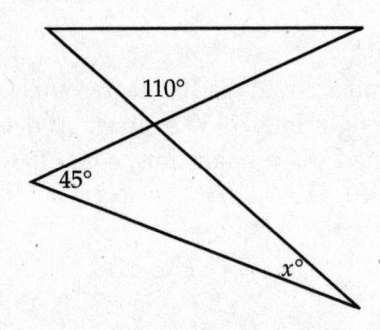

4. In the figure above, what is the value of x?
   (A) 25
   (B) 30
   (C) 35
   (D) 40
   (E) 50

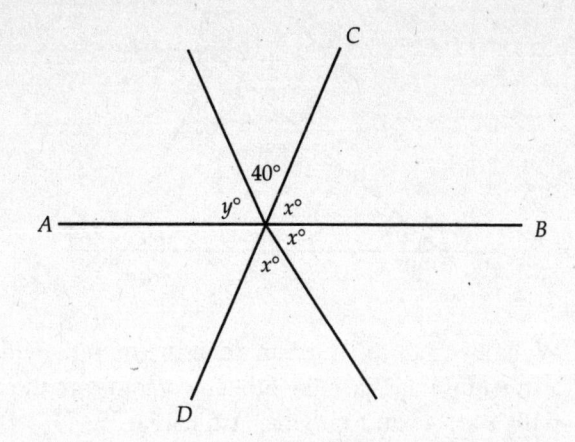

6. In the figure above, if AB and CD are lines, what is the value of y?

   (A) 60
   (B) 70
   (C) 75
   (D) 80
   (E) 85

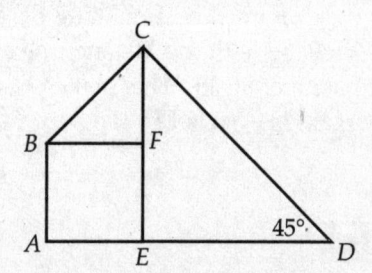

13. If the area of square ABFE = 25, and the area of triangle BCF = 10, what is the length of ED?

    (A) 7
    (B) 8
    (C) 9
    (D) 13
    (E) 14

Answers

a. 180

b. 150

c. $x = 135$, $y = 45$, $z = 135$

d. 180

e. 80

f.

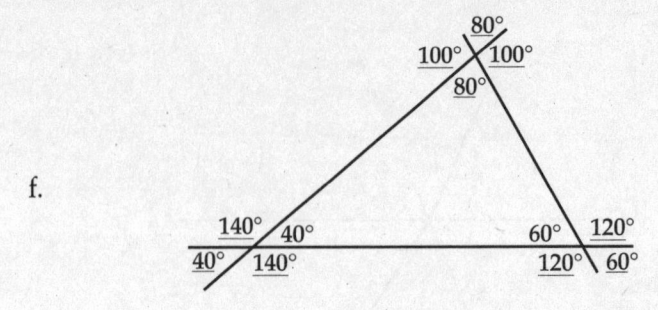

[Triangle figure with exterior angles labeled: top vertex 80°/100°/100°/80°; bottom-left vertex 140°/40°/40°/140°; bottom-right vertex 60°/120°/120°/60°]

4. (A) We know that the third angle in the triangle with 45 and *x* must be 110. Since the other two angles in the triangle with *x* are 45 and 110, then *x* must be 25.

6. (D) We know that the three angles labeled *x* are on a straight line, and therefore must make 180. Since $3x = 180$, $x = 60$. Since the unlabeled angle is opposite an *x*, it too must be 60. And 60, *y*, and 40 lie on the same line, so $60 + y + 40 = 180$. Therefore *y* must be 80.

13. (C) If the area of the square *ABFE* is 25, then each of its sides must be 5. Since *BF* is 5, and the area of triangle *BCF* is 10, then side *CF* must be 4, making *EC* equal to 9. Since *ECD* has one angle that is 90, and one angle that is 45, the other angle must be 45. This makes *ECD* an isosceles triangle. If *EC* is 9, so is *ED*.

THIRD SIDE RULE

One triangle rule that is often tested on the PSAT is the "third side" rule. The rule is:

The sum of every two sides of a triangle must be greater than the third side.

Two Rules

It is impossible for the third side of a triangle to be longer than the total of the other two sides. Nor can the third side of a triangle be shorter than the difference between the other two sides. Imagine a triangle with sides *a*, *b*, and *c*:
$a − b < c < a + b$.

Why? Look at it this way: If you had two sides of a triangle and the sum of their lengths was exactly as big as the third side, they wouldn't be able to make an angle (see the figure below).

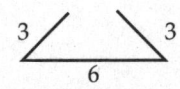

[Figure: two sides of length 3 meeting a base of length 6, flat]

If the sum of two sides of the triangle were equal to the third side, as in the figure, we would not be able to form a triangle. At most we could combine the two short sides to make a straight line of length 6 and place it next to the third side. If we want to "raise" those other two sides to make an angle, they will have to be a bit longer, or else they will separate like a drawbridge and leave a gap. So, to make a triangle, the other two sides will have to have a sum larger than 6.

With this rule in mind, let's look at the following problem:

14. Which of the following is a possible perimeter of a triangle with sides 5 and 8?
    (A) 15
    (B) 16
    (C) 17
    (D) 26
    (E) 30

Here's how to crack it
Let's use POE: Could the answer be (A)? If the perimeter is 15, this means that the sides must be 5, 8, and 2. But this is not a possible triangle, since the sides 5 and 2 don't have a sum that is larger than 8. Choice (B) has the same problem. Choice (C) could work, since a perimeter of 17 would mean that the sides would be 5, 8, and 4. These could be the sides of a triangle, since the sum of any two of them are larger than the third. This makes (C) the answer. Just to be sure, let's see why (D) and (E) don't work. If the perimeter is 26, the sides would have to be 5, 8, and 13. However, the sides 5 and 8 aren't greater than the side of 13, so these can't be the sides of a triangle. Likewise, if the perimeter were 30.

THE PYTHAGOREAN THEOREM

Whenever you have a right triangle, you can use the Pythagorean theorem. The theorem says that the sum of the squares of the legs of the triangle (the sides next to the right angle) will equal the square of the hypotenuse (the side opposite the right angle).

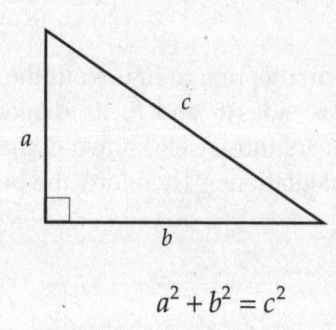

$$a^2 + b^2 = c^2$$

Pythagorean Theorem:
$a^2 + b^2 = c^2$, where c is the hypotenuse of a right triangle. Learn it, love it.

Two of the most common ratios of sides that fit the Pythagorean theorem are 3:4:5 and 5:12:13. Since these are ratios, any multiples of these numbers will also work, such as 6:8:10, and 30:40:50.

Try the following example:

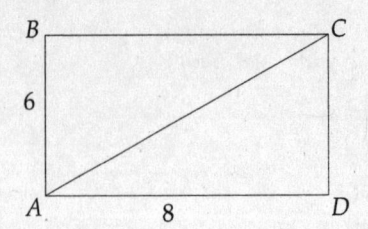

33. If *ABCD* is a rectangle, what is the perimeter of triangle *ABC*?

Here's how to crack it

We can use the Pythagorean theorem to figure out the length of the diagonal of the rectangle—since it has sides 6 and 8, its diagonal must be 10. (If you remembered that this is one of those well-known Pythagorean ratios, you didn't actually have to do the calculations.) Therefore, the perimeter of the triangle is 6 + 8 + 10, or 24.

132 ◆ CRACKING THE PSAT/NMSQT

SPECIAL RIGHT TRIANGLES

There are two right triangles whose properties may play a role in some harder PSAT math problems. They are the right triangles with angles 45–45–90 and the 30–60–90.

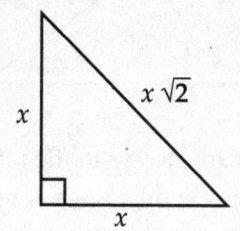

An isosceles right triangle will have angles that measure 45, 45, and 90 degrees. Whenever you have a 45–45–90 triangle, the sides will always be in the proportion $x : x : x\sqrt{2}$. This means that if one of the legs of the triangle measures 3, then the hypotenuse will be $3\sqrt{2}$.

This right triangle is important because it is half of a square. Memorizing the 45–45–90 triangle will allow you to easily find the diagonal of a square from its side, or find the side of a square from its diagonal.

Here's an example:

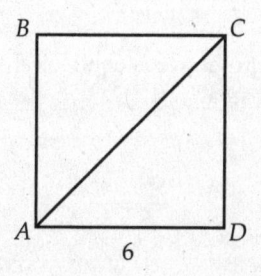

13. In the square above, what is the perimeter of triangle ABC?

    (A) $6\sqrt{2}$
    (B) 8
    (C) $12 + \sqrt{2}$
    (D) $12 + 6\sqrt{2}$
    (E) 18

Here's how to crack it

In this square, we know that each of the triangles formed by the diagonal AC will be a 45–45–90 right triangle. Since the square has a side of 6, using the 45–45–90 right triangle rule, each of the sides will be 6 and the diagonal will be $6\sqrt{2}$. Therefore the perimeter of the triangle will be $6 + 6 + 6\sqrt{2}$, or $12 + 6\sqrt{2}$ and the answer is (D).

The other important right triangle to memorize is the 30–60–90 right triangle.

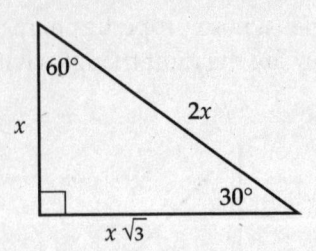

This triangle has sides that are always in the ratio $x : x\sqrt{3} : 2x$. If the smallest side (the x side) of the triangle is 5, then the sides will measure 5, $5\sqrt{3}$, and 10. This triangle is important because it is half of an equilateral triangle, and allows us to find the height of an equilateral triangle.

Try the following:

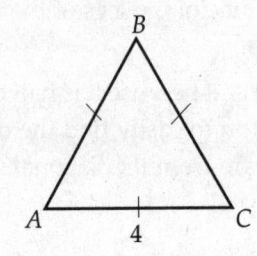

18. Triangle *ABC* above is equilateral, with sides of 4. What is its area?

    (A) 3
    (B) $4\sqrt{2}$
    (C) $4\sqrt{3}$
    (D) 8
    (E) $8\sqrt{3}$

Here's how to crack it

We can divide *ABC* into two equilateral triangles, each with base 2 and hypotenuse of 4. The height of *ABC* will be equal to the remaining side of these triangles. Since we know that the ratio of the sides of a 30–60–90 triangle is always $x : x\sqrt{3} : 2x$, we can figure out that the sides of these smaller triangles must be $2 : 2\sqrt{3} : 4$. So the height of *ABC* is $2\sqrt{3}$. Now we can solve for the area, which is $\frac{1}{2} \times 4 \times 2\sqrt{3}$, or $4\sqrt{3}$. That's choice (C).

OVERLAPPING FIGURES

Very often on a harder geometry problem you'll see two figures that overlap: a triangle and a square, a triangle and a circle, or a square and a circle. The key to solving these problems is figuring out what the two figures have in common.

For instance, the figure below shows a square *ABCD*.

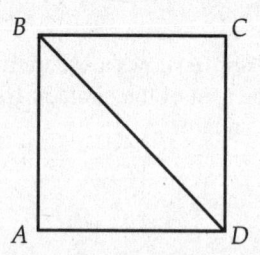

If we know the area or the side of the square, we can figure out its diagonal; since its diagonal is also the hypotenuse of triangles *ABD* and *BCD*, we could figure out the area of these triangles. Likewise, if we know the area of one of these triangles, we can figure out its hypotenuse, from which we could figure out the side or area of the square.

Take a look at the following problem:

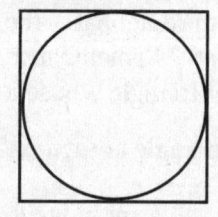

16. The figure above shows a circle inscribed in a square. If the area of the square is 36, what is the area of the circle?

   (A) 3
   (B) 6
   (C) 6π
   (D) 8π
   (E) 9π

Here's how to crack it

First, let's figure out what these two figures have in common. The side of the square is equal to the diameter of the circle. If the area of the square is 36, we know that its side is equal to 6, so the diameter of the circle is also equal to 6. This means that its radius is equal to 3. Now we can solve for the area of the circle, which will be πr^2 or 9π, choice (E). Let's try another one on the next page.

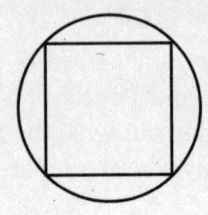

19. The figure above shows a square inscribed in a circle. If the area of the circle is 16π, what is the area of the square?

    (A) 4
    (B) 16
    (C) $16\sqrt{2}$
    (D) 32
    (E) $32\sqrt{2}$

Here's how to crack it

First, what do the circle and the square have in common? The diagonal of the square is the same as the diameter of the circle. So let's find the diameter of the circle. If the area of the circle is 16π, then its radius must be 4, and therefore its diameter is 8. So we know that the diagonal of the square is equal to 8. Now how do we find the side of the square? Remember that the diagonal of 8 is also the hypotenuse of a 45–45–90 right triangle whose legs are the sides of the square.

The ratios of the sides of this triangle are $x : x : x\sqrt{2}$. So we know that the $x\sqrt{2}$ side is equal to 8, and if we solve for x we'll get the side of the square. If $x\sqrt{2} = 8$ then $x = \dfrac{8}{\sqrt{2}}$. Now to get the area of the square, we take length times width or $\dfrac{8}{\sqrt{2}} \times \dfrac{8}{\sqrt{2}}$, which gives us (D) 32.

PROPORTIONALITY IN A CIRCLE

One more rule that plays a role in more advanced circle problems is: Arc measure is proportional to angle measure, which is proportional to sector area. This means that whatever fraction of the circumference of the circle a certain arc describes, the interior angle will be that same fraction of 360, and the sector outlined will be that same fraction of the total area of the circle.

That means that in the figure below:

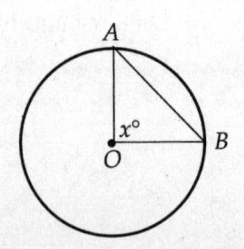

If angle x is equal to 90, which is one-quarter of 360, then the arc AB will be equal to one-quarter of the circumference of the circle and the area of the section of the circle outlined by the radii OA and OB will be equal to one-quarter of the area of the circle.

To see how this works in a question, try the following:

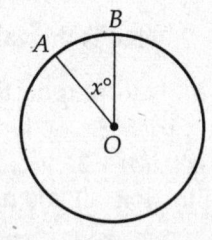

18. The circle above with center O has a radius of 4. If $x = 30$, what is the length of arc AB?

    (A) $\dfrac{\pi}{6}$

    (B) $\dfrac{2\pi}{3}$

    (C) 3

    (D) $\dfrac{3\pi}{2}$

    (E) 3π

Here's how to crack it

Since the interior angle x is equal to 30, which is $\dfrac{1}{12}$ of 360, we know that the arc AB will be equal to $\dfrac{1}{12}$ of the circumference of the circle. Since the circle has radius 4, its circumference will be 8π. Therefore arc AB will measure $\dfrac{1}{12} \times 8\pi$, or $\dfrac{2\pi}{3}$, choice (B).

FUNCTIONS

If you ever see a strange symbol on the PSAT, & or @ for example, don't worry. There are no special symbols you should have learned in school that the PSAT requires you to know. What you're looking at is a function problem.

A function problem is just ETS's way of testing whether you can follow directions. And the answer is always to plug in numbers. For instance, if you see a question like:

If @$x = 2x + 2$, what is the value of @3?

What ETS is asking you to do is to plug in the number that follows the @ symbol everywhere you see the variable x. So to solve for @3, you plug in 3 for x in the expression $2x + 2$, and get $2(3) + 2$, or 8.

To figure out the value of a function, all you have to do is plug in a value for x and solve.

Try the following:

5. If $x \# y = 4x - y$, what is the value of 3 # 4?

(A) 6
(B) 8
(C) 10
(D) 12
(E) 14

Here's how to crack it

In this case, we need to plug in whatever is to the left of the # for x, and whatever is to the right of the # for y. This means that we plug in 3 for x and 4 for y. So 3 # 4 will be equal to $3(4) - 4$, or 8. This makes (B) the answer.

PROBABILITY AND COMBINATIONS

Probability refers to the chance that an event will happen, and is always given as a fraction between 0 and 1. A probability of 0 means that the event will never happen; a probability of 1 means that it is certain to happen.

$$\text{Probability} = \frac{\text{number of outcomes you want}}{\text{number of possible outcomes}}$$

For instance, if you have a cube with faces numbered 1 to 6, what is the chance of rolling a 2? There is one face with the number 2 on it, out of 6 total faces. Therefore the probability of rolling a 2 is $\frac{1}{6}$.

What is the chance of rolling an even number on one roll of this number cube? There are 3 faces of the cube with an even number (the sides numbered 2, 4, and 6) out of a total of 6 faces. Therefore the probability of rolling an even number is $\frac{3}{6}$, or $\frac{1}{2}$.

Let's try one:

> In a jar there are 3 green gumballs, 5 red gumballs, 8 white gumballs, and 1 blue gumball. If one gumball is chosen at random, what is the probability that it will be red?
>
> (A) $\frac{5}{17}$
>
> (B) $\frac{5}{16}$
>
> (C) $\frac{1}{17}$
>
> (D) $\frac{1}{12}$
>
> (E) $\frac{1}{10}$

Here's how to crack it

To solve this problem, we take the number of things we want (the 5 red gumballs) and place it over the number of possible things we have to choose from (all 17 gumballs in the jar). This gives us choice (A).

PROBABILITY OF MORE THAN ONE EVENT

The probability that two events will both happen is always the product of the probabilities of the individual events. For instance, if we flip a coin, the probability that it will land "heads" is $\frac{1}{2}$. What is the chance that on two flips, the coin will land on "heads" twice in a row?

First flip	Second flip	Probability
$\frac{1}{2}$ ×	$\frac{1}{2}$ =	$\frac{1}{4}$

On the first flip, the chance of the coin landing on "heads" is $\frac{1}{2}$. On the second flip, the chance of the coin landing on "heads" is also $\frac{1}{2}$. So the chance that it will land on heads twice in a row is $\frac{1}{4}$.

COMBINATIONS

Combination problems ask you how many different ways a number of things could be chosen or combined. Here's an example:

14. Ms. Grady will choose one boy and one girl from her class to be the class representatives. If there are 3 boys and 7 girls in her class, how many different pairs of class representatives could she pick?

    (A) 10
    (B) 13
    (C) 21
    (D) 23
    (E) 25

Here's how to crack it

There's a very simple rule for combination problems:

The number of combinations is the product of the number of things you have to choose from.

In the problem above, Ms. Grady has 3 boys to choose from and 7 girls to choose from, so the number of different combinations she could choose is 3×7, or 21, choice (C).

Don't forget to watch out for certain cases where some of the choices are fixed, and therefore don't actually count as choices:

Students at Smalltown High	
Eighth Grade	9
Ninth Grade	8
Tenth Grade	10

16. Mr. Livingstone will choose one eighth-grader, one ninth-grader, and one tenth-grader from the students at Smalltown High to be on the student council. If he knows that the ninth-grader on the student council will be Julia Witherspoon, how many different combinations of students could he pick for the student council?

    (A) 72
    (B) 80
    (C) 90
    (D) 720
    (E) 840

Here's how to crack it

Though the problem begins by saying there are 8 ninth-graders, it turns out that there is only one possibility for the ninth-grader. The number of ninth-graders that Mr. Livingstone can choose from is, in fact, only 1. So the correct way to figure out the number of possible combinations is to multiply

Eighth-grade		Ninth-grade		Tenth-grade
9	×	1	×	10

Their product is 90, so the answer is (C).

Now that you've mastered these topics, try the following problems:

Ice Cream	Toppings
Chocolate	Peanuts
Vanilla	Hot Fudge
Strawberry	Chocolate Chips
Wild Berry	
Coffee	

14. Kim is going to buy an ice cream sundae. A sundae consists of one flavor of ice cream and one topping. If she can choose from the kinds of ice cream and toppings above, how many different sundaes could she create?

    (A) 8
    (B) 12
    (C) 15
    (D) 18
    (E) 24

15. At the school cafeteria, students can choose from 3 different salads, 5 different main dishes, and 2 different desserts. If Isabel chooses one salad, one main dish, and one dessert for lunch, how many different lunches could she choose?

    (A) 15
    (B) 30
    (C) 45
    (D) 60
    (E) 80

16. If a drawer contains 6 white socks, 6 black socks, and 8 red socks, what is the probability that a sock drawn at random from the drawer will be red?

   (A) $\dfrac{1}{8}$

   (B) $\dfrac{2}{5}$

   (C) $\dfrac{1}{2}$

   (D) $\dfrac{2}{3}$

   (E) $\dfrac{4}{5}$

17. A bowl of marbles contains 8 blue marbles, 6 green marbles, 10 red marbles, and 1 white marble. If one marble is drawn at random from the bowl, what is the probability that it will be either blue or green?

   (A) $\dfrac{8}{25}$

   (B) $\dfrac{9}{25}$

   (C) $\dfrac{14}{25}$

   (D) $\dfrac{3}{5}$

   (E) $\dfrac{4}{5}$

Answers

14. (C) Since there are 5 kinds of ice cream to choose from, and 3 toppings, the number of different sundaes will be 5×3, or 15.

15. (B) The number of possible combinations is the product of the number of things Isabel can choose from: in this case, 3 different salads × 5 different main dishes × 2 different desserts = 30 possible combinations.

16. (B) The total number of socks in the drawer is 6 + 6 + 8 = 20. The number of socks we want (the red ones) is equal to 8, so the chance of drawing a red sock is 8 out of 20, which reduces to $\frac{2}{5}$.

17. (C) The total number of marbles is 8 + 6 + 10 + 1 = 25. The number of marbles that are blue or green is 8 + 6 = 14. Therefore the chance of drawing either a blue or a green is 14 out of 25.

11
Writing Skills

WSC

The Writing Skills Component contains 39 questions, comprised of 19 Error Identifications (Error ID), 14 Improving Sentences (make the sentence better), and 6 Improving Paragraphs (fix the paragraph). The Writing Skills Component (WSC for short) will be the last section of the PSAT/NMSQT. You will have 30 minutes to answer 39 questions. In other words, you have been allotted less than one minute per question.

How Will You Do Well on the WSC?

- By reviewing/learning PSAT/NMSQT grammar
- By knowing how to attack each type of question
- By knowing which questions to do and which to skip

PSAT/NMSQT Grammar

The grammar ETS chooses to test on the PSAT/NMSQT is pretty basic. Of course, the test writers do their best to trip you up with extraneous phrases and distracting words. Don't sweat it: This chapter will review all the grammar you need to see through ETS's tricks and traps. If, after working through this chapter, you feel particularly weak on any of the areas of grammar discussed here, pick up a copy of The Princeton Review's *Grammar Smart* for a more in-depth review.

Question Strategy

Every question type on the PSAT/NMSQT can be cracked, and WSC questions are no exception. While reviewing the basic grammar you need, you will also learn how to crack Error ID and Improving Sentences questions. After you solidify your approach to these question types, you'll learn how to crack Improving Paragraphs questions by employing the grammar and skills you've already mastered. Of course, you need to practice this stuff to really make it work. After working through the drills in this chapter, be sure to take a full-length PSAT/NMSQT.

To Do or Not To Do

The WSC is not arranged in order of difficulty, therefore, to do well on these questions, you need to determine when a problem is hard and should be skipped. What makes a question hard? It either contains grammar that you don't know, or it's long and time-consuming. As a general rule, you will approach the section in order: Do Error IDs first, since they're quick and POE works well on these; do Improving Sentences questions next, but plan to skip ones in which the entire sentence is underlined; do Improving Paragraphs questions last because they require dealing with an entire passage for only six questions.

SNEAK PREVIEW

Before we begin reviewing ETS's grammar, let's take a peek at the first two question types you'll see on the WSC.

<u>This</u> is an <u>example</u> of an Error ID
  A   B
question <u>that</u> <u>has</u> no error. <u>No error</u>
         C   D   E

An Error ID question gives you a sentence that has four words or phrases underlined, each with a corresponding letter underneath. At the end of each sentence will be "No error"—choice (E). There are some important things you need to know about Error IDs:

- There is never more than one error per sentence.

- If there is an error, it's always underlined.

- Approximately 20 percent of all Error ID questions are correct as written, so don't be afraid to pick choice (E).

- Error IDs are short, and you should usually be able to eliminate at least one answer choice, so guess on all Error ID questions.

- Do Error ID questions first.

IMPROVING SENTENCES

This is an example of an Improving Sentences question <u>that does not contain</u> an error.

(A) that does not contain
(B) that has not been containing
(C) which has not been contain
(D) which is not being with
(E) about which there is nothing to indicate it being with

Improving Sentences questions give you a sentence, part or all of which is underlined. The underlined part may or may not contain a grammatical error. There are some important things you need to know about Improving Sentences questions:

- Answer choice (A) is a reprint of the underlined section. Therefore, if you decide that the sentence contains no error, choose answer choice (A).

- Approximately 20 percent of all Improving Sentences questions are correct as written, so don't be afraid to pick choice (A).

- If you decide the underlined portion of the sentence contains an error, eliminate choice (A). Also, eliminate any other choice that does not fix the error.

- If you are unsure whether the sentence contains an error, look to your answer choices for a clue (more on this later).
- KISS: Keep It Short and Sweet. Concise answers are preferable.

GRAMMAR? UGH!

To do well on the WSC, you need to remember some basic grammar rules. Now, don't get worked up about being tested on grammar. PSAT/NMSQT grammar is not difficult, nor is it extensive. In fact, the WSC really only tests five basic grammatical concepts:

1. verbs
2. nouns
3. pronouns
4. prepositions
5. other little things

These are the five areas in which a sentence can "go wrong." They will function as a checklist for you—every time you read a sentence, you will look at these five areas to find the error. If you don't find one after checking these five things, then there probably isn't one.

NO ERROR?

As we've mentioned, 20 percent of Error ID questions and Improving Sentences questions contain no error. If you've used your checklist and can't find a mistake, chances are there isn't one. Don't be afraid to pick No Error—(E) on Error ID and (A) on Improving Sentences questions.

We will use Error ID questions to illustrate the first four areas of grammar. Before we get going on the grammar stuff, let's learn how to crack an Error ID question.

CRACKING ERROR IDS

As we mentioned, an Error ID question is a short sentence that has four words or phrases underlined and lettered. Your job is to determine if any one of those four underlined segments contains an error. If so, you are to blacken the corresponding oval on your answer sheet. If not, you are to choose "(E) No error."

Let's look at an example of an Error ID to learn how to beat these questions:

The Halloween party was a <u>great</u> success:
                            A

the children <u>enjoyed</u> bobbing <u>for apples</u>,
              B   C

playing party games, and <u>to put</u> on costumes.
                          D

<u>No error</u>
E

THE APPROACH

To solve an Error ID, you need to look at the sentence one piece at a time. As you read through the sentence, pause after each underlined segment and ask, "Is there anything wrong yet?" Run through the first four categories of your grammar checklist. Verb problem? Noun problem? Pronoun problem? Preposition problem? If these four areas check out, cross off the segment (it's not your answer) and move on.

Look at the first segment of this sentence: "The Halloween party was a great success...." Is there a problem with the word *great*? No. Put a slash through answer choice (A). Next segment: "the children enjoyed...." Any problem with this verb? No—it's in the past tense, just like the "was" in the first line, so everything is fine. Cross it off.

Continuing on: "bobbing for apples...." No problem here—cross off (C). Keep going: "playing party games, and to put on costumes." Wait a minute—something doesn't sound right. "To put" is a verb. Notice in this example, ETS gives you a series of activities (verbs): "bobbing," "playing," and "to put." When in a series, all the verbs need to have the same form. Therefore, "to put" should be "putting." The answer is (D).

By the way, you have just learned the first verb rule: When a series of activities is described in a sentence, make sure all the verbs are expressed the same way—make sure they are *parallel*.

TRIM THE FAT

Often an Error ID will contain extraneous phrases that distract from the meat of the sentence and cause you to miss an error. How can you avoid getting waylaid by distracting phrases? "Trim the Fat." As you work through a sentence, cross off anything that is not essential to the sentence: prepositional phrases, phrases offset by commas, etc. Crossing out the distracting phrases puts the important parts of a sentence, the subject and verb for example, together and prevents you from making careless errors.

Let's look at another example:

> Japan, since the early part of the 1980s,
>   A
> have been able to export the high quality
>   B   C
> technology demanded by consumers. No error
>   D   E

Here's how to crack it

First, Trim the Fat. What's the subject of the sentence? *Japan*. Once you see that there is no problem with choice (A), *since*, you can cross off the stuff between the commas—it's there to distract you. What's the verb? *Have been*. "Japan have been?" Don't think so. *Japan* is singular, so it needs a singular verb. The answer is (B).

WRITING SKILLS ◆ 149

BE AGGRESSIVE

Error IDs are typically short and uncomplicated. Be aggressive as you go through these sentences. Read the sentence quickly once, keeping your checklist in mind. If you spot a problem, jump to it—you don't need to labor over the whole sentence if your eye is drawn to a problem right away.

DO I HAVE TO READ THE WHOLE THING?

Once you've found the error, do you need to read the rest of the sentence? Well, if you're sure of the error you've found, a quick read will be easy and reassuring. If you are not so sure, you will need to read the rest of the sentence to be sure you haven't missed anything. Since Error IDs are short and sweet, take a quick second to read them through.

GUESSING

There are three reasons why you should always guess on an Error ID question:

1. **You can always eliminate at least one answer choice.** If you read a sentence that sounds wrong, you can immediately eliminate answer choice (E), even if you are not sure which underlined segment is the culprit.

2. **The odds are with you.** Only one of the four underlined parts of the sentence is wrong, if any at all. You're bound to be able to determine that a few of the segments are correct even if your grammar's not great.

3. **You don't have to fix the error in the sentence; you only have to identify it.** Therefore, guessing is easy. Once you've narrowed it down, take a guess and move on.

As we review the first four areas of grammar, you will work through a bunch of Error ID questions. This will give you a feel for how they work and how easy it is to guess aggressively.

Now that you know how to approach Error IDs, let's work on reviewing ETS's grammar rules.

VERBS

A verb is an action word. It tells what the subject of the sentence is doing. You've already seen two ways in which a verb can "go wrong." There are a total of three things about a verb to check out:

(a) Does it **agree** with its subject?

(b) Is it **parallel** in structure to the other verbs in the sentence?

(c) Is it in the proper **tense**?

Do They Agree?

The rule regarding subject-verb agreement is simple: singular with singular, plural with plural. If you are given a singular subject (he, she, it), then your verb must also be singular (is, has, was). (In case you don't remember, the subject of the sentence is the noun that the verb modifies—the person or thing that is *doing* the action.)

Easy enough, except, as you have already seen, ETS has a way of putting lots of stuff between the subject and the verb to make you forget whether your subject was singular or plural. Remember Japan from the last example? Look at another:

> The statistics <u>released by</u> the state
>   A
> department <u>makes</u> the economic situation
>   B
> look <u>bleaker than</u> it really <u>is</u>. <u>No error</u>
>   C   D E

Here's how to crack it

At first glance, this sentence may appear fine. But let's pull it apart. What is the sentence about? The *statistics*—a plural subject. If the subject is plural, then the verb must be plural, too. *Makes* is the verb modifying *statistics*, but it is a singular verb—no can do. The answer is (B).

Why did the sentence sound okay at first? Because of the stuff stuck between *statistics* and *makes*. The phrase *released by the state department* places a singular noun right before the verb. Get rid of the extraneous stuff (i.e., Trim the Fat) and the error becomes obvious.

Knowing When It's Single

Sometimes you may not know if a noun is singular or plural, making it tough to determine whether its verb should be singular or plural. Of course you know nouns like *he* and *cat* are singular, but what about *family* or *everybody*? The following is a list of "tricky" nouns—technically called collective nouns. They are nouns that typically describe a group of people but are considered singular and thus need a singular verb:

The family *is*

The jury *is*

The group *is*

The audience *is*

The congregation *is*

The United States (or any other country) *is*

The following pronouns also take singular verbs:

Either *is*

Neither *is*

None *is*

Each *is*

Anyone *is*

No one *is*

Everyone *is*

"And" or "Or"

Subjects joined by "and" are plural: Bill and Pat *were* going to the show. However, nouns joined by "or" can be singular or plural—if the last noun given is singular, then it takes a singular verb; if the last noun given is plural, it takes a plural verb.

Pam Cruise and Jim Braswell,

neither of whom takes the bus to work, is
   A   B   C

secretly plotting to take over the world. No error
                      D   E

Here's how to crack it

Once again ETS is trying to trip you up by separating the subject from the verb. You know what to do—Trim the Fat! What's the subject? Pam Cruise *and* Jim Braswell. We know the subject is plural because of the "and." Cross off the stuff between commas and you have "Pam Cruise and Jim Braswell . . . is." Can we use the singular verb "is" with our plural subject? No way—the answer is (C).

Are They Parallel?

The next thing you need to check out about a verb is whether it and the other verbs in the sentence are parallel. In the first example used in this chapter, the children at the Halloween party were "bobbing," "playing," and "to put." The last verb, "to put," is not written in the same form as the other verbs in the series. In other words, it's not parallel. The sentence should read, "the children were *bobbing* for apples, *playing* party games, and *putting* on costumes."

Try another example:

As a competitor in the Iron Man competition,
      A

Scott was required to swim 2.4 miles, to
     B   C

bike 112 miles, and running the last 26 miles. No error
                          D   E

Here's how to crack it

If an Error ID contains an underlined verb that is part of a series of activities, isolate the verbs to see if they are parallel. In this sentence, Scott is required "to swim," "to bike," and "running." What's the problem? He should be required "to swim," "to bike," and "to run"—and then to collapse. The answer is (D).

ARE YOU TENSE?

As you know, verbs come in different tenses—for example, "is" is present tense, while "was" is past tense. You've probably heard of other tenses like "past perfect." Well, first of all, don't worry about identifying the kind of tense used in a sentence—you will never be asked to identify verb tense, only to make sure that the tense is consistent throughout a sentence.

For the most part, verb tense should not change within a sentence. Look at the following example:

> Throughout the Middle Ages, women work
>   A   B
> beside men, knowing that the effort of men and
>   C
> women alike was essential to survival. No error
>   D   E

Here's how to crack it

Our subject? *Women.* Our verb? *Work*—which would be fine if the sentence hadn't started out with "Throughout the Middle Ages. . . ." Is the sentence talking about women working beside men right now? No, it's talking about the Middle Ages. The verb should be *worked*—the answer is (B).

Just the Answer, Please

Remember, when solving Error ID questions, all you have to do is identify the error. Don't worry if you don't know exactly how to fix an error—ETS only cares if you can identify it.

NOUNS

The only thing you really have to check for with nouns is agreement. Agreement is a big thing for most grammarians, ETS included. Verbs must agree with their subjects, nouns must agree with other nouns, and pronouns must agree with the nouns they represent. When you read an Error ID, if you come across an underlined noun, check to see if it refers to or is associated with any other nouns in the sentence. If so, make sure they match in number.

For example:

> As elections approach, campaign managers
>   A
> pay more attention to swing voters, who
>   B   C
> often don't make their decision until the day
>   D
> of the election. No error
>   E

WRITING SKILLS ◆ 153

Here's how to crack it

Take it one piece at a time. "<u>As elections approach</u> . . ." has a subject and a verb, but they agree. No problem here. Cross off (A).

Continuing on, " . . . campaign managers pay more <u>attention to</u>. . . ." No problem we can see. Cross it off. Going on, " . . . swing voters, <u>who</u>. . . ." Hey, is this one of those who/whom things? Maybe you are not too sure about when to use "who" versus when to use "whom." If you aren't sure whether an underlined segment is right, leave it and check out the rest of the sentence. You may get rid of everything else, or you may find an error somewhere else.

Going on: "often don't make their <u>decision</u> . . . ." Is it correct to say "their decision"? Who is being discussed, anyway? The *swing voters*, which is plural. Can all the swing voters make one and the same decision? Of course not. They make *decisions*. The answer is (D).

PRONOUNS

As with verbs, there are three things you need to check when you have pronouns:

(a) Do they **agree**?

(b) Are they **ambiguous**?

(c) Do they use the right **case**?

I AGREE

As you know, a pronoun is a little word that is inserted to represent a noun (he, she, it, they, etc.). As with everything else, pronouns must agree with their nouns: The pronoun that replaces a singular noun must also be singular, and the pronoun that replaces a plural noun must be plural. If different pronouns are used to refer to the same subject or one pronoun is used to replace another, the pronouns must also agree.

This may seem obvious, but it is also the most commonly violated rule in ordinary speech. How often have you heard people say, "*Everyone* must hand in *their* application before leaving." Remember from our list of singular pronouns that "everyone" is singular? But "their" is plural. This sentence is incorrect.

To spot a pronoun agreement error, look for pronouns that show up later in a sentence. If you see a pronoun underlined, find the noun or pronoun it is replacing and make sure the two agree. Let's look at an example:

Everyone <u>on the softball</u> team <u>who came up</u> to bat
              A   B

squinted <u>at the pitcher</u> in order to keep the sun's
            C

glaring rays out of <u>their eyes</u>. <u>No error</u>
               D   E

Here's how to crack it
Is there an underlined pronoun late in this sentence? There sure is: "their eyes." Whose eyes are being referred to? Let's Trim the Fat to check this sentence:

> "**Everyone** . . . squinted . . . to keep the sun's . . . rays . . . out of **their** eyes."

"Everyone" is singular, but "their" is plural, so it cannot replace "everyone."

The answer is (D).

To Whom Do You Refer?
When a pronoun appears in a sentence, it should be infinitely clear which noun it replaces. For example:

> *"After looking over the color samples, Mary agreed with Martha that her porch should be painted green."*

Whose porch is being painted green? Mary's or Martha's? This sentence would be unacceptable to ETS, because it is not perfectly clear to whom the word "her" in the sentence is referring. This is pronoun ambiguity, and it is unacceptable on the PSAT/NMSQT.

If you see a pronoun late in a sentence, check to see if it clearly refers to a noun. Be especially wary if the early part of the sentence contains two singular or two plural nouns. Try the following example:

> The director <u>told</u> the star of the
>   A
>
> production that <u>he</u> was making far too
>   B
>
> much money <u>to tolerate</u> such nasty
>   C
>
> <u>treatment from</u> the producer. <u>No error</u>
>   D   E

Here's how to crack it
Let's take it apart a piece at a time. "The director <u>told</u> . . ." Do a quick tense scan of the sentence. Is it past tense? Yes. Cross off (A) and go on.

Let's Trim the Fat to check the next answer choice:

> *"The director told the star . . . that <u>he</u> was making far too much money. . . ."*

Who was making far too much money? It is not clear whether the pronoun "he" is referring to the director or the star. The answer is (B).

Case? What Case?
Pronouns come in two "flavors," known as cases: subjective or objective. The subject, as you know, is the person or thing performing the action in the sentence. The object is the person or thing *receiving* the action. Think of it this way: An object just sits there. It doesn't *do* anything; rather, things are done to it. The subject, by contrast, does something.

When it comes to pronouns, subjects and objects are represented by different pronouns. For example, "I" is a subjective pronoun, as in "I did it," while "me" is an objective pronoun, as in "it happened to me." Most of the time, you will know if the wrong pronoun case (as it's called) is used because the sentence will sound funny. However, this is another area that is often butchered by our spoken language. When in doubt, Trim the Fat to figure out whether the pronoun is the subject (performing the action) or the object (receiving the action).

SUBJECT PRONOUNS

Singular	Plural
I	We
You	You
He	They
She	They
It	They
Who	Who

OBJECT PRONOUNS

Singular	Plural
Me	Us
You	You
Him	Them
Her	Them
It	Them
Whom	Whom

Try the following example:

The leading roles in the <u>widely acclaimed play</u>, a
                              A
modern <u>version of</u> an Irish folktale, were
        B
<u>performed by</u> Jessica and <u>him</u>. <u>No error</u>
     C   D   E

Here's how to crack it

Read through the sentence, checking each underlined segment. "The leading roles in the <u>widely acclaimed play</u> . . . ." No problem here—cross off (A) and move on. Next segment: " . . . a modern <u>version of</u> . . . ." Again, it seems fine. Cross it out and keep going.

To check the next two, do a little cutting: "The leading roles . . . were <u>performed by</u> Jessica and <u>him</u>." "Performed by" is fine. What about "him"? Get rid of Jessica to check: "The . . . roles . . . were performed by . . . him." "Him" is an objective pronoun and, in this sentence, is used correctly. "He performed" would need the subjective pronoun; "performed by him" is the correct use of the objective pronoun. The answer is (E), No error.

I or Me?

Are you frequently being corrected on the "I" versus "me" thing? If so, you're not alone. In the example we just did, if you were to replace "him" with either "I" or "me," which would it be? You would use "me" since you need an objective pronoun. It is often difficult to tell which case to use when the pronoun is coupled with another noun or pronoun. If you are having trouble deciding which case to use, remember to Trim the Fat: In this case, remove the other person (*Jessica* in the example we just did).

Which one is correct?

The book belongs to Jerry and I.

The book belongs to Jerry and me.

If you're not sure, take Jerry out of the picture:

The book belongs to _____.

Me, of course. It's much easier to tell which is correct if the extraneous stuff is removed. Here's a tricky one:

Clare is more creative than me.

Clare is more creative than I.

Be careful. This may look as though the pronoun is an object, but actually the sentence is written in an incomplete form. What you are really saying in this sentence is, "Clare is more creative than I <u>am</u>." The "am" is understood. When in doubt, say the sentence aloud, adding on the "am" to see whether it is hiding at the end of the sentence.

Don't Be Passive

One final note about subjects and objects: ETS prefers sentences written in the active voice to the passive voice. If a sentence is written in the active voice, the subject of the sentence is doing something. If a sentence is written in the passive voice, the main player becomes an object and things happen to him.

Which of the following is written in the active voice?

She took the PSAT/NMSQT.

The PSAT/NMSQT was taken by her.

She took the PSAT/NMSQT is active because *she* is the subject of the sentence and she is doing something. *The PSAT/NMSQT was taken by her* is passive because *her* is now the object of *by*, not the subject of the sentence. This will be important to know when attacking Improving Sentences questions.

PREPOSITIONS

Remember prepositions? About, above, across, around, along. . . . You use prepositions all the time to add information to a sentence. Using different prepositions can change the meaning of a sentence. For example:

I am standing *by* you.

I am standing *for* you.

I am standing *near* you.

I am standing *under* you.

DRILL 1

In the English language, certain words must be paired with certain prepositions. These pairs of words are called *idioms*. There are really no rules to idioms, so you need to just use your ear and memorize ones that are tricky. Here is a list of some common idioms you may come across. Fill in the blanks with the missing prepositions (some may have more than one possibility). Answers can be found at the end of the chapter.

1. I am *indebted* _____ you.

2. I am *resentful* _____ you.

3. I am *delighted* _____ you.

4. I am *jealous* _____ you.

5. I am *worried* _____ you.

6. I am *astounded* _____ you.

7. The women had a *dispute* _____ politics.

8. You have a *responsibility* _____ take care of your pet.

9. My friends are not so *different* _____ your friends.

Try an Error ID example:

<u>Despite</u> the <u>poor weather</u>, my sister <u>and I</u> were
  A   B   C

planning <u>on attending</u> the festival. <u>No error</u>
           D   E

Here's how to crack it

Let's pull it apart: "<u>Despite</u> the <u>poor weather</u>. . . ." Both of these seem okay, so let's move on. Next phrase: "my sister <u>and I</u> were. . . ." Is the "I" okay? It's the subject, so it's okay (if you can't tell, reword the sentence, leaving out "my sister"). How about the next part: "planning <u>on attending</u> . . . "? You may have heard people say this, but it's wrong. The preposition that should accompany "planning" is "to." The sentence should read, " . . . my sister and I were planning *to attend* the festival." The answer is (D).

ERROR ID AND YOUR GRAMMAR CHECKLIST

Let's do a quick review. On Error ID questions, have your grammar checklist ready (keep it in your head, or jot it on your test booklet). It should look like this:

1. Is there an underlined **verb**? If so,
   (a) Does it **agree** with its subject?
   (b) Is it **parallel** in structure to the other verbs in the sentence?
   (c) Is it in the proper **tense**?

2. Is there an underlined **noun**? If so,
   (a) Does it **agree** in number with any other noun to which it refers?

3. Is there an underlined **pronoun**? If so,
   (a) Does it **agree** with the noun/pronoun it represents?
   (b) Can you tell to which noun it refers or is it **ambiguous**?
   (c) Does it use the right **case** (subjective or objective)?

4. Is there an underlined **preposition**? If so,
   (a) Is it the **right one**?

When you approach Error ID questions, remember to:

- Read them with your checklist in mind
- Cross off underlined stuff that is right
- Trim the Fat
- Not be afraid to pick (E), No error
- Guess if you don't know the answer

Drill 2

Use the following drill to solidify your Error ID strategy. Answers can be found at the end of the chapter.

1. <u>Many</u> young adults find it extremely
     A

   difficult <u>to return</u> home from college
           B

   and <u>abide with</u> the rules <u>set down</u> by
        C   D

   their parents. <u>No error</u>
                E

2. I <u>recently</u> heard an <u>announcement where</u>
      A   B

   the Rangers <u>will be playing</u> a game at
                   C

   home <u>this</u> weekend. <u>No error</u>
        D   E

3. Just <u>last month</u>, two weeks after the
        A

   announcement <u>of elections</u>
                 B

   in Soviet Georgia, 92-year-old Fydor

   <u>has cast</u> his first vote <u>in 70 years</u>.
     C   D

   <u>No error</u>
   E

4. When the student council announced

   its intention <u>to elect</u> a minority
           A

   representative, neither the <u>principal</u>
                         B

   <u>nor</u> the superintendent <u>were</u> willing to
    C   D

   comment on the issue. <u>No error</u>
                       E

5. It is a <u>more difficult</u> task to learn to
          A

   type than <u>mastering</u> a <u>simple</u> word
           B   C

   processing <u>program</u>. <u>No error</u>
           D   E

6. Educators and parents <u>agree</u> that a
   　　　　　　　　　　　　　A

   daily reading time will not only

   enhance a child's education <u>but also</u>
   　　　　　　　　　　　　　　　　B

   <u>encouraging</u> the child to read
   　　C

   <u>independently</u>. <u>No error</u>
   　　D　　　　　　E

IMPROVING SENTENCES

So far we have been concentrating on Error ID questions while reviewing grammar. The good news is Improving Sentences questions test a lot of the same grammar. Let's look at a sample question to see how to crack these questions.

> Although Tama Janowitz and Jay McInerney both have new books on the market, <u>only one of the two are successful</u>.
>
> (A) only one of the two are successful
> (B) only one of the two is successful
> (C) only one of the two books are successful
> (D) only one of the two books is successful
> (E) one only of the books has been successful

Here's how to crack it

There are two ways to go about cracking an Improving Sentences question. The preferable way is for you to identify the error as you read the underlined part of the sentence. How will you do that, you ask? By using your handy-dandy grammar checklist, of course. Let's try it on this example. The underlined portion of the sentence says, "only one of the two are successful." Let's run through your list. Is there an underlined verb? Yes—"are." Does it agree with its subject? What is its subject? If we Trim the Fat—in this case, the prepositional phrase "of the two"—we can easily see the subject is "one." Is it correct to say "one are"? Of course not.

So you've identified the problem—great. However, Improving Sentences questions require you to go farther than just identifying the error—they also require you to fix the error, thus "improving" the sentence. To do this, you will use your old friend: Process of Elimination. First, we know that answer choice (A) is simply a repeat of the underlined portion; therefore, once you've identified an error, cross off answer choice (A).

Next, scan the rest of the answer choices and cross off any answer choices that don't fix the problem you've identified. In our example, we know the verb "are" is wrong. What answer choice can we get rid of? Answer choice (C).

WRITING SKILLS ◆ 161

So far, we have eliminated answer choices (A) and (C). Let's look at the remaining choices to see how they fix the error we found. Answer choice (B) changes "are" to "is," a singular verb. That works. Answer choice (D) does the same thing. Both of these choices are possible. Answer choice (E) changes the verb to "has been." A quick glance at the sentence tells us that this is in the wrong tense—we need present tense. Cross off answer choice (E).

Okay, down to two. The last thing to check is the difference between the two choices that fixed the original problem. Sometimes the underlined portion of the sentence contains a secondary error that also needs to be fixed. Other times, an answer may fix the original problem, but introduce a new error. In this example, the difference between (B) and (D) is that (B) uses the vague language "only one of the two is successful" while (D) clarifies "only one of the two books is successful." We know that ETS hates to be ambiguous, and (B) does not make it as clear that the sentence is referring to one of the two books as opposed to one of the two authors. Therefore, our answer is (D).

Can you say time-consuming?

Wow—that took a while! As you can see, Improving Sentences questions are a bit more work than Error IDs. That's why you want to do all the Error ID questions before you attempt the Improving Sentences questions. Also, you may, on occasion, find it necessary to skip a question, especially one where the whole sentence is underlined. As a general rule, if you can spot the error, you should do the question, since POE is on your side. If you can't spot the error immediately, try the back-up plan, but be ready to back out if you are spending too much time on the question.

BACK-UP PLAN?

What's the back-up plan? Let's say you couldn't tell if there was an error in the example we just did. You thought it might be okay, but you weren't sure. How could you check? By scanning your answer choices. Your answer choices can tip you off to the error contained in a sentence by revealing what is being fixed in each choice. In the example we just did, a quick scan of the answer choices reveals that the verb is being altered:

(A) ... are ...
(B) ... is ...
(C) ... are ...
(D) ... is ...
(E) ... has been ...

Once you pick up on the error being tested, you can try to figure out which form is correct. Let's try another example, using our back-up plan to illustrate how it works.

Whenever people hear of a natural disaster, even in a distant part of the world, <u>you feel sympathy for the people affected</u>.

(A) you feel sympathy for the people affected
(B) people being affected causes sympathy
(C) they feel sympathetic for those people
(D) they feel sympathy for the people affected
(E) you feel sympathetic for the people affected

Here's how to crack it

When you first read this sentence, you may feel that something is wrong, but may not be able to pinpoint what it is. No problem—let your answer choices do the work for you. A quick scan of the answer choices reveals a possible pronoun problem:

(A) you . . .
(B) people . . .
(C) they . . .
(D) they . . .
(E) you . . .

Now that you know what to check, let's Trim the Fat:

Whenever people hear of a natural disaster . . . you . . .

Is *you* the right pronoun to represent people? No. Cross off (A) and any other answer that doesn't fix the *you*. That leaves us with (B), (C), and (D). If you have no idea how the rest of the sentence should read, you've still given yourself great odds of "guessing" this question correctly. But let's forge ahead.

Answer choice (B) doesn't make any sense upon closer inspection. Cross it off. Now you're down to two. Which answer choice is more clear and less awkward? Answer choice (D):

"Whenever people hear of a natural disaster . . . they feel sympathy for the people affected."

OTHER LITTLE THINGS

We mentioned back at the beginning of this chapter that your grammar checklist should include a number 5: Other Little Things. In addition to testing the four main areas we've already reviewed, other little grammar things will be tested on the Improving Sentences questions. Let's look at some of these little grammar tidbits so you are ready for them when they turn up.

If everything else checks out, is the sentence testing other little things like:

- faulty comparisons
- misplaced modifiers
- adjectives/adverbs
- diction

Can You Compare?

There are several little things ETS tries to trip you up with when it comes to comparing. These things are not difficult, but are notoriously misused in spoken English, so you will need to make a note of them. First, when comparing two things, make sure that what you are comparing can be compared. Sounds like double-talk? Look at the following sentence:

> Larry goes shopping at Foodtown because the prices are better than Shoprite.

Sound okay? Well, sorry—it's wrong. As written, this sentence says that the prices at Foodtown are better than Shoprite—the entire store. What Larry means is the prices at Foodtown are better than the *prices* at Shoprite. You can only compare like things (prices to prices, not prices to stores).

While we're on the subject of Foodtown, how many of you have seen this sign?

> Express Checkout: Ten items or less.

Unfortunately, supermarkets across America are making a blatant grammatical error when they post this sign. When items can be counted, you must use the word *fewer*. If something cannot be counted, you would use the word *less*. For example:

> If you eat *fewer* french fries, you can use *less* ketchup.

Other similar words include *many* (can be counted) versus *much* (cannot be counted):

> *Many* hands make *much* less work.

And *number* (can be counted) versus *amount* (cannot be counted):

> The same *number* of CDs played different *amounts* of music.

Two's company; three or more is . . . ?

Finally, the English language uses different comparison words when comparing two things than when comparing more than two things. The following examples will jog your memory:

- **More** (for two things) vs. **Most** (for more than two)
  Given Alex and Dave as possible dates, Alex is the *more* appealing one.
  In fact, of all the guys I know, Alex is the *most* attractive.

- **Less** (for two things) vs. **Least** (for more than two)
  I am *less* likely to be chosen than you are.
  I am the *least* likely person to be chosen from the department.

- **Better** (for two things) vs. **Best** (for more than two)
  Taking a cab is *better* than hitchhiking.
  My Princeton Review teacher is the *best* teacher I have ever had.

- **Between** (for two things) vs. **Among** (for more than two)
    Just *between* you and me, I never liked her anyway.
    Among all the people here, no one likes her.

Try this one:

Jack was disappointed because his score on the test <u>was not as outstanding as Rob</u>.

(A) was not as outstanding as Rob
(B) did not stand out as much as Rob
(C) was not as outstanding as Rob's score
(D) did not surpass Rob
(E) was not as outstanding than Rob's

Here's how to crack it
What is being compared in this sentence? Jack is comparing his score with Rob. Can he do that? No! He really wants to compare his score with Rob's score.

Since you have identified an error, immediately cross off (A). Next, cross off any other answer choice that doesn't fix the error. That gets rid of (B) and (D). Now compare our remaining choices. While (E) technically fixes our problem by inserting the apostrophe (implying Rob's *score*), it makes a new error: "not as outstanding *than*." This is an incorrect idiom (remember those?). ETS's answer is (C).

MISPLACED MODIFIERS
A modifier is a descriptive word or phrase inserted in a sentence to add dimension to the thing it modifies. For example:

Because he could talk, Mr. Ed was a unique horse.

"Because he could talk" is the modifying phrase in this sentence. It describes a characteristic of Mr. Ed. Generally speaking, a modifying phrase should be right next to the thing it modifies. If it's not, the meaning of the sentence may change. For example:

Every time he goes to the bathroom outside, John praises his new puppy for being so good.

Who's going to the bathroom outside? In this sentence, it's John! There are laws against that! The descriptive phrase, "every time he goes to the bathroom outside" needs to be near the *puppy* in order for the sentence to say what it means.

When you are attacking Improving Sentences questions, watch out for sentences that begin with a descriptive phrase followed by a comma. If you see one, make sure the thing that comes after the comma is the person or thing being modified.

Try the following example:

> <u>Perhaps the most beautiful natural vegetation in the world</u>, the West of Ireland explodes each spring with a tremendous variety of wildflowers.

(A) Perhaps the most beautiful natural vegetation in the world
(B) In what may be the world's most beautiful natural vegetation
(C) Home to what may be the most beautiful natural vegetation in the world
(D) Its vegetation may be the world's most beautiful
(E) More beautiful in its natural vegetation than anywhere else in the world

Here's how to crack it

Is the West of Ireland a kind of vegetation? No, so cross off (A). We need an answer that will make the opening phrase modify the West of Ireland. Answer choice (B) is still modifying the vegetation, so cross it off. All three other choices fix the problem, but (C) does it the best. (D) makes the sentence a bit awkward, and (E) actually changes the meaning of the sentence by saying that the West of Ireland definitively has the most beautiful vegetation while the original sentence says "perhaps." ETS's answer is (C).

ADJECTIVES/ADVERBS

Misplaced modifiers aren't the only descriptive errors ETS will throw at you. Another way they try to trip you up is by using adjectives where they should use adverbs and vice versa. Remember that an *adjective* modifies a noun, while an *adverb* modifies verbs, adverbs, and adjectives. The adverb is the one that usually has "-ly" on the end. In the following sentence, circle the adverbs and underline the adjectives:

> The stealthy thief, desperately hoping to evade the persistent police, ran quickly into the dank, dark alley after brazenly stealing the stunningly exquisite jewels.

First, let's list the adjectives along with the nouns they modify: *stealthy* thief, *persistent* police, *dank* alley, *dark* alley, *exquisite* jewels. Now for the adverbs with the words they modify: *desperately* hoping (verb), ran (verb) *quickly*, *brazenly* stealing (verb), *stunningly* exquisite (adjective).

Now try the following Improving Sentences example:

> Movie cameras are no longer particularly costly, but film, development, and editing equipment <u>cause the monetary expense of making a film to add up tremendous</u>.
>
> (A) cause the monetary expense of making a film to add up tremendous
> (B) add tremendously to the expense of making a film
> (C) much increase the film-making expenses
> (D) add to the tremendous expense of making a film
> (E) tremendously add up to the expense of making a film

Here's how to crack it

Hopefully you identified the error as soon as you read the sentence. What should the last word in the sentence be? Tremendous*ly*. Cross off (A), and also (D) since it doesn't fix the error and changes the meaning of the sentence. (C) is way out there, so cross it off too. In (E), the placement of the "tremendously" is awkward and slightly changes the meaning of the sentence. ETS's answer is (B).

DICTION

Finally, ETS may occasionally slip in a diction error just to keep you on your toes. Diction means choice of words. Diction errors are tough to spot because the incorrect word often looks a lot like the word that should have been used.

DRILL 3

Here's a list of some potential diction traps. Indicate the difference between the words in each pair. Answers can be found at the end of the chapter.

1. Imminent _____
   and Eminent _____?

2. Proscribe _____
   and Prescribe _____?

3. Intelligent _____
   and Intelligible _____?

4. Incredible _____
   and Incredulous _____?

5. Irritated _____
   and Aggravated _____?

6. Stationary _____
   and Stationery _____?

7. Illicit _____
   and Elicit _____?

WRITING SKILLS ◆ 167

GIVE IT A SHOT

DRILL 4

Before we move on to Improving Paragraphs questions, try putting together what you've learned. Do the following Error ID and Improving Sentences questions using your grammar checklist. Remember to Trim the Fat and use POE. On Improving Sentences, do not hesitate to check out the answer choices for a clue to help you spot the error. You may wish to jot down your grammar checklist before you begin. Answers can be found at the end of the chapter.

1. Eric's new CD <u>was destroyed</u> when Paula Ann,
                           A

   running <u>quick</u> <u>through the office</u>, stepped on <u>it</u>.
            B   C   D

   <u>No error</u>
     E

2. <u>Because</u> <u>their class</u> was going on a field
      A   B

   trip that day, James and Alice <u>each</u> needed
                                     C

   <u>a lunch</u> to bring to school. <u>No error</u>
     D   E

3. None <u>of the students</u> on the review board
            A

   <u>is qualified</u> to ascertain <u>whether</u> the
      B   C

   money was <u>well spent</u>. <u>No error</u>
              D   E

4. Just <u>between</u> you and <u>I</u>, *Wayne's World 2* was
        A   B

   the dumbest movie I <u>have</u> ever <u>seen</u>. <u>No error</u>
                     C   D   E

5. If you <u>look</u> at the prices <u>close</u>, you'll see that the
        A   B

   "economy size" of detergent is <u>actually</u> more
                                   C

   expensive than the <u>smaller</u> trial sizes. <u>No error</u>
                  D   E

6. The <u>new</u> course schedule worked out
      A

   <u>splendid</u> for all of <u>those students</u> who
     B   C

   <u>had been</u> concerned. <u>No error</u>
     D   E

7. Artists can offer startling representations of the world <u>but with their responsibility</u> to elevate humanity.

    (A) but with their responsibility
    (B) with the responsibility
    (C) having also the responsibility
    (D) but ought also
    (E) their responsibility being as well

8. When the bridge was built in the 1890s, <u>the intention was for two small towns that they once were to be connected, not the large cities that they have become</u>.

    (A) the intention was for two small towns that they once were to be connected, not the large cities that they have become
    (B) it was intended to connect the two small towns that existed at that time, rather than the large cities that the towns have become
    (C) there were not two large cities, like now, but rather two small towns that the bridge was intended to connect
    (D) it was intended to connect not the two large cities that they have become but rather the two small towns that then existed
    (E) the connection was rather between the two small towns then in existence than the two large cities that the two small towns have become

9. The patient began his difficult post-surgery <u>recovery, but he was</u> able to recover from the psychological effects of the injury.

    (A) recovery, but he was
    (B) recovery, where he was
    (C) recovery only when he was
    (D) recovery only when being
    (E) recovery, also he was

10. In 1962 Jackie Robinson gained admission to the National Baseball Hall of Fame, he was the first Black baseball player in the major leagues.

    (A) In 1962 Jackie Robinson gained admission to the National Baseball Hall of Fame, he was the first Black baseball player in the major leagues.
    (B) In 1962 Jackie Robinson, the first Black major-league baseball player, gained admission to the National Baseball Hall of Fame.
    (C) In the National Baseball Hall of Fame in 1962, Jackie Robinson, the first Black baseball player in the major leagues, was admitted to it.
    (D) With admission to the National Baseball Hall of Fame in 1962, he was the first Black major-league player to do it, Jackie Robinson.
    (E) The first Black major-league player was when he was Jackie Robinson, admitted to the national Baseball Hall of Fame in 1962.

11. A well-organized person can go through the day efficiently, wasting little time or they waste none at all.

    (A) wasting little time or they waste none at all
    (B) wasting little or no time
    (C) wasting little time or wasting none at all
    (D) wasting either little time or none
    (E) either little or no time being wasted

12. When Michelle Shocked recorded her *Arkansas Traveler* album, regional American folk songs were used as inspiration, but it was never copied exactly by her.

    (A) regional American folk songs were used as inspiration, but it was never copied exactly by her
    (B) regional American folk songs were used as inspiration, but she never copied them exactly
    (C) regional American folk songs were used as inspiration by her and not copied exactly
    (D) she used regional American folk songs, but they were not exactly copied
    (E) she used regional American folk songs as inspiration, but never copied them exactly

IMPROVING PARAGRAPHS

After you do all of the Error ID and Improving Sentences questions, you'll be left with six Improving Paragraphs questions. Luckily, these questions come last in the section. They are not particularly difficult, but they are more time-consuming than the other two question types.

The six Improving Paragraphs questions require you to make corrections to a replica "first draft" of a student's essay. You will be given a "rough draft" comprised of approximately three paragraphs. Each paragraph contains numbered sentences. Your job is to "edit" the rough draft to make it better.

Here is a sample passage:

(1) Conservation and ecology are the hot topics at our school. (2) Students used to just throw everything out in one big garbage pail. (3) Sure, it was easy. (4) It wasn't good for the environment.

(5) I volunteered to head up the conservation team. (6) My friends and I decided to map out our strategies. (7) First we needed to get students to become aware of the problem. (8) Educating was important. (9) A thing to do was implement a recycling program. (10) We checked with the local town government. (11) They would supply the recycling bins. (12) We had to supply the people who'd be willing to recycle. (13) The most important thing students had to learn to do was to separate their garbage. (14) Glass in one container. (15) Plastic in another.

(16) Our final step was to get the teachers and administrators involved. (17) Paper can be recycled too. (18) We ran a poster contest. (19) The winners are hanging in our halls. (20) Reuse, recycle, renew. (21) That's our school's new motto.

Now, before you get out your red pencil and jump in, there are a few more things you need to know. Your passage may consist of 15–20 or more sentences, each potentially containing some kind of error. However, you will only be asked six questions. Don't spend time fixing errors for which there are no questions.

THE QUESTIONS

There are three basic types of questions that you will be asked:

- **Revision questions:** These questions ask you to revise sentences or parts of sentences in much the same way as Improving Sentences questions do.

- **Combination questions:** These questions ask you to combine two or more sentences to improve the quality and/or flow of the paragraph.

- **Content questions:** These questions ask you about passage content, typically by asking you to insert a sentence before or after a paragraph.

Go to the questions. Go directly to the questions

Instead of wasting a lot of time reading the rough draft, go directly to the questions. There are far more errors in the passage than you'll ever be asked about—reading the passage first will simply waste your time and confuse you.

Also, for many of the questions, the sentences you need to fix are reprinted right under the question, so you won't necessarily need to go back to the paragraph to answer a question. Let's talk about each type of question so you know how to approach it.

REVISION QUESTIONS

As we mentioned, these questions are very similar to Improving Sentences questions. Therefore, you can follow the same basic approach. One warning: *There is normally no such thing as "No error" on Improving Paragraphs questions. Do not assume that (A) is merely a repeat of the given sentence.*

Even though the sentence you are revising is provided for you, you may still need to go back to the passage to gain some context when trying to fix a sentence. Before going back, however, use POE. If you have spotted an error in the given sentence, cross off answers that don't fix it. Also, cross off answer choices that contain obvious errors. After doing some POE, go back and read a few sentences before and after the given sentence. This should be enough context for you to determine the best edit.

Try the following revision question—refer back to the sample passage when needed.

In context, what is the best way to revise sentence 9 (reproduced below)?

A thing to do was implement a recycling program.

(A) Next, we needed to implement a recycling program.
(B) Implementing a recycling program was a thing to do.
(C) A recycling program needed to be implemented.
(D) Implementing a program for recycling was the step that would be next.
(E) A program would need to be implemented next for recycling.

Here's how to crack it
The correct revision will be concise and unambiguous. It will also flow well. We can get rid of choices (B), (D), and (E) before going back to the passage. Choice (B) is as clunky as the given sentence; choices (D) and (E) are awkwardly written.

After doing some elimination, go back and read, beginning with line 7. "First we needed to get students to become aware of the problem. Educating was important. *Next*...." When you read this segment, the word "next" should be jumping into your brain. Sentence 9 seems out of place until you realize that it is a new thought, the next step. ETS's answer is (A).

COMBINATION QUESTIONS
Combination questions are revision questions with a twist: You are working with two sentences instead of one. The sentences are almost always reprinted for you under the question and you can usually answer these questions without going back to the passage at all. As with revision questions, do what you can first, then go back to the passage if necessary.

To combine sentences you will need to work with conjunctions. (Remember *School House Rock's* "Conjunction Junction"?) If the sentences are flowing in the same direction, look for an answer with words like "and," "since," "as well as," etc. If the sentences seem to be flowing in opposite directions, look for trigger words in the answer choices such as "however," "but," "on the contrary," etc.

Try the following without going back to the passage:

> Which of the following represents the most effective way to combine sentences 20 and 21 (reproduced below)?
>
> *Reuse, recycle, renew. That's our school's new motto.*
>
> (A) Reuse, recycle, renew and you know our school's new motto.
> (B) The new motto of our school is that: Reuse, recycle, renew.
> (C) Reuse, recycle, renew are the new motto of our school now.
> (D) The new motto of our school is reusing, recycling, and renewing.
> (E) Reuse, recycle, renew is our school's new motto.

Here's how to crack it
First, the sentences are moving in the same direction. Your job is to find a clear, concise way to combine them. (A) and (B) are out because they are poorly worded. (C) is a trap: "Reuse, recycle, renew" *is* a motto. Don't be fooled into thinking you need a plural verb simply because there is no "and" in answer choice (C). Choice (D) uses the passive voice (doesn't it just *sound* wimpy?) ETS's answer is (E).

Try another:

> Which of the following represents the best revision of the underlined portions of sentences 7 and 8 (reproduced below)?
>
> *First we needed to get students to become aware of the <u>problem. Educating was important</u>.*
>
> (A) problem for educating was important
> (B) problem of educating. It was important
> (C) problem to educate was important
> (D) problem: education was important
> (E) problem for education was important to us

Here's how to crack it

Again, we have a same-direction combination going on. We need something that flows. (A) and (C) are using the wrong prepositions, which slightly change the meaning of the sentence. Cross them off. (B) is as awkward or more awkward than the original sentence. (E) uses the wrong preposition and adds extra awkward stuff. ETS's answer is (D). The colon is a nice, neat way to continue a thought without using two sentences.

CONTENT QUESTIONS

ETS will occasionally ask you a question regarding the content of the passage. These questions may ask:

1. Which sentence should immediately follow or precede the passage?
2. Which sentence should be inserted into the passage?
3. What is the best description of the passage as a whole?

If you are asked the third question, you will need to skim the whole passage. However, you will more likely be asked one of the first two questions. To answer these, you will need to read the relevant paragraph.

Try this example using the sample passage from earlier in this section:

> Which of the following sentences, if added after sentence 4, would best serve to link the first paragraph to the second paragraph?
>
> (A) Unfortunately, the environment suffered.
> (B) Clearly, we had to make a change.
> (C) Easy things are often not good for the environment.
> (D) However, people can be very lazy.
> (E) The school was against any change.

Here's how to crack it

To solve this question, you need to quickly read the first paragraph and the first sentence of the second paragraph. At the end of the first paragraph, something like "something had to be done" may have popped into your head. This is essentially what the connecting sentence needs to say.

(A), (C), and (D) are out because they focus on the "problems" theme from the first paragraph instead of making a transition to the second paragraph. (E) is not implied anywhere in the passage. ETS's answer is (B).

Time Is of the Essence

Now, keep in mind that this is the end of a 30-minute section at the end of a 2+ hour test. Chances are you won't have the time or the gumption to do all the Improving Paragraphs questions. Therefore, reorder the six Improving Paragraphs questions so you are doing the shorter, easier questions first. Then, if you have the time and the inclination, do the longer questions.

The shorter, easier questions are the combination questions and the revision questions that reprint the sentences you need to edit. Do anything that doesn't require you to go back to the passage. Then do questions that require you to go back to specific areas of the passage. Finally, do the ones that require some reading.

Drill 5

Try the following Improving Paragraphs drill to practice what you have learned. Answers can be found at the end of the chapter.

(1) Censorship in the media had been an extremely important issue throughout the twentieth century. (2) In the 1950s television programs and movies had to comply with codes that enforced strict standards of propriety. (3) Couples were shown sleeping in separate beds, and the concept of nudity or verbal profanity was unheard of. (4) In reaction to them, in the 1960s and 1970s the media abandoned the codes in favor of more realistic representations of relationships and everyday life. (5) Filmmakers and songwriters were able to express themselves more honestly and freely. (6) The idea that in the early 1960s the Rolling Stones had to change their lyrics from "let's spend the night together" to "let's spend some time together" seemed almost unlikely by the end of the decade.

(7) Yet in the mid-1980s a period of conservative reaction occurred, turning the cycle around. (8) Explicit song lyrics began to be censored. (9) Warning labels were added to the covers of albums. (10) The labels indicated that some of the language might be "offensive" to the consumer. (11) It is unfortunate that people feel the need to blame the media for societal problems instead of realizing that the media only brings to light the problems that already exist.

(12) Hopefully, our reactions will ultimately break free of all previous patterns. (13) Yet until this happens we must remain content to know that the good parts of the past, as well as the bad, repeat themselves.

1. In context, what is the best version of the underlined portion of sentence 1 (reproduced below)?

    Censorship in the media <u>had been an extremely</u> important issue throughout the twentieth century.

    (A) (As it is now)
    (B) was extremely
    (C) was an extremely
    (D) has been extreme as an
    (E) will be an extremely

2. Which of the following would be the best subject for a paragraph immediately preceding this essay?

    (A) The types of movies most popular in the 1950s
    (B) The changing role of the media over the last ten years
    (C) The ways in which the economy affects society's political views
    (D) The role of the media in European countries
    (E) The roots of media censorship

3. The author wishes to divide the first paragraph into two shorter paragraphs. The most appropriate place to begin a new paragraph would be

    (A) between sentences 1 and 2
    (B) between sentences 2 and 3
    (C) between sentences 3 and 4
    (D) between sentences 4 and 5
    (E) between sentences 5 and 6

4. In sentence 4, the word "them" could best be replaced with which of the following?

    (A) couples
    (B) beds
    (C) nudity and profanity
    (D) relationships
    (E) the codes

5. What word could best replace "unlikely" in sentence 6?

    (A) strange
    (B) conventional
    (C) unpopular
    (D) inconceivable
    (E) unbearable

6. Which would be the best way to revise and combine the underlined portions of sentences 9 and 10 (reproduced below)?

Warning labels were added to the covers of albums. The labels indicated that some of the language might be "offensive" to the consumer.

(A) albums, indicating
(B) albums, which indicated
(C) albums, and they indicated
(D) albums, the indication being
(E) albums, being indicative

Final Words of Wisdom

As with all the sections of the PSAT/NMSQT, you are rewarded for answering the question. Don't be afraid to do some POE and guess. You will almost always be able to eliminate some answer choices, so allow your partial knowledge to earn you credit on the test.

Answers to Drills

Drill 1 (Page 158)

1. to
2. of, for
3. by, for
4. of
5. about, for, by
6. by
7. over
8. to
9. from

Drill 2 (Pages 160–161)

1. C
2. B
3. C
4. D
5. B
6. C

Drill 3 (Page 167)

1. About to happen *versus* prominent or distinguished
2. Forbid, condemn *versus* set down, order (as in medication)
3. Smart *versus* able to be understood
4. Unbelievable *versus* skeptical
5. Annoyed *versus* made worse
6. Fixed, not moving *versus* letter paper
7. Unlawful *versus* draw out

Drill 4 (Pages 168–170)

1. B
2. E
3. E
4. B
5. B
6. B
7. D
8. B
9. C
10. B
11. B
12. E

Drill 5 (Pages 175–177)

1. C
2. E
3. C
4. E
5. D
6. A

12
Vocabulary

VOCABULARY

As you've seen, the Verbal sections of the PSAT are very vocabulary intensive. The Analogies and Sentence Completion questions are, in fact, largely testing the breadth of your knowledge of English words. This makes it very important to begin a vocabulary enrichment program, which is essential to any test-preparation effort.

How to Learn Vocabulary

First, let's talk about how NOT to learn vocabulary. Some people assume that you should take a dictionary, and learn each word, one at a time, starting with the letter "A." This, of course, is not a very well-thought-out plan. The kind of vocabulary that appears on the PSAT is actually a fairly narrow range of what is considered by the test writers to be those words that a well-educated college student should know. These are the words that are typically used by good writers of English prose, scholars, and scientists (when they're writing for the public, and not in scientific jargon).

To help with learning vocabulary, it's extremely important that you carry a pocket dictionary with you all the time so you can look up unfamiliar words. You can find inexpensive paperback dictionaries at any used bookstore. Carry it with you from now until the test!

Flash Cards

Some people like using flash cards as a way to help them learn vocabulary. Flash cards are useful, but be sure to not only to write down the word and its definition, but to also write an example sentence in which you use that word. If you need help, ask a teacher, parent, or friend to help you come up with a sentence.

Some Daily Reading

While preparing for these tests, it's important that you get in the habit of reading. This will not only help you on the reading passages, but will also help you improve your vocabulary. Make sure to set aside 20–30 minutes **every day** to do some reading.

What should you read? Anything. Everything. Pick your favorite magazine or book. Ideally, read something that is just slightly above your current reading level, but **read something every day.** While you're reading, circle any words that you don't understand, and look them up. Then add them to your list of words to learn.

The Hit Parade and Advanced Hit Parade

The Princeton Review's Hit Parade is a list of the words that commonly appear on the PSAT and SAT. This list is useful not only because one or two of these words are likely to appear on your test, but also because it shows you what *kinds* of words are typically tested on the PSAT and SAT. These are the sorts of words that you should pay particular attention to when you're doing your daily reading. Write them down and learn them!

Using These Words

One great way to learn vocabulary is to be annoying. No kidding! Here's how you do it:

Pick 5–10 words each day. Write them down, along with their definitions, on a small note card, which you can refer to if your memory fails you. Now go about your daily business, but use these words every chance you get. Instead of "outgoing," use the word "gregarious." Instead of "funny," use the word "mirthful." You will really annoy your friends, but you will certainly learn those words.

Mnemonics

Another great technique for learning words is to find a mnemonic device. "Mnemonic" is from the Greek word *mneme*, which means "memory," so a mnemonic device is something that is so stupid or funny that it's unforgettable, and will help remind you of the meaning of a word. (By the way—what other common English word comes from that same Greek root *mneme*? We'll tell you in a minute.)

When it comes to mnemonics, the rule is: the weirder, the better. The more off-the-wall your idea, the more likely you'll be to remember it.

For instance, for the word "excavate," which means "to make a hole by digging," you can think of the word *cave*. A cave is a hole underground and part of the word ex**cav**ate.

How about another one? Let's try the word "paramount," which means "of chief importance." You can remember this word because it's like a **mount**ain—it's the biggest and most important thing on the horizon.

Try making mnemonics for each of the following words:

>prosaic
>flagrant
>clandestine
>timorous

Once you've made your own mnemonics for the above words, read our examples below:

Prosaic
Rebecca made a prosaic mosaic—it consisted of only one tile.

Flagrant
Burning the **flag** shows **flag**rant disrespect for the country.

Clandestine
The **clan** of spies planned a **clan**destine maneuver that depended on its secrecy to work.

Timorous
Tiny **Tim** was **tim**orous; he was afraid that one day a giant would crush him.

And the answer to the earlier question: What other common English word has the same root (*mneme*) as the word "mnemonic"? Amnesia (the prefix *a-* meaning "without," the word itself means *without memory*).

If you want more help with mnemonics, check out two other books by The Princeton Review: *Illustrated Word Smart* and *More Illustrated Word Smart*. These both contain some great visuals and mnemonics to help you memorize more words.

THE HIT PARADE

abrogate *v.*
to abolish, repeal, or nullify

abstruse *adj.*
difficult to understand

abysmal *adj.*
extremely hopeless or wretched; bottomless

accolade *n.*
an award or honor

acerbic *adj.*
bitter, sour, severe

acumen *n.*
keenness of judgment, mental sharpness

affable *adj.*
easy to talk to, friendly

afford *v.*
to permit or allow, to enable

aggregate *n., adj.*
collection of things mixed together; the sum total

allocate *v.*
to distribute, assign, or allot

aloof *adj.*
standoffish, uninvolved, keeping one's distance

ameliorate *v.*
to make better or more tolerable

anachronistic *adj.*
out of place in time or history

anathema *n.*
something or someone loathed or detested

ancillary *adj.*
subordinate; providing assistance

annul *v.*
to make void, usu. refers to marriage

anomaly *n.*
an aberration, deviation, or irregularity

anthropology *n.*
the study of human cultures

antithetical *adj.*
in opposition, contrary to

apostate *n.*
one who deserts his or her professed principles or faith

apotheosis *n.*
elevation to divine status; the perfect example of something

appropriate *v.*
to take without permission; to set aside for a particular use

archetype *n.*
an original model or pattern

ardent *adj.*
passionate

arsenal *n.*
a storehouse of weapons

ascertain *v.*
to determine with certainty; to find out definitely

ascetic *adj.*
hermit-like; practicing self-denial

assiduous *adj.*
hardworking, diligent, busy

assuage *v.*
to soothe, pacify, or relieve

attrition *n.*
gradual wearing away, a natural or expected decrease in size or number

augury *n.*
an omen, esp. a good omen

auspices *n.*
protection, support; sponsorship

avarice   *n.*
greed

avuncular   *adj.*
kind, helpful, generous; like a nice uncle

barometer   *n.*
an instrument that measures atmospheric pressure

beguile   *v.*
to delude by guile or craft; to mislead, divert

behest   *n.*
a command or order

beleaguer   *v.*
to surround, besiege, or harass

belie   *v.*
to give a false impression; to contradict

bellicose   *adj.*
warlike, belligerent

bequest   *n.*
something left to someone in a will

blithe   *adj.*
carefree, cheerful

broach   *v.*
to open up a subject, often a delicate one, for discussion

brusque   *adj.*
rough and short in manner, blunt, abrupt

burgeon   *v.*
to expand; to flourish

buttress   *n., v.*
a support for a building or structure; to support

cabal   *n.*
a group of conspirators; the acts of such a group; a clique

cajole   *v.*
to persuade with flattery or gentle urging

calipers   *n.*
a pinching instrument used for determining the thickness of objects or the distance between surfaces

candor   *n.*
sincerity, honesty

canon   *n.*
a rule or law, especially a religious one; a body of rules or laws; an authoritative list; the set of works by an author that are accepted as authentic

cantankerous   *adj.*
ill-natured, contentious

canvass   *v.*
to campaign; to seek or solicit orders, votes, etc.

capacitor   *n.*
a device that stores energy

capitulate   *v.*
to surrender, give up, or give in

capricious   *adj.*
unpredictable, likely to change at any moment

captious   *adj.*
ill-natured, quarrelsome

carp   *v.*
to complain or find fault with someone

cartography   *n.*
the study and creation of maps

castigate   *v.*
to criticize severely; to chastise

catalyst   *n.*
anyone or anything that makes something happen without being directly involved

catharsis   *n.*
purification that brings emotional relief or renewal

cavil   *v.*
to quibble; to raise trivial objections

censure   *v.*
to condemn severely for doing something bad

chagrin   *n.*
humiliation; embarrassed disappointment

chicanery   *n.*
trickery, deceitfulness, artifice (especially legal or political)

chimerical   *adj.*
imaginary, given to fantasy

choleric   *adj.*
hot-tempered, quick to anger

circumvent   *v.*
to go around

closefisted   *adj.*
stingy

coalesce   *v.*
to come together as one, to fuse, to unite

cogitate   *v.*
to ponder; to meditate; to think carefully about

colloquial   *adj.*
ordinary, informal speech

conscript   *v.*
enlisted, drafted, or enrolled; usu. refers to mandatory military service

corroborate   *v.*
to confirm, to back up with evidence

coterie   *n.*
a group of close associates; a circle of friends

coy   *adj.*
shy, reluctant to make a commitment

craven   *adj.*
cowardly, afraid

curmudgeon   *n.*
a greedy, irascible, crotchety old person

dearth   *n.*
a shortage or scarcity of something

debacle   *n.*
a big disaster

deft   *adj.*
very skillful

dehydrate   *v.*
to remove water

deleterious   *adj.*
harmful

demagogue   *n.*
a leader of the people, but more a rabble-rouser

demography   *n.*
the statistical study of the characteristics of populations

desalinate   *v.*
to remove salt from something

desiccate   *v.*
to dry out

diplomatic   *adj.*
tactful; good at negotiating

discomfit   *v.*
to frustrate, to confuse

dither   *v.*
to vacillate between choices; to tremble with excitement

diurnal   *adj.*
occurring every day; occurring during the daytime

divisive   *adj.*
creating conflict and disagreement

draconian   *adj.*
severe, harsh, cruel

ebullient   *adj.*
bubbling with excitement, exuberant

eclectic   *adj.*
drawn from many sources

effigy   *n.*
a likeness of a person, usu. one used to express hatred for that person

egregious   *adj.*
extremely bad, flagrant

elliptical   *adj.*
oval; missing a word or words; obscure

endemic   *adj.*
native, restricted to a particular region or area, indigenous

ephemeral   *adj.*
lasting a very short time

equine   *adj.*
relating to horses, horselike

equivocal   *n.*
ambiguous, intentionally confusing, capable of being interpreted many ways

ersatz   *adj.*
serving as a substitute; synthetic, artificial

ethereal	*adj.*	heavenly, light, insubstantial
etymology	*n.*	the study of words and their meanings
euphonious	*adj.*	pleasant-sounding, opposite of cacophonous; melodious
evanescent	*n.*	fleeting, vanishing, happening only for the briefest period
evince	*v.*	to demonstrate convincingly; to prove
execrate	*v.*	to curse, denounce
exhume	*v.*	to unbury; to dig out of the ground
exonerate	*v.*	to free completely from blame
expeditious	*adj.*	prompt, speedy (to expedite, *v.*)
expiate	*v.*	to make amends, to atone
expunge	*v.*	to erase, obliterate, to blot out
facile	*adj.*	fluent, skillful in a superficial way
fecund	*adj.*	fertile, productive
fervent	*adj.*	having intense feeling, enthusiastic; fervid
feign	*v.*	to pretend; to make a false representation of something
flaccid	*adj.*	soft and limp
florid	*adj.*	very fancy, usu. refers to intangible objects, i.e., *florid speech*
flout	*v.*	to disregard something or someone out of disrespect
ford	*n., v.*	the shallow part of a river; to cross a river at the shallow part

forensics   *n.*
the art or study of argumentation and formal debate

fortuitous   *adj.*
accidental, occurring by chance

fracas   *n.*
a big fight

furrow   *n., v.*
a narrow groove made in the ground; to make wrinkles in the face

gaffe   *n.*
a social blunder, an embarrassing mistake, a faux pas

galvanize   *v.*
to startle into sudden activity; to revitalize

gastronomy   *n.*
the art of eating well

germane   *adj.*
relevant, applicable, pertinent

glower   *v.*
to look or stare with sullen dislike or anger

goldbrick   *v., n.*
to swindle, to sell something worthless as if it were valuable; a swindle

grandiloquent   *adj.*
using a lot of big, fancy words to sound impressive

gratuitous   *adj.*
given freely; uncalled for; unjustified; unprovoked

glut   *n.*
surplus, overabundance

hackneyed   *adj.*
overused, trite, stale

halcyon   *adj.*
peaceful, serene; carefree

harbinger   *n.*
a forerunner, a signal of

hedonism   *n.*
the pursuit of pleasure as a way of life

hegemony   *n.*
leadership, especially of one nation over another

hermetic *adj.*
airtight, impervious to external influence

homily *n.*
a sermon

hubris *n.*
excessive pride

humanist *n.*
one who has great concern for human welfare, values, and dignity; a student of the classics

hybrid *n.*
formed, bred, or composed from different elements

hypodermic *adj.*
beneath the skin

idiosyncratic *adj.*
quirky, peculiar, eccentric

ignominy *n.*
shame, disrepute, disgrace

importune *v.*
to beg, urge, or insist persistently

inane *adj.*
silly, senseless

incantation *n.*
a chant

incarnate *adj.*
in the flesh

incensed *adj.*
very angry

inchoate *adj.*
incomplete; only partially formed

indignant *adj.*
angry or insulted, especially as a result of something unjust or unworthy

indolent *adj.*
averse to activity; habitually lazy

ineffable *adj.*
incapable of being expressed or described

inexorable *adj.*
relentless, inevitable, unavoidable

inoculate *v.*
to protect against disease

insouciant *adj.*
nonchalant, lighthearted, carefree

irascible *adj.*
easily angered or provoked; irritable

jaunt *n.*
a short pleasure trip

jejune *adj.*
lacking maturity or significance; irrelevant

jettison *v.*
to throw or cast off

jingoist *n.*
an excessively vigilant patriot, a bellicose chauvinist, a warmongering nationalist

jurisprudence *n.*
the study of law

karma *n.*
consequences of one's actions; fate; destiny

kudos *n.*
honor, glory, acclaim, compliment

lambaste *v.*
to assault violently with words

lament *v.*
to mourn

laudatory *adj.*
praising

lax *adj.*
not strict; careless or negligent

lexicon *n.*
a glossary or dictionary

limpid *adj.*
transparent; clear; lucid

liniment *n.*
a medicinal liquid or salve for rubbing on the skin

liquidate *v.*
to get rid of; to settle a debt

lugubrious *adj.*
exaggeratedly mournful

luminary *n.*
a person who has attained eminence in his/her field

maudlin *adj.*
silly and overly sentimental

maverick *adj.*
a nonconformist; a rebel

mellifluous *adj.*
flowing sweetly, usu. refers to sounds or voices

mendacious *adj.*
lying, dishonest

meritorious *adj.*
deserving praise or reward

mirth *n.*
amusement or laughter

misanthrope *n.*
one who hates people

mollify *v.*
to soften, soothe, pacify

moribund *adj.*
dying

narcissism *n.*
excessive love of one's body or oneself

nebulous *adj.*
vague, hazy, indistinct

neologism *n.*
a new word or phrase, a new usage of a word

neophyte *n.*
a novice or beginner

noisome *adj.*
offensive or disgusting; stinking, noxious

noxious *adj.*
harmful, offensive

nuance *n.*
a subtle difference or distinction

numerology *n.*
the study of numbers for the purposes of predicting the future

obdurate *adj.*
stubborn, insensitive, unyielding, resistant to persuasion

obeisance *n.*
deep reverence; a bow or curtsy

obfuscate *v.*
to darken or confuse

obsequious *adj.*
fawning, subservient, servile, excessively deferential

odometer *n.*
instrument that measures how many miles one has traveled

olfactory *adj.*
pertaining to the sense of smell

oligarchy *n.*
government by only a very few people

ornate *adj.*
very fancy, usu. refers to tangible objects, i.e., *ornate woodwork*

palliative *adj., n*
to relieve or alleviate something without getting rid of the problem; something that provides temporary relief

paltry *adj.*
insignificant; worthless

panacea *n.*
something that cures everything

panache *n.*
flair, verve; dashing elegance

paragon *n.*
a model of excellence

peccadillo *n.*
a minor offense or error

pedantic *adj.*
boringly scholarly or academic; overconcerned with details

penurious *adj.*
extremely stingy, poor, or miserly

perfidy *n.*
treachery

perfunctory *adj.*
unenthusiastic, careless

pernicious *adj.*
deadly, extremely evil

perquisite	*n.* a privilege that goes along with a job, a "perk"
philistine	*n.* a smugly ignorant person with no appreciation for intellectual or artistic matters
piquant	*adj.* pleasantly sharp in flavor; interestingly provocative or stimulating
pique	*v.* to excite; to arouse an emotion or provoke to action
plebeian	*adj.* common, vulgar, low-class
poignant	*adj.* painfully emotional, extremely moving, sharp, or astute
polemic	*n.* a powerful argument often made to attack or refute a controversial issue
portent	*n.* an omen, a sign of something coming
potentate	*n.* a person who possesses great power
predilection	*n.* a natural preference for something
preempt	*v.* to seize something by prior right
prescient	*adj.* having knowledge of things before they exist or happen
priggish	*adj.* very fussy, self-righteous, high-maintenance, usu. refers to people
profligate	*adj.* extravagantly wasteful; wildly immoral
prolific	*adj.* abundantly productive, fruitful, or fertile
promulgate	*v.* to publicly or formally declare something
prosaic	*adj.* dull, unimaginative

pugnacious *adj.*
quarrelsome, combative, always ready to fight

pulchritude *n.*
physical beauty

queue *n., v.*
a line; to line up

quiescent *adj.*
motionless; at rest; still

quintessential *adj.*
being the most perfect example of

quixotic *adj.*
idealistic to a foolish or impractical degree, like Don Quixote

quotidian *adj.*
daily; everyday; ordinary

raze *v.*
to completely destroy or level something

rebuke *v.*
to criticize sharply

recapitulate *v.*
to review or summarize

recidivism *n.*
the act of repeating an offense

redolent *adj.*
fragrant

renege *v.*
to go back on a bet or promise

retrenchment *n.*
cutting down or off, reduction

rhetoric *n.*
the study or art of using language well; using undue exaggeration

sacrosanct *adj.*
sacred, held to be inviolable

sanguine *adj.*
cheerful, optimistic, hopeful

sardonic *adj.*
mocking, scornful

saturnine *adj.*
gloomy or taciturn

scrupulous	*adj.* strict, careful; hesitant for ethical reasons
semantic	*n.* pertaining to the meaning of words or symbols
semaphore	*n.* a system of signaling, usually through the use of flags
serendipity	*n.* accidental good fortune, discovering good things without looking for them
skinflint	*n.* a mean, penny-pinching person
smidgen	*n.* a very small amount
somber	*adj.* depressing, dismal, gloomy
specious	*adj.* deceptively plausible or attractive; misleading; like an answer choice Joe Bloggs would fall for
stand	*n.* a group of trees
sublime	*adj.* of great intellectual, moral, or spiritual value
subsidy	*n.* a gift of money
subterfuge	*n.* deceptive strategy used to conceal, escape, or evade
supercilious	*adj.* haughty, patronizing
supplicate	*v.* to ask or beg humbly
tenable	*adj.* valid, capable of being argued successfully
threadbare	*adj.* falling apart, meager, poor, old
truculent	*adj.* fierce, cruel, savagely brutal
turbid	*n.* unclear or opaque; lacking clarity or purity

uncanny *adj.*
extraordinary, mysterious, uncomfortably strange

unilateral *adj.*
involving one side only; done on behalf of one side only

usury *n.*
the practice of lending money at a high rate of interest

vacuous *adj.*
empty of content; lacking in ideas or intelligence

vapid *adj.*
dull, spiritless

verdant *adj.*
covered with green plants; leafy; inexperienced

vernacular *n.*
everyday speech, slang, idiom

vestige *n.*
a remaining bit of something, a last trace

vilify *v.*
to say vile things about, to defame

wane *v.*
to decrease in strength or intensity; to fade away; to decline in power

wanton *adj.*
malicious, unjustifiable, unprovoked, egregious

wizened *adj.*
shriveled; withered; shrunken

zeitgeist *n.*
the mood or spirit of the times

zenith *n.*
the highest point; peak; pinnacle

PART III

The Princeton Review Practice Tests and Explanations

13

Practice Test 1

Time—25 Minutes
25 Questions
(1–25)

For each question in this section, select the best answer from among the choices given and fill in the corresponding oval on the answer sheet.

Each sentence below has one or two blanks, each blank indicating that something has been omitted. Beneath the sentence are five words or sets of words labeled A through E. Choose the word or set of words that, when inserted in the sentence, **best** fits the meaning of the sentence as a whole.

Example:

Medieval kingdoms did not become constitutional republics overnight; on the contrary, the change was -------.

(A) unpopular (B) unexpected (C) advantageous

(D) sufficient (E) gradual

Ⓐ Ⓑ Ⓒ Ⓓ ●

---

1. While its unique eating habits make the mountain gorilla a fascinating subject for observations, its small population and its shyness serve to ------- many potential studies.

    (A) inspire (B) release (C) fortify

    (D) hinder (E) extenuate

2. Originally designed as work clothes for miners, jeans are now worn by all segments of society, their appeal ------- by their comfort and affordability.

    (A) overwhelmed (B) corroded (C) broadened

    (D) lessened (E) complicated

3. While many consumer electronics are ------- in a very short time by newer technologies, it will be many years before the home computer becomes -------.

    (A) supplanted..obsolete
    (B) popularized..uncommon
    (C) noticeable..forgotten
    (D) discovered..disparaged
    (E) replaced..remembered

4. Although many believed that the problems of the community were -------, the members of the governing council refused to give up and devised several ------- solutions.

    (A) indomitable..ingenious
    (B) intractable..inconsequential
    (C) exorbitant..promising
    (D) irrelevant..lofty
    (E) obscure..meager

5. So ------- were the voters of Winsburg that, despite the blizzard, 2,500 of the 3,200 residents made their way to the voting sites.

    (A) endemic (B) relenting (C) ephemeral

    (D) resolute (E) erratic

GO ON TO THE NEXT PAGE

Each question below consists of a related pair of words or phrases, followed by five pairs of words or phrases labeled A through E. Select the pair that best expresses a relationship similar to that expressed in the original pair.

Example:

CRUMB : BREAD ::

(A) ounce : unit
(B) splinter : wood
(C) water : bucket
(D) twine : rope
(E) cream : butter

Ⓐ ● Ⓒ Ⓓ Ⓔ

6. STABLE : HORSE ::

    (A) jungle : ape
    (B) ranch : cowboy
    (C) trunk : tree
    (D) sky : eagle
    (E) sty : pig

7. AXE : WOOD ::

    (A) coin : metal
    (B) knife : blade
    (C) spade : shovel
    (D) notch : screw
    (E) cleaver : meat

8. COWARD : INTIMIDATED ::

    (A) egoist : humbled
    (B) dupe : deceived
    (C) politician : opinionated
    (D) child : punished
    (E) celebrity : educated

9. INSENSITIVE : FEELING ::

    (A) inedible : taste
    (B) inevitable : event
    (C) infinite : end
    (D) incorrigible : child
    (E) incompetent : help

10. INTRACTABLE : GOVERN ::

    (A) unfaithful : promise
    (B) hopeful : anticipate
    (C) immobile : motivate
    (D) obstinate : persuade
    (E) pretentious : achieve

11. MELLIFLUOUS : EUPHONY ::

    (A) monotonous : lecture
    (B) belligerent : hostility
    (C) offensive : language
    (D) agile : weakness
    (E) turbulent : calm

GO ON TO THE NEXT PAGE

Questions 12–16 are based on the following passage.

Jazz represents one of the most significant elements in America's musical history. The following passage concerns Duke Ellington, one of the preeminent figures in American jazz.

In the years following 1940, the Duke Ellington Band was on a crest. Ellington grossed more than a million dollars in 1940. He was broadcasting every
Line night, and making movies and playing major
5 locations, such as the Hurricane Club on Broadway.
In 1940, a new generation of jazz fans, brought to the music by swing bands, was discovering Ellington's music. Many of these new fans were too young to have been caught up in the excitement of
10 the early discovery of Ellington's "Black and Tan Fantasy" and "Creole Love Call." In the annual poll conducted by the magazine *Down Beat* in 1938, the Ellington band's alto saxophonist, Jonny Hodges, was named the second leading swing musician in
15 the country. Ellington himself won fifth for his arrangements, and other Ellington band members appeared further down the list. By 1940, however, the Ellington band came in second to Benny Goodman in the hot-band category; Hodges was
20 ranked number-one; four Ellingtonians were third on their respective instruments; and six others ranked in the top ten, meaning that two-thirds of the band members were given high ratings, a distinction that no other band could claim. In the years
25 following, the Ellington band was near the top in the swing-band category year after year, beating out Benny Goodman for the number-one position in 1942. Several of the band members were always near the top of the ratings for their instruments, and
30 Jonny Hodges was named best jazz alto saxophone player in the country almost automatically, year after year.
Down Beat readers were somewhat more sophisticated about swing music than the mass
35 audience, and more committed to their passions. The Duke Ellington Band was probably never the second or even third most popular swing band in the country, as far as the ordinary fan was concerned. But during this period, Ellington's was among the
40 most talented bands of the day, generally playing much more complex music than other bands. As live recordings from clubs and ballrooms show, Ellington featured his most difficult works as matter of course in his standard program. For example, at a
45 dance in Fargo, North Dakota, in November 1940, Ellington presented such complicated pieces, today considered among his finest works, as "Ko Ko," "Harlem Airshaft," "Warm Valley," and "Clarinet Lament." This, mind you, was not New York or
50 Los Angeles, but a small city far removed from a major center of jazz music. The point is that by 1940 jazz had moved into the center of American popular culture, and Ellington was one of its most prominent musicians.

12. The primary purpose of the passage is to

   (A) commemorate a particular event in Ellington's life
   (B) discuss the interaction between Ellington and his band
   (C) identify enduring works of jazz music
   (D) discuss the appeal of Ellington's band during a particular period
   (E) detail the awards given to various jazz musicians

13. In line 2, the word "crest" is used to mean

   (A) emblem
   (B) peak
   (C) brush
   (D) downturn
   (E) cloud

14. The songs "Black and Tan Fantasy" and "Creole Love Call" were most likely to have been embraced by

   (A) the most sophisticated jazz aficionados
   (B) the first generation of Ellington followers
   (C) Benny Goodman fans
   (D) devotees of the swing era
   (E) *Down Beat* staff writers

GO ON TO THE NEXT PAGE

15. In emphasizing the sophistication of *Down Beat* readers in lines 32–34, the author seeks primarily to

(A) demonstrate the fine-tuned musical sensibilities of jazz enthusiasts
(B) explain the limited appeal of jazz during its early days
(C) recognize the role of New York and Los Angeles jazz fans in promoting the art of jazz
(D) suggest that popular opinion is not the only way to judge the skill or greatness of musicians
(E) argue that *Down Beat* polls were probably inaccurate

16. The author distinguishes the Duke Ellington Band from other popular swing bands primarily on the basis of

(A) Ellington's appeal to diverse audiences
(B) the amount of money the band earned
(C) the complexity of its music
(D) its meteoric rise following 1940
(E) its extensive national tours

The passage below is followed by questions based on its content. Answer the questions on the basis of what is stated or implied in the passage and in any introductory material that may be provided.

Questions 17–25 are based on the following passage.

Though slang may appear on the surface to be unworthy of serious study, Mario Pei in his 1954 book All About Language *offers an astute examination of the history of slang and its significance in modern society.*

Dialects are a matter of geography. Slang is nationwide. There are some who think that only poorer and less educated people use slang. This is
Line not necessarily true. A little bit of slang, in fact, is
5 used by practically everybody. Slang is a departure from standard, accepted language, but it may easily turn into standard language if it meets with enough favor. Or it may die out and leave little or no trace.
   English is a language very rich in slang, but the
10 mortality among slang words is very high. People who make up our dictionaries usually admit slang expressions on probation. They are either placed in a separate section of the dictionary, or marked "colloquial" or "vulgar" or "slang." If they survive
15 a certain number of years, the label is removed, and they are admitted on a basis of equality with other words. If they disappear from use, they vanish also from the dictionaries.
   In a many good cases, slang words and uses can
20 be traced to one individual. Dizzy Dean, of baseball fame, is responsible for "goodasterous" as the opposite of "disastrous," and "slud" as the past of "slide." Walter Winchell started the expression "making whoopee," and Shakespeare himself was
25 the first to use, at least in writing "beat it" and "not so hot." But far more often the creator of the slang expression is unknown.
   Slang as we said before is nationwide. The expressions we see would be understood pretty
30 much anywhere in America. Dialect is local, as where sections of the Midwest use "mango" in the sense of "green pepper." Two other items that call for discussion are cant and jargon. Jargon is a form of speech current in a given class or profession and
35 hardly understood on the outside. Cant, the language of the underworld, is a variety of jargon. A French poet of the fifteenth century, François Villon, used in many of his poems a type of Paris underworld cant that cannot be understood today.
40 American and British cant has been mysterious in the past, but today large segments of it are known, having been spread by detective stories, and many of its expressions have become general slang and even regular language. "Sawbuck" for "$10" and
45 "grand" for "$1,000" are generally understood and even used, though they are not the best language in the world. Other cant expressions that have acquired a measure of respectability are "take the rap," "take for a ride," "throw the book at," "blow
50 one's top," "frisk," and "gat." But there are many others not so well known, like "quizmaster" for "District Attorney."
   There are jargons of the various professions and trades, even jargons of the sexes and age-levels.
55 Bankers, lawyers, doctors will talk among themselves in specialized languages which people on the outside have difficulty following. So do scientists, technicians, teachers, scholars in every field. But it is not only the intellectual professions
60 that have jargons; it is also the manual trades and occupations. From them too, many words have come into the general language. Shipboard terminology is very extensive and complicated, as you know if you have read stories about ships,
65 particularly the old sailing vessels. When you speak of "knowing the ropes," "keeping on an even keel," "keeping a weather eye open," "giving plenty of leeway," you are using sailors' expressions that have become general. But there are many more
70 such expressions that have not entered the general language, and that you have to look up in the dictionary if you want to understand all the details of a sea story.
   There is a jargon for the military, railroad
75 workers, rodeo people, truck drivers, and soda fountain attendants. In short, there is no occupation that doesn't have its own special terminology, which baffles outsiders. Though linguists might condemn the investigation of slang as unworthy of legitimate
80 study, there is certainly the possibility that its widespread use might cause some of it to become part of the standard language sooner than they think.

17. In lines 1–2, the phrase "Slang is nationwide" refers to the view that
    (A) the use of slang is not restricted to a particular group of people
    (B) slang is considered equivalent to standard English
    (C) dictionary writers often accept slang on a trial basis
    (D) the controversy over slang's popularity is not just a local problem, but also a national concern
    (E) jargon is something that both professional and non-professional people have in common

18. In line 9, the word "rich" most nearly means
    (A) wealthy
    (B) abundant
    (C) entertaining
    (D) seasoned
    (E) productive

19. In the third paragraph, the author refers to Dizzy Dean and Shakespeare in order to
    (A) present the reader with some of the more amusing examples of slang
    (B) show how slang became popular both in sports and literature
    (C) illustrate how both men shared similar phrases in their everyday speech
    (D) explain that slang can usually be traced back to a single person
    (E) offer examples of single individuals who were responsible for certain expressions

20. It can be inferred from the beginning of the passage that "cant," as mentioned in line 35, was most popularly used by
    (A) criminals
    (B) French aristocracy
    (C) midwestern farmers
    (D) bankers and doctors
    (E) the military

21. It can be inferred from the passage that François Villon provides an example of
    (A) how slang adds a unique quality to any piece of literature
    (B) why certain slang expressions seem to enter into standard, accepted language
    (C) how some expressions become part of common usage but later pass out of use
    (D) how slang can make the difference in a writer's career
    (E) why the French underworld during the fifteenth century was able to thrive for so long

22. The author describes certain examples of cant as "not the best language in the world" in lines 46–47 so as to
    (A) convey his opposition to the popular belief that cant has become one of the most accepted dialects
    (B) describe the overwhelming popularity that cant seems to possess
    (C) find a reason why cant is generally understood and even used
    (D) communicate that such speech is not acceptable in some settings
    (E) imply his distaste for the use of cant in society

23. The word "measure" in line 48 most nearly means
    (A) rhythm
    (B) meter
    (C) degree
    (D) melody
    (E) regulation

GO ON TO THE NEXT PAGE

24. The author mentions "shipboard terminology," in lines 62–63 in order to illustrate

   (A) that slang evolved within manual trades as well as intellectual fields
   (B) the intellectual background that inspired such general terms as "keeping on an even keel"
   (C) the complications that often followed sailors who worked on old sailing vessels
   (D) the distinction between complicated nautical terms and more general terms like "knowing the ropes"
   (E) the importance of understanding phrases like "keeping a weather eye open" in order to become an accomplished sailor

25. The author is primarily concerned with

   (A) defining the importance of jargon in intellectual professions
   (B) explaining the origins of slang and its different variations
   (C) tracing the history of slang
   (D) discussing how certain professions have been affected by the popularity of cant
   (E) describing the effect that a single individual can have on slang

STOP
**If you finish before time is called, you may check your work on this section only.
Do not turn to any other section in the test.**

NO TEST MATERIAL ON THIS PAGE.

| 2 | □ | □ | 2 | □ | □ | 2 |

Time—25 Minutes
20 Questions
(1–20)

In this section, solve each problem using any available space on the page for scratchwork. Then decide which is the best of the choices given and fill in the corresponding oval on the answer sheet.

Notes:
1. The use of a calculator is permitted. All numbers used are real numbers.
2. Figures that accompany problems on this test are intended to provide information useful in solving the problems. They are drawn as accurately as possible EXCEPT when it is stated in a specific problem that the figure is not drawn to scale. All figures lie in a plane unless otherwise indicated.

Reference Information

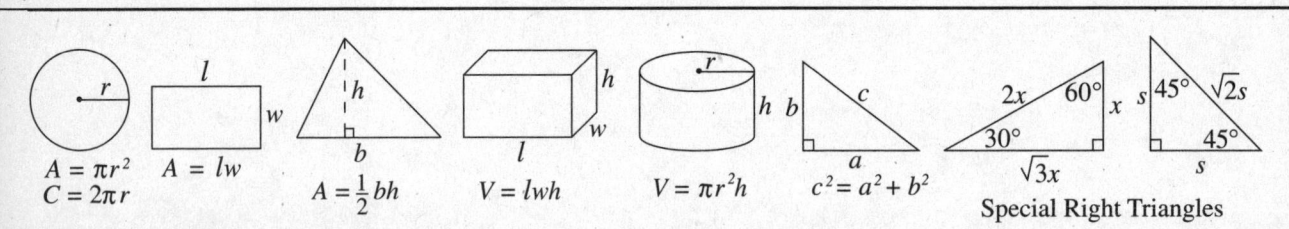

$A = \pi r^2$
$C = 2\pi r$

$A = lw$

$A = \frac{1}{2}bh$

$V = lwh$

$V = \pi r^2 h$

$c^2 = a^2 + b^2$

Special Right Triangles

The number of degrees of arc in a circle is 360.
The measure in degrees of a straight angle is 180.
The sum of the measures in degrees of the angles of a triangle is 180.

---

1. If $12b - 4 = 0$, then $b =$

   (A) 4
   (B) 3
   (C) 0
   (D) $\frac{1}{3}$
   (E) $\frac{1}{4}$

2. If an oil tank contains 60 gallons of fuel and is $\frac{5}{12}$ full, how many gallons would the tank hold when full?

   (A) 72
   (B) 84
   (C) 128
   (D) 144
   (E) 720

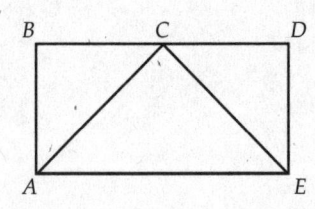

3. If the area of rectangle ABDE is 16 square inches, and C is the midpoint of BD, what is the area of triangle ACE?

   (A) 2
   (B) 4
   (C) 6
   (D) 8
   (E) 16

4. An integer that is a multiple of 32 must also be a multiple of which of the following integers?

   (A) 11
   (B) 9
   (C) 8
   (D) 5
   (E) 3

GO ON TO THE NEXT PAGE

210 ◆ CRACKING THE PSAT/NMSQT

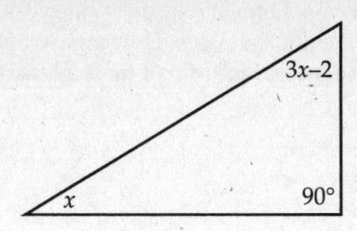

5. In the figure above, what is the value of x?

   (A) 18
   (B) 23
   (C) 32
   (D) 38
   (E) 42

6. If x, y, and z are consecutive integers where x < y < z, what is the sum of y and z in terms of x?

   (A) 2x + 6
   (B) 2x + 4
   (C) 2x + 3
   (D) 2x − 2
   (E) 2x − 1

7. If $(2^a)^b = 64$, then what is $a \times b$?

   (A) 2
   (B) 3
   (C) 4
   (D) 5
   (E) 6

8. What is the average (arithmetic mean) of x, 3x, and 8x?

   (A) 3x
   (B) 4x
   (C) 5x
   (D) 6x
   (E) 8x

9. In the regular hexagon above, how many diagonals can be drawn that have negative slope?

   (A) 0
   (B) 1
   (C) 2
   (D) 3
   (E) 4

10. If a certain number is 3 more than 7 times itself, what is the number?

    (A) −3
    (B) $-\frac{3}{2}$
    (C) $-\frac{1}{2}$
    (D) $-\frac{3}{8}$
    (E) $\frac{1}{2}$

11. Which of the following is equivalent to $-12 \leq 3b + 3 \leq 18$?

    (A) $-5 \leq b \leq 5$
    (B) $-4 \leq b \leq 6$
    (C) $-5 \leq b \leq 6$
    (D) $3 \leq b \leq 5$
    (E) $5 \leq b \leq 5$

GO ON TO THE NEXT PAGE

12. If x is an odd integer divisible by 3, which of the following must be divisible by 4?

    (A) $x + 1$
    (B) $x + 2$
    (C) $x + 3$
    (D) $2x$
    (E) $2x - 2$

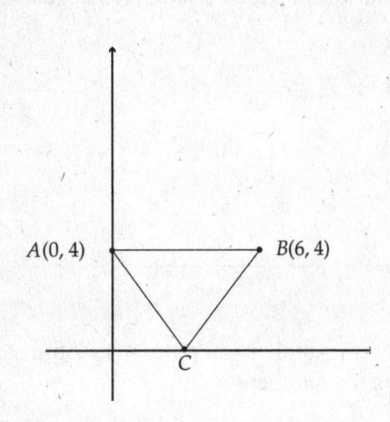

13. If $AC = BC$ in the figure above, what is the perimeter of triangle ABC?

    (A) 14
    (B) 15
    (C) 16
    (D) 18
    (E) $10 + 3\sqrt{3}$

14. For any two integers x and y, $x\Phi y = \dfrac{2x + y}{2x - y}$. What is the value of $4\Phi 6$?

    (A) –3
    (B) 0
    (C) 7
    (D) 8
    (E) 10

15. A bottle containing c ounces of juice can be emptied to fill g identical glasses. How many such bottles would be needed to fill n of these glasses with juice?

    (A) $\dfrac{gn}{c}$
    (B) $\dfrac{cn}{g}$
    (C) $\dfrac{g}{n}$
    (D) $\dfrac{n}{g}$
    (E) $\dfrac{c}{n}$

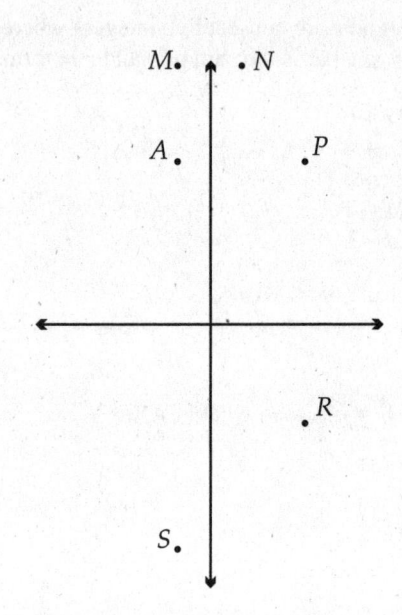

16. Six points are shown on the standard (x, y) coordinate plane as above. If the coordinates of point A are (x, y), which of the following points could have the coordinates $(2x, -y)$?

    (A) M
    (B) N
    (C) P
    (D) R
    (E) S

GO ON TO THE NEXT PAGE

212 ◆ CRACKING THE PSAT/NMSQT

17. A large cubical block of cheese measures 8 inches on each edge. If a small rectangular piece measuring 4 inches by 2 inches by 2 inches is cut out and thrown away, the volume of the remaining block of cheese is what fraction of its original volume?

(A) $\frac{1}{32}$

(B) $\frac{3}{4}$

(C) $\frac{7}{8}$

(D) $\frac{15}{16}$

(E) $\frac{31}{32}$

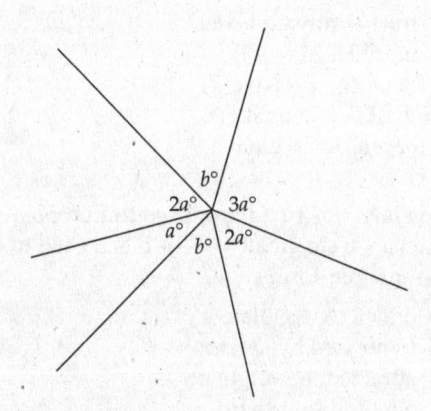

19. If x and y are integers and $y = 4x$, which of the following could be the average (arithmetic mean) of x and y?

(A) −36
(B) −35
(C) 4
(D) 12
(E) 28

20. If 2000 gallons of paint are needed to cover a surface of m square feet, and Marie's house has a surface area of t square feet, how many gallons of paint will she need to paint her house?

(A) $\frac{m}{2000t}$

(B) $\frac{t}{2000m}$

(C) $\frac{mt}{2000}$

(D) $\frac{2000m}{t}$

(E) $\frac{2000t}{m}$

Note: Figure not drawn to scale

18. In the figure above, what is the measure of b in terms of a?

(A) $90 + 2a$
(B) $180 - 4a$
(C) $180 - 8a$
(D) $360 - 8a$
(E) $360 - 12a$

STOP

If you finish before time is called, you may check your work on this section only. Do not turn to any other section in the test.

**Time—25 Minutes
25 Questions
(26–52)**

For each question in this section, select the best answer from among the choices given and fill in the corresponding oval on the answer sheet.

Each sentence below has one or two blanks, each blank indicating that something has been omitted. Beneath the sentence are five words or sets of words labeled A through E. Choose the word or set of words that, when inserted in the sentence, best fits the meaning of the sentence as a whole.

Example:

Medieval kingdoms did not become constitutional republics overnight; on the contrary, the change was -------.

(A) unpopular (B) unexpected (C) advantageous

(D) sufficient (E) gradual

Ⓐ Ⓑ Ⓒ Ⓓ ●

26. Though many people are willing to ------- saving the environment when speaking in public, they are often not willing to ------- their lifestyles to help protect the earth.

(A) promote..maintain
(B) condone..justify
(C) advocate..alter
(D) denounce..adjust
(E) champion..substantiate

27. Due to his ------- personality, Prince Klemens von Metternich dominated the Congress of Vienna after the defeat of Napoleon.

(A) amiable (B) pleasant (C) commanding

(D) duplicitous (E) sympathetic

28. The ancient forest's landscape is enlivened by ------- hues whenever the lush canopy is ------- by the strong rays of the sun.

(A) vibrant..blemished
(B) muted..overwhelmed
(C) threatening..enveloped
(D) mellow..blanketed
(E) vivid..pierced

29. The reclusive nature of the iguana helps to explain the long-standing ------- of fruitful investigations of its behavior in the wild.

(A) constancy (B) notoriety (C) necessity

(D) paucity (E) probity

30. The aim of the governor's plan was to make more housing available for middle-income families, but unfortunately she only ------- the problem by making such housing even more scarce.

(A) repealed (B) exacerbated (C) abolished

(D) hoisted (E) ingratiated

31. Many people consider Dana ------- because of her friendly and honest manner, but she is actually a ------- negotiator.

(A) trustworthy..relaxed
(B) gullible..shrewd
(C) taciturn..decisive
(D) vigilant..lenient
(E) eccentric..secluded

32. When jazz was first introduced to Europe, many musicians were greatly ------- it and tried to ------- its free-form style.

(A) drawn to..emulate
(B) impressed by..reject
(C) attracted to..originate
(D) opposed to..adopt
(E) afraid of..accept

33. The senator's aide claimed that even though the United States was established by rebellion, it is now inclined to view ------- in other nations with -------.

(A) reactionaries..adoration
(B) misers..disdain
(C) insurgents..animosity
(D) autocrats..malevolence
(E) revolutionaries..indifference

GO ON TO THE NEXT PAGE

> Each question below consists of a related pair of words or phrases, followed by five pairs of words or phrases labeled A through E. Select the pair that best expresses a relationship similar to that expressed in the original pair.
>
> Example:
>
> CRUMB : BREAD ::
>
> (A) ounce : unit
> (B) splinter : wood
> (C) water : bucket
> (D) twine : rope
> (E) cream : butter
>
> Ⓐ ● Ⓒ Ⓓ Ⓔ

34. WATER : THIRST ::

    (A) spasm : discomfort
    (B) rest : exhaustion
    (C) debate : resentment
    (D) sedative : sleep
    (E) sight : understanding

35. OIL : LUBRICATE ::

    (A) thermometer : cure
    (B) antidote : poison
    (C) message : transmit
    (D) boat : swim
    (E) ornament : decorate

36. EPILOGUE : PLAY ::

    (A) aria : opera
    (B) director : movie
    (C) afterword : book
    (D) act : scene
    (E) comedy : drama

37. RUDE : TACT ::

    (A) treacherous : loyalty
    (B) transparent : sight
    (C) naïve : innocence
    (D) regretful : memory
    (E) sympathetic : compassion

38. MOLLIFY : INTENSITY ::

    (A) liberate : freedom
    (B) predict : future
    (C) harass : injury
    (D) soothe : discomfort
    (E) protect : opportunity

39. ILLUSORY : DECEPTION ::

    (A) realistic : photograph
    (B) eclectic : viewpoint
    (C) didactic : instruction
    (D) intrinsic : value
    (E) majestic : view

40. IMPERVIOUS : PENETRATED ::

    (A) categorized : stored
    (B) irresponsible : finished
    (C) interminable : defeated
    (D) studious : educated
    (E) indefatigable : exhausted

GO ON TO THE NEXT PAGE →

Questions 41–52 are based on the following passages.

The following passages, written one hundred years apart, are both attempts to justify resistance to an act of government. The first passage, which is from Martin Luther King's "Letter from Birmingham Jail," concerns the injustice of law, while the second, Henry David Thoreau's "On Civil Disobedience," explores the foundation and the limits of democratic government.

Passage 1

One may well ask: "How can you advocate breaking some laws and obeying others?" The answer lies in the fact that there are two types of laws: just and
Line unjust. I would be the first to advocate obeying just
5 laws. One has not only a legal but also a moral responsibility to disobey unjust laws. I would agree with St. Augustine that "an unjust law is no law at all." To put it in the terms of St. Thomas Aquinas: an unjust law is a human law that is not rooted in eternal
10 law and natural law. Any law which uplifts human personality is just. Any law that degrades human personality is unjust. All segregation statutes are unjust because segregation distorts the soul and damages the personality.
15 One who breaks an unjust law must do so openly, lovingly, and with a willingness to accept the penalty. I submit that an individual who breaks a law that conscience tells him is unjust, and who willingly accepts the penalty of imprisonment in order to arouse
20 the conscience of the community over its injustice is in reality expressing the highest respect for the law.
Actually, we who engage in nonviolent direct action are not the creators of tension. We merely bring to the surface the hidden tension that is already alive. We
25 bring it out into the open, where it can be seen and dealt with. Like a boil that can never be cured so long as it is covered up but must be opened with all its ugliness to the natural medicines of air and light, injustice must be exposed, with all the tension its
30 exposure creates, to the light of human conscience and the air of national opinion, before it can be cured.

Human progress never rolls in on wheels of inevitability; it comes through the tireless efforts of men willing to be co-workers with God, and without
35 this hard work, time itself becomes an ally of the forces of stagnation. We must use time creatively, in the knowledge that the time is always ripe to do right. Now is the time to make real the promise of democracy and transform our national elegy into a
40 creative psalm of brotherhood. Now is the time to lift our national policy from the quicksand of racial injustice to the solid rock of human dignity.

Passage 2

I heartily accept the motto "That government is best which governs least," and I should like to see it acted
45 up to more rapidly and systematically. Carried out, it finally amounts to this, which I also believe, "That government is best which governs not at all," and when men are prepared for it, that will be the kind of government which they will have. Government is at
50 best expedient; but most governments are usually, and all governments are sometimes, inexpedient. This American government, what is it but a tradition, endeavoring to transmit itself unimpaired to posterity, but each instant losing some of its integrity.
55 But, to speak practically, and as a citizen, unlike those who call themselves no-government men, I ask for, not at once no government, but at once a better government. Let every man make known what kind of government would command his respect, and that will
60 be one step toward obtaining it. After all, the practical reason why, when the power is once in the hands of the people, a majority is permitted, and for a long period continue, to rule is not because they are most likely to be in the right, nor because this seems fairest
65 to the minority, but because they are physically the strongest.

But a government in which the majority rule in all cases cannot be based on justice, even as far as men understand it. Can there not be government in which
70 majorities do not virtually decide right and wrong, but conscience? In which majorities decide only those questions to which the rule of expediency is applicable? Must the citizen ever for a moment, or in the least degree, resign his conscience to the
75 legislator? Why has every man a conscience then? I think that we should be men first and subjects afterward. It is not desirable to cultivate a respect for the law, so much as for the right. The only obligation which I have a right to assume is to do at any time
80 what I think right.

41. In the first paragraph, the author of Passage 1 suggests that every law has the possibility of being

   (A) valid or invalid, depending upon the method by which it is created
   (B) beneficial to the society that it is meant to govern
   (C) just or unjust, depending on its effect on human personality
   (D) expedient or inexpedient, depending on the intended goal of the act
   (E) detrimental to certain individuals in a society

42. In Passage 1, the author refers to St. Augustine (line 7) and St. Aquinas (line 8) in order to

   (A) use religious authority to place his argument on a theological basis
   (B) further define the distinction between a just and an unjust law
   (C) suggest that this categorization of law has been in existence for over fifteen hundred years
   (D) discuss the various ways laws are written and passed
   (E) respond to critics who argue that any law that is passed by an elected legislature must be just

43. With which one of the following individuals would the author of Passage 1 most likely agree?

   (A) The person who, after careful reflection, determines that a given law accords with his or her sense of morality and therefore should be obeyed.
   (B) The person who, without any thought or contemplation, decides that a given law should be disobeyed because it is inconvenient.
   (C) The person who always follows the letter of the law, out of respect for the rule of law.
   (D) The person who, after hearing a legislator's opinion, obeys or disobeys the law based on the opinion of the legislator.
   (E) The person who always chooses to disregard any governmental authority.

44. In lines 22–31, the author's discussion of the results of "nonviolent direct action" suggests that the society in which the author lives

   (A) allows the majority, through the use of force, to rule unjustly over various minority groups
   (B) lives under a system of laws that is primarily unjust
   (C) is not a well-disciplined, law-abiding society
   (D) exhibits injustice that may be exposed by an open refusal to obey certain laws
   (E) is restricted in its movement toward a just society by the forces of immorality and stagnation

45. The final paragraph of Passage 1 is an attempt to point out that "injustice" (line 42)

   (A) can be reduced, so long as individuals act according to their beliefs and resist the complacency that allows injustice
   (B) is a necessary evil that has existed since the earliest human societies
   (C) can only be fought by appealing to governmental authorities
   (D) is but one stage of human development, which will naturally and gradually give way to a more just society
   (E) is a natural consequence of people coming together in society, and to escape it requires people to seek new forms of social organization

GO ON TO THE NEXT PAGE

46. The primary purpose of Passage 2 is to

    (A) show why every government is unjust
    (B) lay down a principle of government in order to support the author's critique of current unjust acts
    (C) suggest that not all governments are capable of protecting the rights of its citizens
    (D) support an argument for the overthrow of the current government
    (E) describe an ideal toward which the current government should strive

47. In the second paragraph (lines 58–60), the author of Passage 2 suggests that the first step toward improving government is

    (A) an understanding of what kind of government would be worthy of respect
    (B) a commitment to the basic principles of democracy
    (C) an acceptance of the injustice inherent in democratic government
    (D) the elimination of governmental control of the economy
    (E) the removal of moral issues from politics

48. In developing the argument in the last paragraph of Passage 2, the author is primarily concerned with

    (A) comparing the American government with the government of other European countries
    (B) discussing the limits of governmental authority over the individual
    (C) demonstrating a flaw that appears in every social organization
    (D) pointing out the need for nonviolent direct action against unjust laws
    (E) establishing the authority of majority rule

49. According to the author of Passage 2, majority rule serves as the basis for the form of government in certain societies because

    (A) the majority generally knows what is right, and so their decisions have greater moral authority
    (B) majority rule is the ideal system of government
    (C) the conscience of each individual is always expressed through the views of the majority
    (D) the majority can use the strength of their greater numbers to carry out their wishes
    (E) even minority groups believe that majority rule is the most fair system of government

50. It can be inferred that the authors of Passages 1 and 2 agree that

    (A) people are obliged to obey every law of the country they reside in
    (B) individuals should consult their lawmakers when judging whether an act would be just
    (C) in some cases the majority may be treating a minority group unfairly
    (D) disobeying an unjust law requires that one accept punishment for breaking the law
    (E) some forms of government are far superior to democracy

51. The author uses the phrase "that we should be men first, and subjects afterward" in lines 76–77 in order to

    (A) demonstrate the isolation of the individual in society
    (B) argue that humans have a need for government
    (C) explain the need for nonviolent direct action
    (D) further the claim that each individual must follow his or her own conscience
    (E) draw a distinction between the legislator and the citizen

52. Which of the following best illustrates an important difference between Passage 1 and Passage 2?

(A) Passage 1 advocates a certain manner of action, while Passage 2 is more theoretical
(B) Passage 1 discusses the rights of the individual to disobey an unjust law, whereas Passage 2 is only concerned with the rights of minority groups
(C) Passage 2 is concerned with discussing specific forms of nonviolent direct action, whereas Passage 1 is not
(D) Passage 2 bases its argument in religious doctrine, whereas Passage 1 does not
(E) Passage 1 argues, in contrast to Passage 2, that citizens have certain responsibilities that non-citizens do not

STOP
**If you finish before time is called, you may check your work on this section only.
Do not turn to any other section in the test.**

4 4 4 4 4 4 4

Time—25 Minutes
20 Questions
(21–40)

In this section, solve each problem using any available space on the page for scratchwork. Then decide which is the best of the choices given and fill in the corresponding oval on the answer sheet.

Notes:
1. The use of a calculator is permitted. All numbers used are real numbers.
2. Figures that accompany problems in this test are intended to provide information useful in solving the problems. They are drawn as accurately as possible EXCEPT when it is stated in a specific problem that the figure is not drawn to scale. All figures lie in a plane unless otherwise indicated.

Reference Information

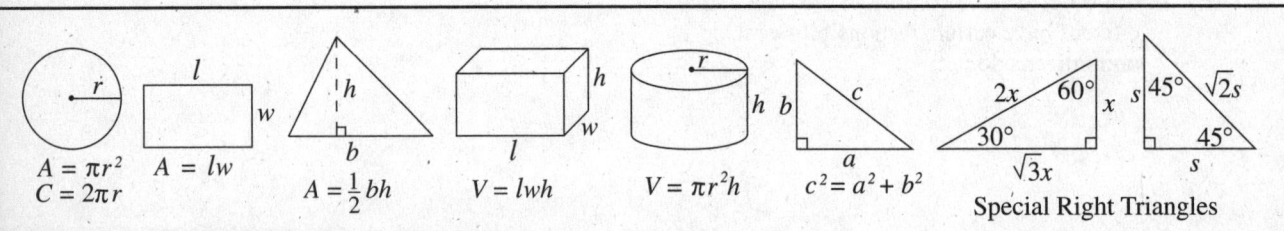

$A = \pi r^2$
$C = 2\pi r$

$A = lw$

$A = \frac{1}{2}bh$

$V = lwh$

$V = \pi r^2 h$

$c^2 = a^2 + b^2$

Special Right Triangles

The number of degrees of arc in a circle is 360.
The measure in degrees of a straight angle is 180.
The sum of the measures in degrees of the angles of a triangle is 180.

Directions for Quantitative Comparison Questions

Questions 21–32 each consist of two quantities in boxes, one in Column A and one in Column B. You are to compare the two quantities and on the answer sheet fill in oval

A if the quantity in Column A is greater;
B if the quantity in Column B is greater;
C if the two quantities are equal;
D if the relationship cannot be determined from the information given.

AN E RESPONSE WILL NOT BE SCORED.

Notes:
1. In some questions, information is given about one or both of the quantities to be compared. In such cases, the given information is centered above the two columns and is not boxed.
2. In a given question, a symbol that appears in both columns represents the same thing in Column A as it does in Column B.
3. Letters such as x, n, and k stand for real numbers.

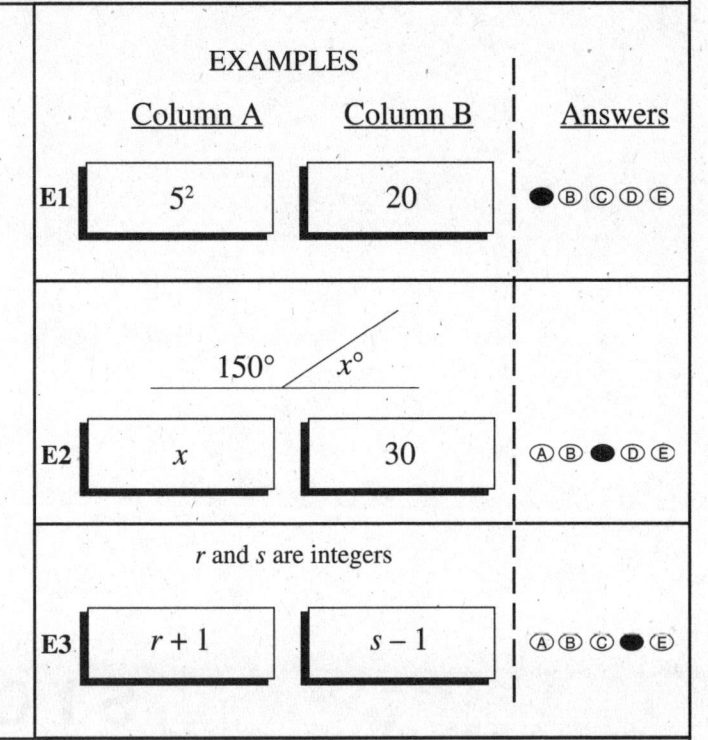

EXAMPLES

	Column A	Column B	Answers
E1	5^2	20	● Ⓑ Ⓒ Ⓓ Ⓔ
E2	(150° / x°) x	30	Ⓐ Ⓑ ● Ⓓ Ⓔ
E3	*r and s are integers* $r + 1$	$s - 1$	Ⓐ Ⓑ Ⓒ ● Ⓔ

220 ◆ CRACKING THE PSAT/NMSQT

4 4 4 4 4 4 4

SUMMARY DIRECTIONS FOR QUANTITATIVE COMPARISON QUESTIONS

Answer: A if the quantity in Column A is greater;
B if the quantity in Column B is greater;
C if the two quantities are equal;
D if the relationship cannot be determined from the information given.

AN E RESPONSE WILL NOT BE SCORED.

	Column A	Column B
21.	6% of 5	4% of 7

22. n is a positive integer

	Column A	Column B
	3^n	n^3

23. $a < b - 3$

	Column A	Column B
	a	b

24. The length of segment WZ is 5

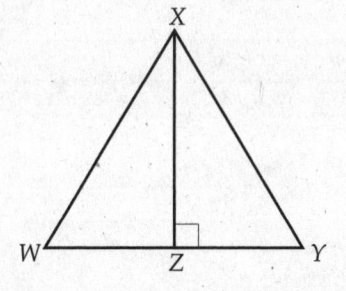

	Column A	Column B
	Length of WX	Length of XY

25. The ratio of 18 to 6 is the same as the ratio of y to 4

	Column A	Column B
	10	y

26. Segment EH bisects $\angle DHG$
Segment FH bisects $\angle EHG$

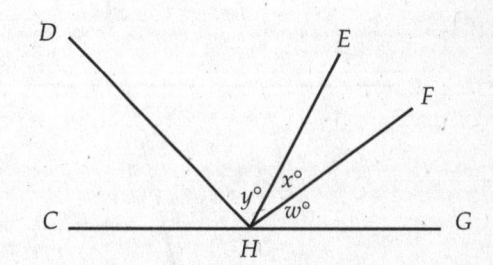

	Column A	Column B
	y	$2w$

27. $a^3 = 3$
$b^4 = 4$

	Column A	Column B
	$a^6 + b^8$	24

GO ON TO THE NEXT PAGE

PRACTICE TEST 1 ◆ 221

4 4 4 4 4 4 4

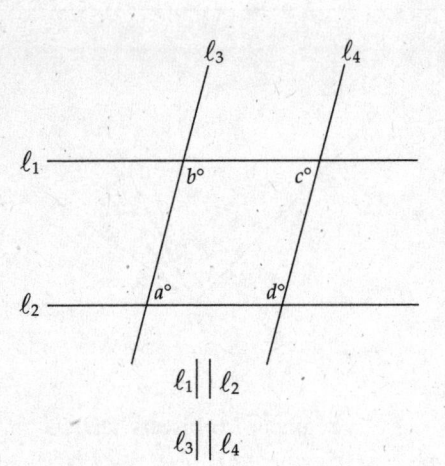

SUMMARY DIRECTIONS FOR QUANTITATIVE COMPARISON QUESTIONS

<u>Answer</u>: A if the quantity in Column A is greater;
B if the quantity in Column B is greater;
C if the two quantities are equal;
D if the relationship cannot be determined from the information given.

AN E RESPONSE WILL NOT BE SCORED.

	Column A	Column B		Column A	Column B
	$r^2 - 3r = 10$			$6a - 8b = 4$	
28.	r	0	31.	$3a - 2$	$4b$

				$a < b < 0$	
	(figure: lines ℓ_3, ℓ_4 crossing ℓ_1, ℓ_2 with angles $b°, c°, a°, d°$; $\ell_1 \parallel \ell_2$; $\ell_3 \parallel \ell_4$)		32.	$a^2 + b^2$	$(a+b)^2$
29.	$a + b$	$c + d$			

	$x \neq 0$				
30.	$x \cdot 2x$	$\dfrac{x}{2x}$			

GO ON TO THE NEXT PAGE →

Directions for Student-Produced Response Questions

Each of the remaining questions (33–40) requires you to solve the problem and enter your answer by marking the ovals in the special grid, as shown in the examples below.

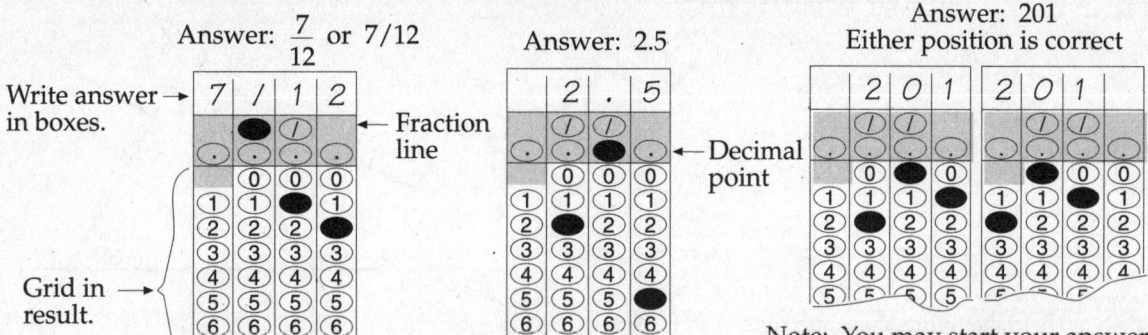

Answer: $\frac{7}{12}$ or 7/12

Write answer in boxes. ← Fraction line

Grid in result.

Answer: 2.5 ← Decimal point

Answer: 201
Either position is correct

Note: You may start your answers in any column, space permitting. Columns not needed should be left blank.

- Mark no more than one oval in any column.
- Because the answer sheet will be machine-scored, **you will receive credit only if the ovals are filled in correctly.**
- Although not required, it is suggested that you write your answer in the boxes at the top of the columns to help you fill in the ovals accurately.
- Some problems may have more than one correct answer. In such cases, grid only one answer.
- No question has a negative answer.
- **Mixed numbers** such as $2\frac{1}{2}$ must be gridded as 2.5 or 5/2. (If $2\,1\,/\,2$ is gridded, it will be interpreted as $\frac{21}{2}$, not $2\frac{1}{2}$.)

- **Decimal Accuracy:** If you obtain a decimal answer, **enter the most accurate value the grid will accommodate.** For example, if you obtain an answer such as 0.6666..., you should record the result as .666 or .667. **Less accurate values such as .66 or .67 are not acceptable.**

Acceptable ways to grid $\frac{2}{3}$ = .6666...

GO ON TO THE NEXT PAGE

PRACTICE TEST 1 ◆ 223

33. If 20 percent of a number n is 36, what is 0.2 percent of n?

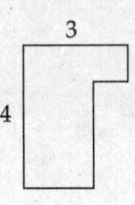

34. If all of the angles in the figure above are right angles, what is the perimeter of the figure above?

35. If $x - 8 = 5y$ and $x = 23$, then $x - y =$

36. What is the product of all the positive integer factors of 20?

37. Marcia can type 18 pages per hour, and David can type 14 pages per hour. If they work together, how many <u>minutes</u> will it take them to type 24 pages?

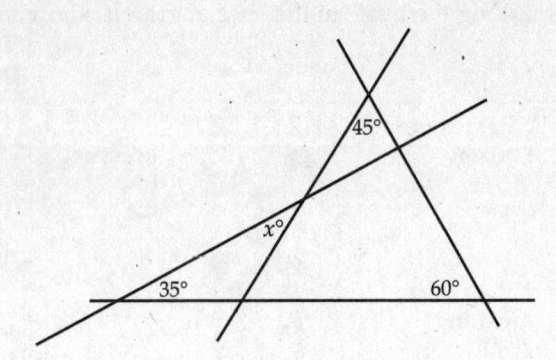

38. What is the value of x in the figure above?

39. The operation # is defined by the equation $\#x = x^2 - x + 4$ for all nonzero integers x. If $\#x = 10$, what is the value of x?

40. A box contains only large marbles and small marbles. There are twice as many large marbles as small marbles in the box. The large marbles are all either blue or red, and there are 5 times as many blue marbles as red marbles. If one marble is drawn from the box at random, what is the probability that it will be a large blue marble?

STOP
**If you finish before time is called, you may check your work on this section only.
Do not turn to any other section in the test.**

NO TEST MATERIAL ON THIS PAGE.

Time—30 Minutes
39 Questions
(1–39)

For each question in this section, select the best answer from among the choices given and fill in the corresponding oval on the answer sheet.

Directions: The following sentences test your knowledge of grammar, usage, word choice, and idiom.
Some sentences are correct.
No sentence contains more than one error.

You will find that the error, if there is one, is underlined and lettered. Elements of the sentence that are not underlined will not be changed. In choosing answers, follow the requirements of standard written English.

If there is an error, select the one underlined part that must be changed to make the sentence correct and fill in the corresponding oval on your answer sheet.

If there is no error, fill in oval Ⓔ.

EXAMPLE:

The <u>other</u> delegates and <u>him</u> <u>immediately</u>
    A   B   C

accepted the resolution <u>drafted by</u> the
                           D

neutral states. <u>No error</u>
                   E

SAMPLE ANSWER

Ⓐ ● Ⓒ Ⓓ Ⓔ

---

1. <u>Revered as</u> one of the world's most versatile
    A

   geniuses, Leonardo da Vinci excelled <u>in every</u>
                                                 B

   endeavor he attempted and <u>serving</u> as <u>a prototype</u>
                               C   D

   for the Renaissance man. <u>No error</u>
                               E

2. The twins wanted to be <u>a member</u> of the team, <u>but</u>
                               A   B

   the captain <u>had already made</u> <u>her selections</u>.
                   C   D

   <u>No error</u>
   E

3. Of the nominees <u>for</u> the Nobel Prize in literature
   A   B

   this year, <u>few</u> are <u>as qualified as</u> the English
           C   D

   novelist Anthony Powell. <u>No error</u>
                              E

4. The recent production <u>of</u> Arthur Miller's *A View*
                       A

   From the Bridge exemplifies the strength of this

   unsung masterpiece <u>and demonstrates</u> that the work
                          B

   has been <u>ignored</u> <u>unjust</u>. <u>No error</u>
        C   D   E

GO ON TO THE NEXT PAGE

5. Yoga is <u>more than</u> simply a <u>series of</u> stretches and
         A   B
poses; it is a means of centering oneself spiritually
and <u>focus</u> in such a way <u>as to</u> put one's life in
       C   D
order. <u>No error</u>
         E

6. <u>Prior to</u> the Industrial Revolution, children and
     A
parents <u>spend</u> a great deal <u>of time</u> working
          B   C
together to meet the needs <u>of the family</u>. <u>No error</u>
                                D   E

7. The fund-raising campaigns <u>of many</u> public radio
                                 A
and television stations <u>are</u> often <u>viewed by</u>
                          B   C
subscribers as a necessary, <u>albeit</u> undesirable, evil.
                              D
<u>No error</u>
  E

8. Neither the president <u>nor</u> the CEO of the three sister
                           A
companies <u>was</u> able to determine why the last
            B
quarter's financial reports <u>were</u> so inconsistent with
                              C
previous <u>years</u>. <u>No error</u>
           D   E

9. If one is interested <u>in</u> learning more about Jacob
                         A
Lawrence, <u>you should</u> visit the Metropolitan
             B
Museum of Art when next <u>his</u> work <u>is exhibited</u>.
                          C   D
<u>No error</u>
  E

10. In many colleges in the Northeast, it is <u>necessarily</u>
                                               A
for students <u>to wear</u> snowshoes to get from the
                B
dormitory to <u>their</u> classes <u>during</u> the winter
                C   D
months. <u>No error</u>
          E

11. <u>Just as</u> parents vary in their readiness to have their
      A
babies learn <u>to</u> walk, babies vary in <u>their</u> readiness
                B   C
to take <u>his or her</u> first steps. <u>No error</u>
           D   E

12. While in training, each member of the team <u>were</u>
                                                  A
required to focus exclusively on the tasks associated
<u>with</u> <u>her</u> position, and therefore had little sense of
  B   C
the functioning of the team <u>as a whole</u>. <u>No error</u>
                              D   E

13. The gift that Karen and Mary ultimately purchased for **her**(A) mother was much **less**(C) expensive than the gift they originally intended **to purchase**(D). **No error**(E)
    - B: was

14. Vocalists **are**(A) often able **to sing**(B) oratorios in flawless Latin, even if none of them **have**(C) ever **studied**(D) Latin in school. **No error**(E)

15. Thomas Pynchon's novel *The Crying of Lot 49* **has been**(A) lauded for **it's**(B) satirical prose and **favorably**(C) described as **akin to**(D) Joyce's *Ulysses*. **No error**(E)

16. John knew he **should've went**(A) home on the team's bus when he **had**(B) the chance **instead of**(C) waiting **for**(D) the bus to return to bring home the spectators. **No error**(E)

17. **Many**(A) students find Shakespeare's *Richard III* impossible **to understand**(B); yet, when it is **proper**(C) conveyed, students can often learn from the familial turmoil and inner conflict **that occurs**(D) in the play. **No error**(E)

18. Many scholars **agree**(A) that there **has been**(B) no greater contributor to the advancement **of architecture**(C) in the twentieth century than **that of**(D) Frank Lloyd Wright. **No error**(E)

19. Constructing a fence **ought not to be**(A) seen as an insurmountable task; **rather**(B), it should be viewed as a challenge **that**(C) can be accomplished by a **combination of**(D) perseverance and patience. **No error**(E)

GO ON TO THE NEXT PAGE

Directions: In each of the following sentences, some part or all of the sentence is underlined. Below each sentence you will find five ways of phrasing the underlined part. Select the answer that produces the most effective sentence, one that is clear and exact, without awkwardness or ambiguity, and fill in the corresponding oval on your answer sheet. In choosing answers, follow the requirements of standard written English. Choose the answer that best expresses the meaning of the original sentence.

Answer (A) is always the same as the underlined part. Choose answer (A) if you think the original sentence needs no revision.

20. After visiting their friends in Paris, my parents told me that <u>in France they sometimes</u> do not wear bathing suits on the beach.
    (A) in France they sometimes
    (B) in France some people
    (C) some French people
    (D) in France there are some who
    (E) in France, men and women

21. Today's computers <u>are becoming not only more varied and powerful, but also less expensive</u>.
    (A) are becoming not only more varied and powerful, but also less expensive
    (B) not only are becoming more varied and powerful, they cost less
    (C) become not only more varied and powerful, they become less expensive
    (D) becoming more varied and powerful, but also less expensive
    (E) become more varied and powerful, not only, but also less expensive

22. <u>Getting off the chairlift, Neil adjusted his boot buckles, polished his goggles, and skied down the slope</u>.
    (A) Getting off the chairlift, Neil adjusted his boot buckles, polished his goggles, and skied down the slope.
    (B) He got off the chairlift, Neil adjusted his boot buckles, polished his goggles, and skied down the slope.
    (C) After getting off the chairlift, Neil adjusted his boot buckles, polished his goggles, and then he went skiing down the slope.
    (D) Neil, after getting off the chairlift, adjusted his boot buckles, polished his goggles, and was skiing down the slope.
    (E) After he got off the chairlift, Neil adjusted his boot buckles, polished his goggles, and skied down the slope.

23. Since they have been told not to do so in their school books, students often hesitate to write in their personal books; yet, circling an unknown word or underlining an important phrase <u>is critically when one wishes to truly learn something</u>.
    (A) is critically when one wishes to truly learn something
    (B) is critically being as one might wish to truly learn something
    (C) is critical when one wishes to truly learn something
    (D) is critical when you truly want to learn that something has been
    (E) can only be seen as critical when one wishes to truly learn something

GO ON TO THE NEXT PAGE

24. One of Humphrey Bogart's earlier movies, Samuel Spade is a detective trying to solve the mystery of his partner's death in *The Maltese Falcon*.
    (A) One of Humphrey Bogart's earlier movies, Samuel Spade is a detective trying to solve the mystery of his partner's death in *The Maltese Falcon*.
    (B) One of Humphrey Bogart's earlier movies, *The Maltese Falcon* is a movie in that Samuel Spade, detective, tries to solve the mystery of his partner's death.
    (C) One of Humphrey Bogart's earlier movies, *The Maltese Falcon* is a mystery in which Samuel Spade tries to solve his partner's death.
    (D) In *The Maltese Falcon*, one of Humphrey Bogart's earlier movies, Samuel Spade is a detective trying to solve the mystery of his partner's death.
    (E) In *The Maltese Falcon*, one of Humphrey Bogart's roles is that of Samuel Spade, a detective trying to solve the mystery of his partner's death, and it was also one of his earlier movies.

25. While Boudin's own paintings have never been held in that high regard, he is seen as having played a critical role in the education of Impressionist painter Monet.
    (A) While Boudin's own paintings have never been held in that high regard, he is seen as having played a critical role in the education of Impressionist painter Monet.
    (B) While Boudin's own paintings were never regarded highly, Monet is seen as having been one of his most educated students.
    (C) It is seen that Boudin's critical role in educating the Impressionist painter Monet was held in higher regard than his paintings.
    (D) Since Boudin's own paintings have never been held in that high regard, he has been seen as having played a critical role in the education of Impressionist painter Monet.
    (E) Since Boudin's own paintings, which were never held in that high regard, were seen as having played a critical role in the education of Impressionist painter Monet.

26. Although everyone was forewarned about the upcoming exam, yet only three students out of the entire class passed it.
    (A) yet only three students out of the entire class
    (B) only three students out of the entire class
    (C) only three students, which was out of the entire class,
    (D) yet only three students that were forewarned out of the entire class
    (E) but only three students out of the entire class

27. The committee chairpersons agreed to return to their respective committees and they would discuss the proposals made by the executive board.
    (A) to return to their respective committees and they would discuss
    (B) upon return to their respective committees, thereby discussing
    (C) to return to her respective committees and discuss
    (D) to return to their respective committees discussing
    (E) to return to their respective committees and discuss

28. The clog has come back into fashion recently, yet few people know that originally it was called the sabot, made by hollowing a single piece of wood, and was worn by peasants in Europe.
    (A) it was called the sabot, made by hollowing a single piece of wood, and was worn by peasants in Europe
    (B) it was called the sabot, making it by hollowing a single piece of wood, and worn by peasants in Europe
    (C) it was called the sabot, made by hollowing a single piece of wood, and worn by peasants in Europe
    (D) it was called the sabot, making it by hollowing a single piece of wood, and was worn by peasants in Europe
    (E) it was called the sabot, and the peasants made it by hollowing a single piece of wood, and wore it in Europe

GO ON TO THE NEXT PAGE

29. Many say that, after inventing an explosive more powerful than any then known, Alfred Nobel instituted the Nobel Peace Prizes to atone for his "accomplishment" and relieve his conscience.

   (A) after inventing an explosive more powerful than any then known
   (B) after inventing an explosive that was more powerful than any that were then known
   (C) after he invented an explosive more powerful than he or any others had then known
   (D) after he invented an explosive, it being more powerful than any then known
   (E) after inventing an explosive more powerful then any than known

30. For many a brilliant actor, being free to interpret their character as they wish is more important than being well paid.

   (A) being free to interpret their character as they wish
   (B) being free to interpret his or her character as they wish
   (C) being free to interpret their character as they wishes
   (D) being free to interpret his or her character as he or she wishes
   (E) being free to interpret his or her character as he or she wish

31. On Sunday afternoons, Omar and his family enjoy playing Monopoly with the neighbors, and they always win.

   (A) and they always win
   (B) even though they always win
   (C) even though the neighbors always win
   (D) and the neighbors, they always win
   (E) it being that the neighbors always win

32. Although he was not an advocate of psychiatrists, Sigmund Freud was respected by Albert Einstein as a social philosopher, and worked with him to promote peace during the Nazi uprising.

   (A) Sigmund Freud was respected by Albert Einstein as a social philosopher, and worked with him to promote peace
   (B) Sigmund Freud was respected by Albert Einstein, since he was a social philosopher, and they worked to promote peace
   (C) Albert Einstein respected Sigmund Freud as a social philosopher, and they together worked to promote peace
   (D) Albert Einstein respected Sigmund Freud as a social philosopher who was working with him to promote peace
   (E) Albert Einstein respected Sigmund Freud as a social philosopher, and worked with him to promote peace

33. After getting her driver's license, Jenny used her father's car as often as possible, and her father said to put less miles on it by walking to school and work.

   (A) as often as possible, and her father said to put less miles on it
   (B) as often as possible; eventually her father told her to put fewer miles on it
   (C) as often as possible, but then eventually her father told her to be putting fewer miles on it
   (D) as often as possible; eventually her father told her to put less miles on it
   (E) as often as possible, and her father said to be putting less miles on it

GO ON TO THE NEXT PAGE

Directions: The following passage is an early draft of an essay. Some parts of the passage need to be rewritten.

Read the passage and answer the questions that follow. Some questions are about particular sentences or parts of the essay or the entire essay and ask you to consider organization and development. In making your decisions, follow the conventions of standard written English. After you have chosen your answer, fill in the corresponding oval on your answer sheet.

(1) Our town needs to make more of an effort to make its museums accessible to children. (2) Raised with frequent exposure to sculpture and paintings, it is much more likely that young people will mature into artists and patrons of the arts.

(3) It is often quite easy to accomplish a great deal simply. (4) Placed slightly lower on the walls, paintings become more visible to children. (5) But extensive programs to encourage children to appreciate art are often not a necessity. (6) Children have a natural enjoyment of art. (7) A museum is an excellent place for a child. (8) We must only understand that these young museum patrons can not help acting like them. (9) Children should not be asked to be silent, or spend long periods of time in front of any one piece. (10) If necessary, museums should set up special "children's times" during which young people may roam through the building, enjoying the artwork in their own way. (11) A wonderful learning experience! (12) Children can have a great time, and at the same time gain an appreciation of art. (13) Precautions could be taken to make sure that no damage was done.

(14) This is necessary because places like museums must be available for everyone. (15) These changes can not happen overnight, but if we volunteered and were helping to make these changes in our town's museums, we can realize the goal of making them accessible to people of all ages.

34. Which of the following could best replace the word "But" in sentence 5 (reproduced below)?

    But extensive programs to encourage children to appreciate art are often not a necessity.

    (A) However,
    (B) Rather,
    (C) Indeed,
    (D) Notwithstanding,
    (E) And yet,

35. Which version of the underlined portion of sentence 8 (reproduced below) provides the most clarity?

    We must only understand that these young museum patrons can not help acting like them.

    (A) (as it is now)
    (B) like it
    (C) as if they were
    (D) like what they are
    (E) like children

36. Sentence 13 could be best improved if the author were to

    (A) describe possible damage
    (B) explain the precautions to be taken
    (C) give a historic precedent
    (D) extend her argument to include other institutions
    (E) explain the mission of a museum

37. Which of the following represents the best revision of sentence 4 (reproduced below)?

    Placed slightly lower on the walls, paintings become more visible to children.

    (A) (As it is now)
    (B) Placing them slightly lower on the walls, the paintings become more visible to the children.
    (C) For example, placing paintings slightly lower on the walls makes them more visible to children.
    (D) For example, when placed slightly lower on the walls, children can see the paintings better.
    (E) Placed paintings that are lower on the walls are more visible to children.

GO ON TO THE NEXT PAGE

38. Which of the following is the best way to revise sentences 10 and 11 (reproduced below)?

    If necessary, museums should set up special "children's times" during which young people may roam through the building, enjoying the artwork in their own way. A wonderful learning experience!

    (A) To avoid disrupting everyone else, create "children's times" in the museum, during which children could roam throughout the building, enjoying the artwork in their own way and a wonderful learning experience.
    (B) Museums should set up "children's times." This would be a wonderful learning experience. Children could roam through the museum. Children could enjoy the artwork in their own way.
    (C) If necessary, museums should set up a wonderful learning experience called "children's times." During it, young people could roam throughout the building, enjoying the artwork in their own way.
    (D) To enjoy artwork in their own way, children should be given the freedom to roam throughout the building. This would be a wonderful learning experience, and it could be called "children's times."
    (E) To avoid disrupting other museum-goers, museums should set up special "children's times." During these times, children would be allowed to roam throughout the building and enjoy the artwork in their own way. What a wonderful learning experience!

39. In context, sentence 14 could be made more precise by changing the phrase "*This is*" to which of the following?

    (A) That is
    (B) These changes are
    (C) The reasons for these changes is that they are
    (D) It is
    (E) These changes, as mentioned above, are also

STOP
**If you finish before time is called, you may check your work on this section only.
Do not turn to any other section in the test.**

PRACTICE TEST 1 ANSWERS

Section 1	Section 2	Section 3	Section 4	Section 5
1. D	1. D	26. C	21. A	1. C	31. C
2. C	2. D	27. C	22. D	2. A	32. E
3. A	3. D	28. E	23. B	3. E	33. B
4. A	4. C	29. D	24. D	4. D	34. A
5. D	5. B	30. B	25. B	5. C	35. E
6. E	6. C	31. B	26. C	6. B	36. B
7. E	7. E	32. A	27. A	7. E	37. C
8. B	8. B	33. C	28. D	8. D	38. E
9. C	9. D	34. B	29. C	9. B	39. B
10. D	10. C	35. E	30. D	10. A	
11. B	11. A	36. C	31. C	11. D	
12. D	12. E	37. A	32. B	12. A	
13. B	13. C	38. D	33. 0.36	13. A	
14. B	14. C	39. C	34. 14	14. C	
15. D	15. D	40. E	35. 20	15. B	
16. C	16. E	41. C	36. 8000	16. A	
17. A	17. E	42. B	37. 45	17. C	
18. B	18. B	43. A	38. 40	18. D	
19. E	19. B	44. D	39. 3 or −2	19. E	
20. A	20. E	45. A	40. $\frac{5}{9}$ or .55	20. B	
21. C		46. E		21. A	
22. D		47. A		22. E	
23. C		48. B		23. C	
24. A		49. D		24. D	
25. B		50. C		25. A	
		51. D		26. B	
		52. A		27. E	
				28. C	
				29. A	
				30. D	

You will find a detailed explanation for each question beginning on page 240.

SCORING YOUR PRACTICE PSAT

VERBAL

After you have checked your answers against the answer key, you can calculate your score. For the two Verbal sections (Sections 1 and 3), add up the number of correct answers and the number of incorrect answers. Enter these numbers on the worksheet on the next page. Multiply the number of incorrect answers by .25 and subtract this result from the number of correct answers. Then round this to the nearest whole number. This is your Verbal "raw score." Next, use the conversion table to convert your raw score to a scaled score.

MATH

Figuring your Math score is a bit trickier, because some of the questions have 5 answer choices (for these, the incorrect answer deduction is .25), some have 4 answer choices (for these, the incorrect answer deduction is .33), and some are Grid-Ins (which have no deduction for wrong answers).

First, check your answers on Sections 2 and 4. For Section 2 and questions 21–32 of Section 4, put the number of correct answers and the number of incorrect answers into the worksheet on the next page. For questions 33–40 of Section 4, simply put in the number of correct answers. For Section 2, multiply the number of incorrect answers by .25 and subtract this total from the number of correct answers. For Section 4, multiply the number of incorrect answers by .33, and subtract this from the number of correct answers. For the Grid-In questions, simply put the number of correct answers into the box. Now, add up the totals for all three types of math questions to give you your total Math raw score. Then you can use the conversion table to find your scaled score.

WRITING SKILLS

The Writing Skills section should be scored just like the Verbal sections. Add up the number of correct answers and the number of incorrect answers from Section 5, and enter these numbers on the worksheet on the next page. Multiply the number of incorrect answers by .25 and subtract this result from the number of correct answers. Then round this to the nearest whole number. This is your Writing Skills raw score. Next, use the conversion table to convert your raw scores to scaled scores.

WORKSHEET FOR CALCULATING YOUR SCORE

Verbal

		Correct		Incorrect		
A.	Sections 1 and 3	_____	− (.25 ×	_____) =		A
B.	Total rounded Verbal raw score					B

Mathematics

		Correct		Incorrect		
C.	Section 2	_____	− (.25 ×	_____) =		C
D.	Section 4 (Questions 21–32)	_____	− (.33 ×	_____) =		D
E.	Section 4 (Questions 33–40)	_____	=			E
F.	Total unrounded Math raw score (C + D + E)					F
G.	Total rounded Math raw score					G

Writing Skills

	Correct		Incorrect		
Section 5	_____	− (.25 ×	_____) =		
Total rounded Writing Skills raw score					

SCORE CONVERSION TABLE

Math Raw Score	Math Scaled Score	Verbal Raw Score	Verbal Scaled Score	Writing Skills Raw Score	Writing Skills Scaled Score
0	25	0	20	0	33
1	28	1	23	1	34
2	30	2	24	2	36
3	31	3	26	3	37
4	33	4	28	4	38
5	34	5	29	5	39
6	36	6	30	6	40
7	37	7	32	7	42
8	38	8	33	8	43
9	40	9	34	9	44
10	41	10	35	10	45
11	42	11	36	11	46
12	43	12	38	12	47
13	44	13	39	13	48
14	45	14	40	14	49
15	46	15	41	15	51
16	48	16	42	16	52
17	49	17	43	17	53
18	50	18	44	18	54
19	51	19	45	19	55
20	52	20	46	20	56
21	53	21	47	21	57
22	55	22	48	22	59
23	56	23	49	23	60
24	57	24	50	24	62
25	58	25	51	25	63
26	59	26	52	26	64
27	61	27	53	27	66
28	62	28	54	28	67
29	63	29	55	29	69
30	64	30	56	30	70
31	65	31	57	31	72
32	66	32	58	32	73
33	67	33	59	33	73
34	68	34	60	34	74
35	70	35	61	35	76
36	72	36	61	36	78
37	73	37	62	37	79
38	75	38	63	38	80
39	78	39	64	39	80
40	80	40	65		
		41	66		
		42	68		
		43	69		
		44	70		
		45	71		
		46	73		
		47	75		
		48	77		
		49	78		
		50	80		
		51	80		
		52	80		

14
Practice Test 1: Answers and Explanations

Section 1

1. **D** This sentence begins with the trigger word "while," so we know that the sentence is going to change direction. The first part of the sentence says that the gorilla is interesting to study, so we will need to finish the sentence with something that contrasts with this. Perhaps the gorilla is, in fact, difficult to study or unsuitable. This would make a word like "stop" or "prevent" a good choice for this blank. The closest choice available is choice D.

2. **C** A good clue in this sentence is "now worn by all segments of society." This means that the word in the blank should be a word like "widened" or "made more popular." Choices A, B, D, or E don't match this meaning, so we're left with C.

3. **A** With a two-blank SC like this one, start with the blank that seems easier for you. In this case, let's try the second blank. (Often, the second blank will be easier because you'll have more information by the time you get to it.) We have the trigger word "while" in this sentence, which tells us there will be a contrast between many newer technologies and computers—while the former may only last a short time, it will be a long time before the computer goes away. So something like "goes away" would be good for the second blank. Choices D and E definitely don't fit, so we can cross those out. Now let's look at the first blank. In fact, the word in the first blank should also have a meaning similar to "goes away," which will allow us to eliminate B and C.

4. **A** Using the trigger word "although" and the clue "refused to give up," we know that the meaning of the first blank should be a word that means something like "difficult." If we cross off the words that won't work for the first blank, that will eliminate choices C, D, and E. Now we're down to A and B. Because the council refused to give up, they must have come up with some helpful, or clever, or complicated solution. So the word for the second blank should mean something positive. This means we can eliminate choice B, and we're left with choice A as the answer.

5. **D** The sentence says that the voters managed to vote despite the blizzard. This is our clue: that the people managed to vote even under very difficult circumstances. So a good word for the blank would be something like "strong" or "hardy." Remember that this is a difficult question, so we should expect the answer choices to be difficult words. If you don't know a word, don't cross it off! (After all, it might be right.) But if you know any of the words in choices A, B, C, or E, you'll know that they don't mean "strong." So we can cross them off. If you don't cross off every one of these, that's okay—you'll still be making an intelligent guess if you can cross off any of them.

6. **E** We can make a sentence using the words in reverse: A horse lives in a stable. Does an ape live in a jungle? Maybe. So let's leave this choice for later. Does a cowboy live in a ranch? A cowboy works on a ranch, but doesn't really live in one. So let's cross off B. Does a tree live in a trunk? Definitely not. So we can cross off choice C. Does an eagle live in the sky? Nope. Eliminate choice D. Does a pig live in a sty? Yes. So we're down to choices A and E. Now we need to make a more specific sentence. A horse lives in a man-made structure called a stable. Does an ape live in a man-made structure called a jungle? No. But a pig does live in a man-made structure called a sty. This makes E a better choice than A.

7. **E** An ax is used to cut wood. Is a coin used to cut metal? No, so we can eliminate choice A. Is a knife used to cut a blade? Nope—a knife has a blade, and the blade does the cutting. Is a spade used to cut a shovel? No, a spade is a kind of shovel. Is a notch used to cut a screw? No, so we can eliminate D also. Is a cleaver used to cut meat? Yes. Since we've crossed off A, B, C, and D, the best answer must be E.

8. **B** A coward is someone who is easily intimidated. Is an egoist someone who can be easily humbled? (If you're not sure of one of the words, remember—you have to leave it in!) In fact, an egoist is someone who is not at all humble, so we can eliminate A. Is a dupe easily deceived? Yes, so let's leave it in. Is a politician easily opinionated? Maybe, but that's not really a clear defining sentence. Being a politician doesn't really have anything to do with being opinionated. Is a child easily punished? Maybe, but as with choice C, that's not a defining sentence. Is a celebrity someone easily educated? A celebrity is someone who is well known; this doesn't have much to do with whether he or she is educated. So we should eliminate A, C, D, and E. This leaves us with B as the best answer.

9. **C** Insensitive means lacking feeling. (For instance, when you are given an anaesthetic before surgery, it makes you insensitive to pain.) Does inedible mean lacking taste? Not really—something inedible might just taste terrible. So we can eliminate A. Does inevitable mean lacking event? That doesn't make much sense, so eliminate B. Does infinite mean lacking an end? Yes, so let's leave this choice in. Does incorrigible mean lacking a child? Probably not, so let's eliminate it. Does incompetent mean lacking help? Nope. (In fact, someone incompetent probably needs a great deal of help.) This leaves us with C as our best answer.

10. **D** Now that we're into the harder questions, the words are getting harder; if you don't know the word "intractable" then try Working Backward. Even if you don't know the word "intractable" you can still eliminate some choices: Immobile means impossible to move, but that doesn't really have much to do with motivating. And being pretentious doesn't have much to do with what you achieve, so we can eliminate C and E as well. If you do know the words, try making a sentence. One possible sentence would be this: Someone intractable is difficult to govern. Is someone unfaithful difficult to promise? Or someone hopeful difficult to anticipate? These don't seem to make much sense, so let's eliminate A and B. Someone obstinate is difficult to persuade, so our best choice is D.

11. **B** These words are really tough. If you don't know them, work backward and see if you can cross off any choices, or try using Side of the Fence. If you have any sense of the words, you may know that both of these words are positive words, so we will need to look for a pair that is also a same-side relation. Choices D and E, however, are opposite-side relations: Agile is roughly the opposite of weak, and turbulent is roughly the opposite of calm. Even if we get no further, we can cross off these choices, and take a guess. Further, choices A and C don't really have strong relationships: Being monotonous doesn't have much to do with a lecture, and language might or might not be offensive. In fact, mellifluous speech is characterized by euphony, and belligerent speech is characterized by hostility. This makes B the best choice. But you'll probably get it right by POE.

12. **D** From the blurb, we know that this is a passage primarily about Duke Ellington. Choices C and E don't mention him; they are much too broad, and we can cross them off. While the interaction between Ellington and his band is mentioned in the passage, it is only discussed in one paragraph, so choice B is too specific to be correct. Likewise, there is a great deal of discussion about Ellington's music in general, so choice A is also too specific to be correct. Once we've eliminated these choices, we're left with D as the answer.

13. **B** This is a Vocab-in-Context question, so we should cover the word "crest" with our finger and try to put our own word in for it in the sentence (just as if we were doing a Sentence Completion question). We know that at this time Ellington was making a great deal of money and broadcasting every night; the word we'd probably put in place of the word "crest" would be a word like "on top" or "at his best." Of the answer choices, B comes closest to this idea.

14. **B** The lead words for this question are "Black and Tan Fantasy" and "Creole Love Call." We can find these songs mentioned at the beginning of the second paragraph, so that's where we should look for our answer. The opening lines of this paragraph say that, "In 1940, a new generation of jazz fans, brought to the music by swing bands, was discovering Ellington's music. Many of these new fans were too young to have been caught up in the excitement of the early discovery" of these songs. This tells us that people who were fans of these songs must have been from an earlier generation of listeners to Ellington's music. Now let's look at our answer choices and try to find a choice that conveys this idea. Choice B says exactly this.

15. **D** The line numbers in this question take us back to the first line of the third paragraph, where the readers of *Down Beat* are said to be more sophisticated than the average fan. To understand this statement, let's read it in context, by reading the lines above and below it. Above these lines, in the second paragraph, the author says that the readers of *Down Beat* ranked many of Ellington's musicians as the best at their art. Below these lines the author states that, "The Duke Ellington Band was probably never the second or even third most popular swing band in the country, as far as the ordinary fan was concerned." This tells us that the opinion of the average person doesn't quite agree with the opinions of the more sophisticated readers of *Down Beat*. Now we need to look for a choice that says something like this. Choices A, B, and C definitely don't say anything like this idea. It's a little unclear what E says, but choice D seems to be a paraphrase of the idea that we got from the evidence we found in the passage. Therefore it's our answer.

16. **C** Remember that it's important to always look back to the passage for evidence to support your answer. On the PSAT every answer is somewhere in the passage, in black and white, so be sure to find it. If we look for a sentence in the passage that discusses other bands, we find on lines 39–41 that Ellington's band was "generally playing a much more complex music than other bands." Choice C is a paraphrase of this line, so it must be the answer.

17. **A** If we go back and read the lines immediately following the idea that slang is nationwide, we find what Pei means by this: "There are some who think that only poorer and less educated people use slang. This is not necessarily true. A little bit of slang, in fact, is used by practically everybody." That is, that slang is used by everyone, both educated people and less educated people. Now we need to find a choice that is a close paraphrase of this idea, which is choice A. Choice E is tempting, but the notion of jargon is not addressed until the fourth paragraph, so it can't be the correct answer to a question about the first paragraph.

18. **B** To solve this Vocab-in-Context question, cover the word "rich" with your finger and use the same technique you learned for Sentence Completion: Read the sentence, and figure out what the meaning of the word should be from the context. In this case, we'd probably put in a word like "has a lot." The choice that comes closest to this in meaning is B.

19. **E** This question not only gives us the lead words Dizzy Dean and Shakespeare, but also tells us where the answer will probably be found: in the third paragraph. Let's go back to that part of the passage and see what it is says. The first line states that, "In a many good cases, slang words and uses can be traced to one individual." Shakespeare and Dizzy Dean are given as examples, so our answer should be a paraphrase of this line. The other choices are claims that are not addressed in the third paragraph.

20. **A** According to line 36, the word "cant" was the "language of the underworld." This has to be our answer; now we need to find the choice that best paraphrases "underworld," which is choice A.

21. **C** We can use the lead words "François Villon" to find the place in the passage where the answer to this question will be found. François Villon is mentioned in the fourth paragraph, around lines 37–38. The passage states at that point that he "used in many of his poems a type of Paris underworld cant that cannot be understood today." Evidently the passage cites him in order to show that some kinds of popular speech can no longer be understood in modern times. Now let's look for a choice that paraphrases this idea. Choice C says exactly this: that some kinds of speech are no longer current usage. None of the other choices have evidence to support them from this part of the passage.

22. **D** Let's go back to the line in question and read what the author says at that point in the passage. He says that some examples of cant "are generally understood and even used, though they are not the best language in the world." That is to say that even if the expressions aren't always appropriate, they are almost always understood. Now we need to find a paraphrase among the answer choices. Choices A and E are a little negative—the author doesn't show opposition or distaste, so these can be eliminated. Choices B and C aren't really stated, either. Choice D is a fair paraphrase of what is stated in the passage, so it's the best answer.

23. **C** Here's another Vocab-in-Context question. If we cover up the word "measure" and use context to put our own word in the blank, we'd probably choose something like "a certain amount." Choice C comes closest to this in meaning.

24. **A** Let's go back to the passage, around the middle of the fifth paragraph, where these lines appear. The passage states, "But it is not only the intellectual professions that have jargons; it is also the manual trades and occupations," and then goes on to cite the example of shipboard terminology. This means that shipboard terminology is cited as an example of how jargon has evolved in manual trades and occupations, as well as in other places. Now let's find a choice that paraphrases this idea, which is what choice A does.

25. **B** According to the blurb, this passage is about the history and significance of slang. Already this should make B and C look like a good choices, but let's see why the others can be eliminated. Choices D and E are too narrow—cant and important individuals are mentioned only in one paragraph each, so they couldn't be the main idea. Likewise, jargon is only discussed in one paragraph, so choice A can be eliminated. Now we're down to B and C. This is a tough choice, but C is a little too broad—it's very difficult to do a complete history of slang in only a few paragraphs. But to discuss some of the origins and variations is more feasible, and this what the passage tries to do.

SECTION 2

1. **D** To solve for b, our first move should be to move the 4 to the other side of the equation by adding 4 to both sides. This will give us $12b = 4$. Now we divide each side by 12, and get $b = \frac{1}{3}$.

2. **D** Before doing any math on this problem, we should guesstimate and eliminate answers we know are wrong. The question tells us that 60 gallons represents $\frac{5}{12}$ of the full tank—or a little less than half. So the full tank will need to be a little more than twice 60 gallons, or something a little larger than 120. This makes choices A, B, and E unreasonable, so let's eliminate those choices. The answer has to be either C or D. To figure out which, let's try plugging in the answer choices. Is $\frac{5}{12}$ of 128 equal to 60? Nope, that's equal to 10.67. So let's try choice D. Is $\frac{5}{12}$ of 144 equal to 60? Yes, so D is the answer.

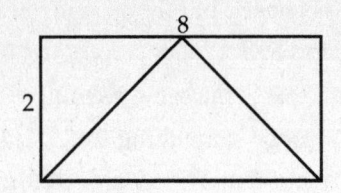

[Figure: a rectangle with top side labeled 8 and left side labeled 2, containing a triangle whose base is the bottom of the rectangle and whose apex touches the top side.]

3. **D**   To make this problem easier, let's plug in some numbers for the sides of this rectangle. We can pick whichever numbers we want, as long as they make the area equal to 16. So let's assume that the rectangle has dimensions 8 and 2. This makes the base of the triangle 8 and the height 2, so the area of the triangle will be $\frac{1}{2} \times 8 \times 2$, or 8. (Even if we made the dimensions of the rectangle 16 and 1, we'd still get the same answer!) You may also know the rule that a triangle inscribed in a rectangle will have exactly half the area of that rectangle; but even without knowing the rule, by plugging in some values we can figure it out.

4. **C**   The first multiple of 32 is 32, so the correct choice must divide evenly into 32. In other words, 32 must be a multiple of the correct choice. Is 32 a multiple of 11? No; nor is it a multiple of 9, 5, or 3. So we can eliminate A, B, D, and E.

5. **B**   This question is testing your knowledge of the rule of 180. We know that all the angles in a triangle have to add up to 180. Since one of the angles is 90 degrees, we know that the others must add up to 90 also. This means that the two angles x and $3x - 2$ must have a sum of 90 degrees. So we can write the equation $x + 3x - 2 = 90$. By adding the xs together, we get $4x - 2 = 90$. Now we can solve for x. By adding 2 to each side, we get $4x = 92$; then we divide each side by 4 to get $x = 23$.

6. **C**   Since we've got variables in the answer choices, we should plug in. We can plug in whatever numbers we want for x, y, and z, provided that we obey the rule that $x < y < z$. Let's choose 2 for x, 3 for y, and 4 for z, since those are easy numbers. The question then asks: What is the sum of y and z? Using our numbers, the answer will be $3 + 4$, which makes 7. Now the question is: Which of the answer choices gives 7, using our value of 2 for x? Choice C gives $2(2) + 3$, which equals 7.

7. **E** This question looks nasty, but if you remember your exponent rules it won't be too bad. Whenever you raise an exponent to another exponent, this is the same as multiplying the exponents together. So $(2^a)^b$ is the same thing as $2^{a \times b}$. Using your calculator you can figure out that $2^6 = 64$, so $a \times b$ must be equal to 6.

8. **B** We know that the formula for average is $\frac{Total}{Number\ of\ Things}$. The total will be $x + 3x + 8x$, or $12x$. The number of things we have to average is 3. So our average will be $\frac{12x}{3}$, or $4x$.

9. **D** A line with negative slope is one that you can draw going down and to the right from any starting point. Lines *AE* and *BD* won't count, since they have no slope. The only ones we can draw are *AC*, *FD*, and *AD*.

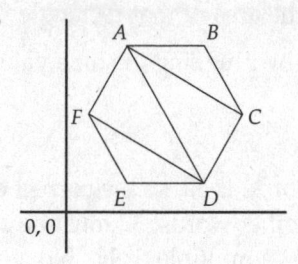

10. **C** The best way to approach this question is to try plugging in the answer choices and see which fits the description "3 more than 7 times itself." Let's start with C. If we multiply $-\frac{1}{2}$ times seven and then add 3, we get $-\frac{1}{2}$, so C is our answer.

11. **A** Like many problems on the SAT, this question will be difficult if we try to do it all at once. Instead, let's break it down into bite-sized pieces. Let's start with just part of the inequality, $-12 \leq 3b + 3$. Remember that we can solve inequalities just like equations—provided that if we multiply or divide by a negative value, we swap the direction of the inequality sign. To solve this part of the inequality, though, we just need to subtract 3 from each side (giving us $-15 \leq 3b$), and then divide 3 from each side, which leaves us with $-5 \leq b$. Now we can eliminate several choices that we know won't work: B, D, and E don't have -5 in them. Now let's take the other part of the inequality: $3b + 3 \leq 18$. If we subtract 3 from each side and then divide by 3, we get $b \leq 5$. Now we can cross of C, and we're left with A.

12. **E** Let's start by plugging in a number for x. We need an odd integer divisible by 3, so let's pick $x = 9$. The question asks us which of the following must be divisible by 4. Choice A says $x + 1$, or 10, which is not divisible by 4. Choice B says $x + 2$, or 11, which is also not divisible by 4. This allows us to eliminate A and B. Choice C says $x + 3$, or 12, which is divisible by 4, so we should leave C in. Choice D says 18, which is not divisible by 4, so we can eliminate this choice too. Choice E says 16, which can be divided by 4, so we should leave it in. Now we're down to C and E. Let's pick another number for x and keep working. How about $x = 15$? In this case, choice C gives us 18, which is not divisible by 4. This knocks off C, so the answer must be E.

13. **C** To find the perimeter, we need to find the lengths of each of the sides of this triangle. Side AB is fairly easy, since we can just count the points: from (0, 4) to (6, 4) is a length of 6. However, finding sides AC and BC is a little more difficult. The problem tells us that $AC = BC$, so we know that point C must be on the x-axis right in between points A and B—which places it at coordinate (3, 0).

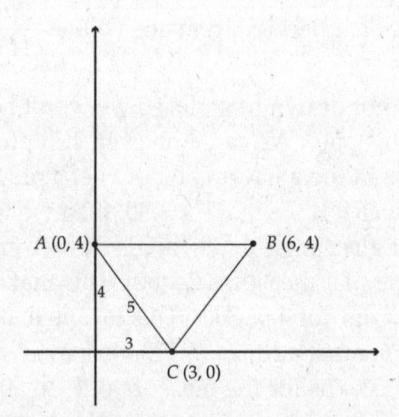

Now to find the length of AC, we can look at the triangle formed by A, C, and the origin. This triangle has a base of 3, since point C is at (3, 0), and a height of 4, since point A is at (0, 4). This makes a right triangle with sides 3 and 4, so side AC must be equal to 5. We can do the same thing to solve for side BC. So we know that the sides of this triangle are 6, 5, and 5 for a total perimeter of 16.

14. **C** For a function problem like this one, we need to follow the rule given to us in the problem. To solve for $4\Phi6$, we need to put 4 in the place of x, and 6 in the place of y in the expression $\frac{2x+y}{2x-y}$. This then becomes $\frac{2(4)+6}{2(4)-6}$, which equals 7.

15. **D** Since we have variables in the answer choices, we should plug in on this problem. To make the math work easily, let's pick 5 for c, 10 for g, and 20 for n. If 1 bottle containing 5 ounces will fill 10 glasses, then how many bottles will be needed to fill 20 glasses? Two bottles. So now we need to figure out which choice says two. Using 5 for c, 10 for g, and 20 for n, choice A reads 40, which is too large. Choice B gives 10, which is also too large. Choice C gives 0.5, which is too small. Choice D gives 2, which is our answer. Choice E gives .25, which is too small.

16. **E** Let's plug in some numbers to make this problem easier. Point A looks like it's approximately at (–1, 5), so let's plug in –1 for x and 5 for y. Now let's use these values to plug in for 2x and –y in the question, so that our question now reads: Which point could have coordinates (–2, –5)? The only one that would be in this area is point S.

17. **E** This question is testing volume. The volume of the original block of cheese is 8 x 8 x 8, or 512. The piece that we cut out measures 4 x 2 x 2, so its volume is 16. If we take away 16 from 512, we get 496. The fractional part that remains will be $\frac{496}{512}$, or $\frac{31}{32}$.

18. **B** This figure is not drawn to scale, so we won't be able to trust our eyes on this one. We can, however, still plug in, since we have variables in the answer choices. Let's plug in 30 for a and see what happens. If we make a = 30, then we will have values for 4 of our angles: angle a (30), angle 2a (60), angle 3a (90), and the other angle that measures 2a (60). This makes a total of 240 degrees out of our total of 360. This means that the other angles, b and b, must add up to 120. So b must be equal to 60. The question asks us for the measure of b, so 60 is our answer. Now we just see which choice (remembering that a = 30) gives 60. This shows us that B is the answer. This problem could also have been solved algebraically, of course—and on a hard problem it's a good idea to try it both ways to double-check your work.

19. **B** If we're averaging two numbers x and y, then this average will always be half of the sum of these numbers. Let's try some values for x and y and see what kind of numbers we get. Since $y = 4x$, if $x = 5$ then $y = 20$, and their sum is 25. If $x = 6$ then $y = 24$, and their sum is 30. If $x = 7$ then $y = 28$, and their sum is 35. It looks like the sum of x and y will always be a multiple of 5. Now let's look at the choices we have, starting with C. If the average of x and y is 4, then their sum total will be 8. But we know that the sum of x and y will always be a multiple of 5, so C can't be right. Likewise for choices D and E. If the average is 12, the sum of x and y will be 24; if their average is 28, their sum would have to be 56. So neither of these could be right. The only choice that would give us a sum of x and y as a multiple of 5 is choice B.

20. **E** Even though this is a hard problem, it will be relatively easy if we plug in. Let's try plugging in 10 for m and 20 for t. If 2000 gallons of paint will cover 10 square feet, and we have 20 square feet to cover, then we'll need 4000 gallons of paint. Now we just need to figure out which choice says 4000. Using 10 for m and 20 for t, check each of the choices. Choice E gives $\frac{2000}{10} \times 20$, which is 4000.

Section 3

26. **C** For an easier question, reading the sentence will probably allow you to put your own words into the blank—just be sure to pay particular attention to the clues and trigger words in the sentence. In this case, the trigger word "though" indicates a change of direction: On the one hand, people are willing to speak about saving the environment, but they are often not willing to change their lifestyles. Let's start eliminating choices by using the second blank: A word like "change" or "improve" would be good here. This allows us to eliminate A, B, and E. Now for the first blank, a word like "support" would fit. This will eliminate D, so C is the best choice.

27. **C** The clue in this sentence is "dominated the Congress of Vienna." The blank should be a word that describes a dominating person. We can just recycle the clue, and use the word "dominating" in the blank. Now let's see which word comes closest to "dominating": Choices A and B are both words that mean "nice," so we can cross them off. Likewise for choice E. If you're not sure of choice D, leave it in; but if you know the word, you know that it means "lying" or "deceitful," which is not quite the same thing as dominating.

28. **E** A good clue for the first blank is "enlivened"—the word in the blank should go along with this idea. This will eliminate choices B, C, and D. Now we're down to choices A and E. Remember that you don't need to think of the exact word for the blank; a general idea will do just fine. You can even recycle the clue. In this case, for the second blank, a word like "enlivened" would also fit nicely. This makes E a better choice than A.

29. **D** The clue in this sentence is "reclusive." If the animal is reclusive, that will make it difficult to investigate, so the word in the blank should be a word like "lack" or "difficulty." Choices A, B, C, and E don't mean anything like "lack," so we can eliminate them. This leaves D as our best choice.

30. **B** In this sentence we've got a great trigger word, "but." The aim of the plan was to solve a problem, but in fact the plan made it worse. So a word that means "made it worse" would fit in this blank. If you don't know some of these words, you'll have to leave them in (and take your best guess) but if you do know the words in A, C, D, and E, you know that none of them mean to make something worse. This is, however, exactly the meaning of the word "exacerbate," which makes B the best answer.

31. **B** Let's start with the first blank. The clue here is "friendly and honest." Choices C, D, and E definitely don't match this idea, which leaves us with A and B. Now note that the trigger word "but" signals that the sentence is changing direction after the first blank. Therefore, the word in the second blank should mean nearly the opposite of the one in the first blank. This leaves us with B as the best choice.

32. **A** For this question, the best help is the trigger word "and." We know that the meanings of the two words in the blanks need to be similar. However, many of the answer choice pairs are opposites: You wouldn't reject something you were impressed by, or adopt something you were opposed to, so we can eliminate choices B, D, and E. Further, the words in choice C really aren't similar in meaning. Therefore A is our best answer.

33. **C** This sentence has the trigger "though" in it, so we should expect a reversal of direction in the sentence. The clue is "established by rebellion." So if the US was originally on the side of rebellion, and we have the trigger word "though," we should expect that the sentence finishes by saying that the US is now *opposed* to rebellion. This means that in the first blank we need a word that deals with rebellion. Neither misers (choice B) or autocrats (choice D) have much to do with rebellion, so we can cross them off. Because of our trigger word, we know that the US is now opposed to rebellion, so we need a word like "dislike" in the second blank. This will eliminate A and E, which leaves us with choice C as our answer.

34. **B** We can make a sentence like "water removes thirst." Does a spasm remove discomfort? No, so we can cross off choice A. Does rest remove exhaustion? Yes, so let's leave it in. Does a debate remove resentment? Not really. Does a sedative remove sleep? A sedative actually causes sleep. Does sight remove understanding? Doesn't sound too promising. This leaves B as our best choice.

35. **E** A good sentence for this pair would be "oil is used to lubricate" or "oil serves to lubricate." Is a thermometer used to cure? Not really; a thermometer is used to tell temperature, or perhaps diagnose. Is an antidote used to poison? Definitely not. Is a message used to transmit something? No; a message is something that gets transmitted. Is a boat used to swim? Nope. Is an ornament used to decorate? Definitely.

36. **C** An epilogue comes at the end of a play. Does an aria come at the end of an opera? No, an aria comes somewhere in the middle. (If you don't know the word "aria" you should, of course, leave this choice as it is and come back to it later.) Does a director come at the end of a movie? That doesn't make any sense. Does an afterword come at the end of a book? Absolutely. Does an act come at the end of a scene? Nope. Does a comedy come at the end of a drama? That doesn't work either. Our best answer is therefore C.

37. **A** Someone rude lacks tact. Does someone treacherous lack loyalty? Yes, that sounds promising. Does someone transparent lack sight? No. Does someone naïve lack innocence? Exactly the opposite: Naïve means having a great deal of innocence. Does someone regretful lack memory? Nope. Does someone sympathetic lack compassion? Exactly the opposite. This makes A the answer. You could also approach this problem by using Side of the Fence; these words are roughly opposite in meaning, so we could cross off the answer choices that are not also opposite in meaning.

38. **D** To mollify means to reduce intensity. Does liberate mean to reduce freedom? No, exactly the opposite. Does predict mean to reduce the future? Definitely not. Does harass mean to reduce injury? Nope. Does soothe mean to reduce discomfort? Yes. Does protect mean to reduce opportunity? Doesn't sound too plausible. D is our best choice.

39. **C** Sometimes it's easier to make a sentence using the words in reverse direction: A deception has the property of being illusory. Does a photograph have the property of being realistic? Usually, but there might also be photographs that are artistic and not terribly realistic. Let's leave it in, but this isn't the strongest relationship and maybe we'll find something better. Does a viewpoint have the property of being eclectic? That's not part of the meaning of the word viewpoint, so we should eliminate it. Does instruction have the property of being didactic? Yes, that's what didactic means. Does value have the property of being intrinsic? Not all values are intrinsic, so we can cross off D. Does a view have the property of being majestic? That's not part of the meaning of the word view. Choice C has the strongest relationship here, so it's the one we should pick. You could also use Side of the Fence on this one: These words are similar in meaning, so we could eliminate any choices that were not also similar in meaning.

40. **E** Something impervious cannot be penetrated. Can we say that something categorized cannot be stored? That doesn't make much sense. How about this: Something irresponsible cannot be finished? There are no relationships here at all (in choices A and B), so we can definitely eliminate them. Is it true to say that something interminable cannot be defeated? If you don't know the word "interminable" you should leave it in, but if you know it (it means "without end"), you can eliminate this choice. Is someone studious unable to be educated? Definitely not. But something indefatigable cannot be exhausted, so E is our answer.

41. **C** Like most reading questions on the PSAT, this question tells us about where to find the answer: It will be somewhere in the first paragraph of Passage 1. The answer has to be there somewhere, so be sure to find some evidence that supports one of the answer choices. If we go back to the first paragraph, we find the statement, "Any law which uplifts human personality is just. Any law that degrades human personality is unjust." This is paraphrased by choice C, which makes C the best answer.

42. **B** If we look back to the lines of the passage where these figures are mentioned, we see that they both discuss the difference between a just law and an unjust law. This already makes B look like the best choice. We can be sure of this if we look at the others. The author doesn't discuss the writing of laws, so we can eliminate D. Since the author doesn't go on to talk about religion, we can eliminate A. Finally, we aren't given any dates for these two saints (do we know they are fifteen hundred years old?), nor are any critics discussed; this means we can cross off C and E as well.

43. **A** Though this question doesn't give us a specific line reference to help us find the answer, we can still look for a discussion about how individuals should act, which we can find in the second paragraph of the passage. There, the author states that, "an individual who breaks a law that conscience tells him is unjust…is in reality expressing the highest respect for the law." So we need to look for an example of someone who acts according to his or her conscience. The only choice that is an example of this is choice A.

44. **D** Let's go back to the third paragraph where "nonviolent direct action" is discussed. At the end of this paragraph the author says that the point of such action is to expose injustice, because "injustice must be exposed…before it can be cured." This is about what is said in choice D, which makes it the best answer. Don't forget to use POE on this question if it gives you difficulty. Choice A can't be right because while the author of Passage 2 discusses majority and minority groups, the author of Passage 1 does not. Choice B is really quite strong, but does the author say that the society is "primarily unjust"? Not really.

45. **A** In the final paragraph of Passage 1, the author tells us that, "Human progress…comes through the tireless efforts" of people willing to act according to their moral conscience. This tells us that C and D are wrong, since the author doesn't discuss appeals to government, or a natural decline in injustice (in fact, the author says that people need to act, or else injustice won't go away). Choices B and E are too extreme (a "necessary evil"?), which leaves us with A as our best answer.

46. **E**   This main point question is probably best saved for last—by the time you answer the other questions, this one will probably be easier. The most reliable way to approach this sort of question is by POE. The author says, in the second paragraph, "I ask for, not at once no government, but at once a better government." That is, the author is not out to abolish the government but to show how it can be improved. This eliminates choices A and D. While the author is certainly concerned about justice, there is no case of an actual unjust law that is criticized in the passage, so choice B can be crossed off. Finally, choice C doesn't really capture the author's attempt to show how government can improve itself by making more room for conscience. This makes E the best choice.

47. **A**   Let's go back to the second paragraph of Passage 2, and read just those lines carefully. The author says on lines 58–60, "Let every man make known what kind of government would command his respect, and that will be one step toward obtaining it." Now we need to find a paraphrase of this sentence somewhere in the answer choices. Of the choices given, choice A comes closest to what this sentence says.

48. **B**   This is another great question for POE. It may not be obvious why the right answer is right, but if we can find reasons to eliminate the other four choices, we will know which answer to pick. There is definitely no discussion of European governments in the last paragraph of Passage 2, so we can eliminate A. The discussion in this final paragraph is only about democracies where the majority rules, and not about all social organizations, so choice C is too strong to be correct. And nonviolent direct action isn't mentioned here, so choice D can also be crossed off. Finally, we can see that the author here is criticizing majority rule in some fashion, so E couldn't be right. That leaves us with B as the best answer.

49. **D**   Let's look back to a line in the passage and find a statement that will answer this question. In the second paragraph, the author states, "the practical reason why…a majority is permitted…to rule is not because they are most likely to be in the right, nor because this seems fairest to the minority, but because they are physically the strongest." This states that the basis for majority rule isn't rightness or fairness, but simply strength. This will allow us to eliminate A, B, C, and E, so we're left with D.

50. **C** When it comes to the toughest questions, expect to solve them by POE. We can eliminate choice A, because both authors claim that people are not obliged to obey laws that they believe to be unjust. And while it's clear that the author of Passage 1 states that one must accept the punishment for such refusal to obey, the author of Passage 2 doesn't say this. So we can eliminate D as well. The author of Passage 2 does seem to think that less government is better, but neither author says that some specific form is better than democracy. This will allow us to cross off E. Finally, both authors claim that individuals should consult their own consciences, and not lawmakers, so choice B can be eliminated.

51. **D** According to the final paragraph of Passage 2, "The only obligation which I have a right to assume is to do at any time what I think right." That is, each person needs to act according to his or her conscience, obeying those laws that he or she considers just. The choice that best paraphrases this idea is D.

52. **A** Again, let's approach this by POE. It may not be obvious why the right answer is right, but we can at least find definite reasons why the wrong answers are wrong. While the author of Passage 2 does discuss the majority and the minority, he does not restrict himself simply to the rights of minority groups—he also discusses the rights of individuals to consult their own conscience. This allows us to eliminate B. Choice C can be eliminated, because it is Passage 1 that discusses nonviolent direct action, and not Passage 2. While Passage 1 does mention religious figures, neither passage is actually based on religious doctrine. Therefore choice D can be crossed off. Finally, neither passage discusses the distinction between citizens and non-citizens, so choice E can also be eliminated.

Section 4

21. **A** We can translate column A into arithmetic as $\frac{6}{100} \times 5$, which is .30. We can translate column B as $\frac{4}{100} \times 7$, which equals .28. This means that column A is greater, so choice A is correct.

22. **D** Let's try plugging in a number for n. If $n = 2$, then column A is equal to 9, and column B is equal to 8. This will allow us to cross off choices B and C. If $n = 3$, then column A is equal to 27, and column B is equal to 27. This will allow us to cross off choice A, so our actual answer must be D.

23. **B** Let's try plugging in some numbers for a and b. Remember that we need to obey the restriction that $a < b - 3$. So what numbers could we plug in? How about 2 for a and 8 for b. In this case, column B is larger than column A, so we can cross off choices A and C. Are there other numbers we could plug in for a and b? Yes, but they must always obey the rule that $a < b - 3$, so b will always be larger than a.

24. **D** This is a tricky problem, because the triangle *looks* like it's isosceles, so it looks like WX and XY are equal. But nothing in the problem tells us that the triangle is isosceles. So we really can't tell whether one side is larger or smaller than the other.

25. **B** To solve this ratio we can set up a ratio box or use a proportion. Let's try doing it as a proportion:

    $$\frac{18}{6} = \frac{y}{4}$$

    We can now cross-multiply to solve for y. $6y = 18 \times 4$, so $6y = 72$, and y must therefore be 12. This makes column B bigger than column A.

26. **C** Let's plug in a value for the size of angle DHG, so we can work with actual numbers. Let's suppose that it measures 120 degrees. If EH bisects DHG, then it cuts that angle into two equal parts, each of which measures 60 degrees. This means that $y = 60$, and $x + w = 60$. If FH bisects angle EHG, then it splits that 60 degrees into two angles of 30 degrees. This means that both x and w are equal to 30. So column A equals 60, and column B also equals 60. That means our answer must be C.

27. **A** There's no easy way to solve for a or b alone, but we don't actually need to know the values of a or b to solve this problem. Since we know a^3, we can solve for a^6, since $a^6 = a^3 \times a^3$, which in this case will be 9. Likewise, since we know b^4, we can solve for b^8, since $b^8 = b^4 \times b^4$, which in this case will be 16. This makes column A 25, so the answer is A.

28. **D** The equation $r^2 - 3r = 10$ looks a lot like a quadratic equation. We can rewrite it as $r^2 - 3r - 10 = 0$. Now let's factor. Since 10 can be factored as 5 times 2, and the difference between those two digits is 3, we can factor this equation as $(r - 5)(r + 2) = 0$. This means that r could equal 5 or –2. Since r could equal 5, it might be larger than zero; in this case column A would be larger. However, r could also equal –2, in which case it would be smaller than zero and column B would be larger. Therefore the answer is D.

29. **C** This figure shows a parallelogram, so we know that the opposite angles are equal and the adjacent angles add up to 180. Therefore, $a + b = 180$, and $c + d = 180$. So the two columns are equal, and the answer is C.

30. **D** This is a great example of how Plugging In can be helpful on Quant Comp questions. Let's start by plugging in an easy number for x. Let's say that $x = 2$. In this case, column A becomes 8, and column B becomes $\frac{1}{4}$. In this case, column A is larger than column B, which means that we can eliminate choices B and C. Now let's try some other numbers for x. What if x were a very small fraction, such as $\frac{1}{8}$? In this case, column A would be equal to $\frac{1}{8} \cdot 2\left(\frac{1}{8}\right)$, or $\frac{2}{64}$ (which reduces to $\frac{1}{32}$). Column B would then become $\frac{\frac{1}{8}}{2\left(\frac{1}{8}\right)}$, which is equal to $\frac{1}{8} \div \frac{2}{8}$, or $\frac{1}{2}$. In this case, column B is bigger than column A, so we can eliminate choice A, and the answer to the question must be D.

31. **C** One way we could solve this problem is by Plugging In—we could find values for a and b that make $6a - 8b = 4$. (For instance, using $a = 2$ and $b = 1$ would work). In this case, we could also notice that the terms in columns A and B look suspiciously like our original statement, but slightly modified. In fact, if we remove a factor of 2 from the equation $6a - 8b = 4$, we get $3a - 4b = 2$. If we rearrange the terms in this equation, we get $3a - 2 = 4b$. This means that columns A and B are equal.

32. **B** This is a difficult problem, but since we have variables in it, we can plug in. Let's start by plugging in some easy numbers: Let's try -2 for a and -1 for b. Using these values, column A becomes 5, and column B becomes 9. In this case, column B is larger than column A, so we can eliminate choices A and C. Try some other numbers (remembering that $a < b < 0$) and see what happens—in every case, you'll find that column B is larger. So B must be the answer.

   We could also solve this algebraically in the following way: We can expand column B to read $a^2 + 2ab + b^2$. The only difference between column A and column B will be the term $2ab$. Since both a and b are negative, we know that $2ab$ must be positive; this means that column B will always be larger than column A.

33. **.36** Let's start with the first part of the question. 20% of n is 36. If we translate this into math, it becomes $\frac{20}{100}n = 36$. Now we can solve for n by reducing $\frac{20}{100}$ to $\frac{1}{5}$, and by moving the $\frac{1}{5}$ to the other side: $\frac{1}{5}n = 36$, so $n = 36 \times 5$. This gives us $n = 180$. Now we translate the other part. What is 0.2 percent of 180 becomes: $x = \frac{.2}{100} \times 180$. Now we solve for x, and get that $x = .36$

34. **14** While we don't know the exact lengths of the bottom or right side of the figure, we don't need to know them. We know that the lengths of the unknown horizontal surfaces must have a length of 3, and the lengths of the unknown vertical surfaces have to have a length of 4.

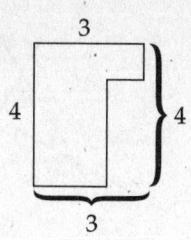

Therefore we know that the total perimeter of the object is
$4 + 3 + 4 + 3 = 14$.

35. **20** Since the problem tells us the value of x, which is 23, we can put this into the equation and solve for y. $23 - 8 = 5y$, so we know that

$$15 = 5y \text{ and } 3 = y$$

Now we know the value of y. However, on this problem, don't forget that we're not just solving for y; we're solving for $x - y$. So the correct answer is $23 - 3$, or 20.

36. **8000** Let's start by finding all of the positive integer factors of 20. We can factor 20 into 1×20, 2×10, and 4×5. The question asks for the product of these numbers, which will be $1 \times 20 \times 2 \times 10 \times 4 \times 5$, or 8000.

37. **45** If Marcia types 18 pages per hour, and David can type 14 pages per hour, then together they will be able to type $18 + 14$, or 32 pages per hour. To see what fraction of an hour it will take them to type 24 pages, we can set up a proportion:

$$\frac{pages}{hour} \frac{32}{1} = \frac{24}{x}$$

If we solve for x, we can see that they can type 24 pages in .75 of an hour. But that isn't our answer! The question asks for the answer in minutes. Three-quarters of an hour is equal to 45 minutes, so the answer is 45.

38. **40** With a geometry question like this, it's best to just start filling in what you know. Since we know that the angles in a triangle always add up to 180, we can figure out the third angle of the triangle with angles 45 and 60. The sum of these angles is 105, so the third angle must measure 75. This means that the angle on the line next to it must also measure 105. Now in the triangle on the left, we have angles 105 and 35. Together these angles make 140, so we know that the third angle (marked with an x) is equal to 40. (See the figure on the following page.)

PRACTICE TEST 1: ANSWERS AND EXPLANATIONS ◆ 261

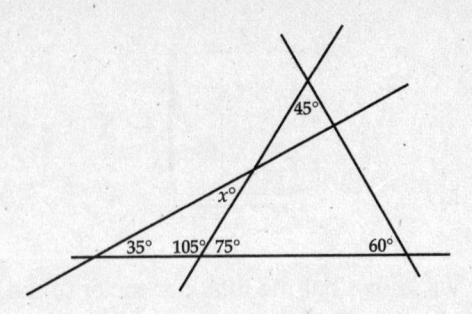

39. **3 or −2** Since the problem tells us that #$x = 10$, and that #$x = x^2 - x + 4$, we can set these two equal to each other and say that $x^2 - x + 4 = 10$. Now we need to factor to solve for x. If we move the 10 to the left side of the equation, we get

$$x^2 - x - 6 = 0$$

which we can factor as

$$(x - 3)(x + 2) = 0$$

This tells us that the value of x could be 3 or −2.

40. $\dfrac{5}{9}$ **or .55** This problem is tricky more because of its wording than the actual math involved. But let's break it down into Bite-Sized Pieces. First, we know that there are twice as many large marbles as small marbles. This means, for instance, that there could be 4 large and 2 small marbles (or 6 large and 3 small, etc.). If we have 4 large marbles and 2 small marbles, then 4 out of 6 (or two-thirds) are large marbles. So if we were to pick a marble at random, we'd have a $\dfrac{2}{3}$ chance of picking a large marble. Now of those large marbles, 5 times as many are blue as are red. This means that we might have 5 blue and 1 red, or 10 blue and 2 red marbles. If we have 5 blue and 1 red marble, then five out of six would be blue. So we have a $\dfrac{2}{3}$ chance of picking a large marble, and then a $\dfrac{5}{6}$ chance that this marble would be blue. The total probability of picking a large blue marble is $\dfrac{2}{3} \times \dfrac{5}{6}$, or $\dfrac{5}{9}$.

Section 5

1. **C** <u>Revered as</u> is fine, so cross it off. *Leonardo da Vinci excelled <u>in</u>* (that's correct, so cross it off)... *and <u>serving</u> as...*. Your verbs are not parallel. It should be *excelled in* and *served as*.

2. **A** The twins are two people who wanted to be *members*...they cannot be <u>a member</u>. Subject-verb agreement.

3. **E** No error.

4. **D** *Production <u>of</u>* is fine, so cross it off. <u>And demonstrates</u> is also fine. The work <u>has been</u> (no problem here) ignored how? *Unjustly*. You need an adverb to modify the verb *ignored*.

5. **C** *Yoga is <u>more than</u> simply a <u>series of</u> stretches and poses*—no problems in the first phrase, so cross off A and B. Now pull the verbs out: *It is a means of centering...and <u>focus</u>...*. They are not parallel. *Focus* should be *focusing*.

6. **B** <u>Prior to</u> *the Industrial Revolution*...no problem here, so cross off A. *Children and parents <u>spend</u>...*. *Spend* is present tense, but we are talking about the past. It should be *spent*.

7. **E** No error.

8. **D** *Neither...<u>nor</u>* is fine, so cross off A. *The CEO...<u>was</u>* is also fine. *Financial reports <u>were</u>* (no problem) *inconsistent with previous <u>years</u>*. Not with previous *years*, with previous *years' financial reports*.

9. **B** *If one is interested <u>in</u> learning* is fine (cross it off). *You should ...* The subject of the first phrase is *one*, so one it should stay. *You* is incorrect.

10. **A** *It is <u>necessarily</u> for students <u>to wear</u>...*no, it is *necessary* for students to wear something.

11. **D** <u>Just as</u> *parents* is fine (eliminate it). *Babies learn <u>to</u> walk*—no problem here. *Babies vary in <u>their</u> readiness* (okay) *to take <u>his or her</u> first steps*. Pronoun problem...*babies* and *their* are plural, so they must be taking *their* first steps.

12. **A** *Each member... <u>were</u>*—don't think so. *Each member was*.

13. **A** *The gift that Karen and Mary purchased for <u>her</u> mother*.... Whose mother? This is a case of pronoun ambiguity.

14. **C** *Vocalists <u>are</u> often able <u>to sing</u> oratorios in flawless Latin*...A and B are both fine, so cross them off. *Even if none ... <u>have</u> ... None* is a singular noun, so it needs a singular verb. It should be *has*.

15. **B** *Thomas Pynchon's novel...<u>has been</u>* is fine, so cross it off. *Lauded for <u>it's</u>*....Lauded for *it is*? The correct form is *its*.

16. **A** *John knew he <u>should've went</u> home*.... Actually, John *should have gone* home.

17. **C** *<u>Many</u> students find*...so far, so good. *Impossible <u>to understand</u>*... no problem, so cross off A and B. *When <u>proper</u> conveyed... properly* conveyed. You need an adverb to modify a verb.

18. **D** Pull it apart: *Scholars <u>agree</u>* is fine so cross off A. *There <u>has been</u> no greater contributor* is also fine. *Advancement <u>of architecture</u>*...no problem. *No greater contributor...than <u>that of</u> Frank Lloyd Wright.* The *that of* is incorrect—it should say *no greater contributor than Frank*....

19. **E** No error.

20. **B** Ambiguous pronoun. Who doesn't wear bathing suits on the beach? Eliminate A. E changes the meaning of the sentence. C and D are not as well written as B.

21. **A** This sentence is correct as written.

22. **E** Neil did not do all this while he was getting off the chairlift. Eliminate A. B and D are poorly written. C is not parallel (*adjusted, polished* and *he went skiing*...).

23. **C** *Critically* is the error in the sentence. Cross off A and B since they don't fix the error. D and E both add extra stuff that makes the sentence awkward.

24. **D** The original error is a misplaced modifier. The opening phrase modifies the movie *The Maltese Falcon*, not Samuel Spade. Cross off A. All the other answer choices fix this error but introduce new ones. E is out because it is so poorly written. B is also awkward. Be careful on C—can Sam Spade *solve* his partner's *death*?

25. **A** The sentence is correct as written.

26. **B** Because the opening phrase of the sentence begins with the trigger word "although," it is incorrect to begin the second half of the sentence with another trigger word. Eliminate A, D, and E. B and C fix the original problem, but C is poorly worded.

27. **E** The *they would* makes the underlined phrase incorrect. *The committee agreed to return...and discuss.* Eliminate A and B. D implies the chairpersons are discussing the proposals as they walk in the door. Be careful on C—it fixes the original error but uses the singular pronoun "her" to describe the plural subject.

28. **C** The verbs in the sentence are not parallel (*called*, *made*, and *was worn*). Eliminate A and D. B fixes the original error, but makes a new error by changing *made* to *making*. E is a big mess.

29. **A** The sentence is correct as written.

30. **D** The sentence incorrectly uses plural pronouns to represent the singular subject. Eliminate A, B, and C for not fixing the error. E fixes the error, but then makes a subject-verb agreement error at the end.

31. **C** Who always wins? Pronoun ambiguity is the first problem here. Eliminate A and B. D and E are awkward and missing the appropriate trigger words.

32. **E** Misplaced modifier. *Einstein* was not an advocate of psychiatrists (Freud *was* a psychiatrist). Eliminate A and B. D is poorly worded. C is not consistent with the opening phrase and is therefore not as good a choice as E.

33. **B** Lots of problems here. First, the wrong quantity word is used— it should be *fewer* miles, not *less* miles. Eliminate A, D, and E. C is poorly worded.

34. **A** All the other choices are weak when compared with *however*.

35. **E** You must clarify who *them* is. E is the only choice that says *like children*.

36. **B** All the other answer choices are too far out of the scope of this passage.

37. **C** The sentence is not well written, so cross off A. D places the children on the walls. B and E are awkward.

38. **E** Answer choice A is worse than the original because it is a long, run-on sentence. B is just the opposite—several short, non-cohesive sentences. C and D are awkward and do not convey the exact meaning of the original sentence.

39. **B** The *this* in the sentence needs to be clarified. Get rid of A and D. Choices C and E are long and awkward.

15

Practice Test 2

Time—25 Minutes
25 Questions
(1–25)

For each question in this section, select the best answer from among the choices given and fill in the corresponding oval on the answer sheet.

Each sentence below has one or two blanks, each blank indicating that something has been omitted. Beneath the sentence are five words or sets of words labeled A through E. Choose the word or set of words that, when inserted in the sentence, best fits the meaning of the sentence as a whole.

Example:

Medieval kingdoms did not become constitutional republics overnight; on the contrary, the change was -------.

(A) unpopular (B) unexpected (C) advantageous

(D) sufficient (E) gradual

Ⓐ Ⓑ Ⓒ Ⓓ ●

1. Though he is usually very ------- at such occasions, John was surprisingly quiet at his engagement party.

    (A) reserved (B) outgoing (C) successful

    (D) irreverent (E) vague

2. Although a few critics loved Isabel's new play, it never achieved the ------- success necessary for a long run in the theaters.

    (A) intellectual (B) eccentric (C) persuasive

    (D) dignified (E) popular

3. Despite their very ------- cultural and religious backgrounds, the leaders of the civil rights march were able to put their differences behind them and fight for a ------- goal.

    (A) diverse..common
    (B) different..poetic
    (C) similar..joint
    (D) indifferent..impossible
    (E) incompatible..remote

4. The ------- water made it extremely difficult for the divers to search for the sunken treasure, as they couldn't see more than a few feet in front of their faces.

    (A) transparent (B) murky (C) malodorous

    (D) turgid (E) noxious

5. She was a very ------- student; she checked every reference in her papers and always used the correct form in her footnotes.

    (A) prodigious (B) supercilious (C) punctilious

    (D) acute (E) inspirational

GO ON TO THE NEXT PAGE

268 ◆ CRACKING THE PSAT/NMSQT

Each question below consists of a related pair of words or phrases, followed by five pairs of words or phrases labeled A through E. Select the pair that best expresses a relationship similar to that expressed in the original pair.

Example:

CRUMB : BREAD ::

(A) ounce : unit
(B) splinter : wood
(C) water : bucket
(D) twine : rope
(E) cream : butter

Ⓐ ● Ⓒ Ⓓ Ⓔ

6. HOUR : TIME ::

(A) kilogram : scale
(B) length : yardstick
(C) meter : unit
(D) index : encyclopedia
(E) mile : distance

7. VACCINE : INFECTION ::

(A) guard : prison
(B) vault : theft
(C) army : war
(D) alcohol : intoxication
(E) antiseptic : cleanliness

8. JUBILATION : HAPPINESS ::

(A) mine : force
(B) unity : disagreement
(C) decency : trickery
(D) agony : pain
(E) hallway : light

9. GARBLED : CLARITY ::

(A) priceless : value
(B) shallow : depth
(C) displaced : immigrant
(D) copied : reproduction
(E) soft : texture

10. CAPACIOUS : VOLUME ::

(A) pale : color
(B) precious : value
(C) muffled : detail
(D) servile : bureaucracy
(E) garish : shape

11. EMACIATED : THIN ::

(A) audacious : bold
(B) humid : foggy
(C) courageous : benevolent
(D) radiant : subtle
(E) pathetic : contrite

GO ON TO THE NEXT PAGE

Questions 12–19 are based on the following passage.

This passage discusses the introduction of the common currency in Europe. It was written in 1997.

With less than two years remaining before the introduction of the new European common currency, dubbed the "euro," businesses and governments of the European Community are preparing for sweeping changes in the way that business will be conducted both nationally and internationally among the member states—changes which will fundamentally change the nature of business in Europe. During the three-year transition period, scheduled to last from 1999 to mid-2002, the euro will coexist with national currencies; afterwards, the national currencies will be phased out, leaving the euro as the single European currency. The transition to the common currency will be a difficult one, not only due to its high cost to governments (which will have to print millions of new banknotes) and to businesses (which will need to completely revise their accounting practices and cash handling systems) but also because many businesses will find that they cannot compete in the new, more open, European market. This openness, however, will be a boon for many businesses and particularly for consumers, who will benefit from a wider choice of products and services. Additionally, the new single currency will allow both businesses and individual consumers to save billions of dollars annually in transaction costs associated with the current multi-currency system.

One factor that has been largely ignored by businesses and governments alike is consumers' reaction to this switch to the common currency, which will be imposed on them largely without their input and, in many cases, without their even understanding the reasons for this change. People may be reluctant to accept the euro for several reasons: an attachment to their national currency as a symbol of their homeland, the potential mistrust of a currency not controlled by their own national bank, or a feeling of complete disorientation when faced with the conversion to a new standard. When the French supermarket chain E. Leclerc decided, as an experiment, to print several million dollars' worth of mock "euro" bills for use in its stores, it discovered that the majority of consumers were simply confused by the new currency and preferred paying with bank cards.

One of the biggest advantages brought by the euro will be its convenience for tourists and business travelers, who will no longer have to change money from one currency to another while traveling across different European countries. As income from tourism is a major part of the economies of many European countries, this may have the effect of bolstering the tourist industry across Europe, especially in the smaller countries such as Belgium and the Netherlands. However, most experienced tourists will feel a bit of nostalgia for the old days, when part of the fun of traveling was having to figure out the little pieces of coinage that one received at the window upon entering each different country.

12. The passage is primarily concerned with

    (A) The difficulties of changing from one currency to another
    (B) The impact of the euro on cash-handling and accounting systems
    (C) The importance of a national currency for consumer confidence
    (D) Why the euro will be good for European business
    (E) Some of the advantages and problems of the conversion to the euro

13. The author's use of the word "sweeping" (line 5) most closely means

    (A) enormous
    (B) clean
    (C) local
    (D) hardworking
    (E) intelligent

14. It can be inferred from the second paragraph that

    (A) having a currency controlled by a national bank gives some consumers a sense of security
    (B) consumers often prefer paying with bank cards than with cash
    (C) many consumers do not yet know about the conversion to the euro in 1999
    (D) The euro should not be introduced without a concurrent public information campaign
    (E) The introduction of the euro will entail less national sovereignty for the member states of the European Union

15. The author's use of the word "boon" (line 22) is most accurately described by which of the following?

    (A) certainty
    (B) challenge
    (C) mild difficulty
    (D) advantage
    (E) necessity

16. It can be inferred from the passage that the author believes which of the following statements:

    (A) The three-year transition period currently scheduled for the conversion to the euro should be considerably lengthened.
    (B) The conversion to a single currency will have some effect on competitive pressures on the European common market.
    (C) Many companies for whom the commission on currency transactions is a substantial part of their income will no longer be profitable after the introduction of the euro.
    (D) If people educated themselves about the euro before its introduction in 1999, the transition period would be made substantially easier.
    (E) The number of new businesses that will be created after the introduction of the euro will be greater than the number of businesses that will be forced to cease their operations because of the introduction of the euro.

17. According to the author, experienced tourists will probably greet the euro with

    (A) mild ambivalence
    (B) strong disappointment
    (C) general amusement
    (D) zealous support
    (E) ardent research

18. Which of the following is NOT cited as a drawback to the conversion to the euro?

    (A) The need for businesses to substantially modify their accounting systems
    (B) The difficulties that European consumers may have in adapting to the new currency
    (C) The cost of printing and minting new euro bills and coins
    (D) The fact that bank cards will have to be adapted to operate with the new currency
    (E) The fact that many companies may have trouble surviving greater international competition

19. The author's attitude in the passage above is best described as one of

    (A) enthusiastic support
    (B) sharp criticism
    (C) scholarly objectivity
    (D) indifference
    (E) mild distaste

GO ON TO THE NEXT PAGE

The passage below is followed by questions based on its content. Answer the questions on the basis of what is stated or implied in the passage and in any introductory material that may be provided.

Questions 20–25 are based on the following passage.

The following passage is an excerpt from Thomas Paine's "Common Sense," a political treatise first published in 1776 that served as a precursor to the Declaration of Independence.

I have as little superstition in me as any man living, but my secret opinion has ever been and still is that God Almighty will not give up a people to
Line military destruction or leave them unsupportedly to
5 perish who have so earnestly and repeatedly sought to avoid the calamities of war by every decent method which wisdom could invent. Neither have I so much of the infidel in me as to suppose that He has relinquished the government of the world and
10 given us up to the care of devils, and as I do not I cannot see on what grounds the King of Britain can look up to heaven for help against us; a common murderer, a highwayman, or a housebreaker has as good pretense as he.
15 And what is a Tory? I should not be afraid to go with a hundred Whigs* against a thousand Tories, were they to attempt to get into arms. Every Tory is a coward; for a servile, slavish, self-interested fear is the foundation of Toryism, and a man under such
20 influence, though he may be cruel, never can be brave.
  I once felt all that kind of anger which a man ought to feel against the mean principles that are held by the Tories: a noted one, who kept a tavern
25 at Amboy, was standing at his door with as pretty a child in his hand, about eight or nine years old, as I ever saw, and after speaking his mind as freely as he thought was prudent, finished with this unfatherly expression, "Well! Give me peace in my day." Not
30 a man lives on this continent but fully believes that a separation must some time or other finally take place, and a generous parent should have said, "If there must be trouble, let it be in my day, that my child may have peace." This single reflection, well
35 applied, is sufficient to awaken every man to duty.
  Not a place upon this earth might be so happy as America. Her situation is remote from all the wrangling world, and she has nothing to do but trade with them. A man can distinguish himself between
40 temper and principle, and I am confident that America will never be happy until she gets clear of foreign dominion. Wars without ceasing will break out until that period arrives, and the continent must in the end be conqueror; for though the flame of
45 liberty may sometimes cease to shine, the coal can never expire.

  *Whigs and Tories were rival eighteenth-century political factions. Whigs favored breaking away from British rule, while Tories remained loyal to King George III.

20. From the first sentence of the passage, it can be inferred that the author thinks Americans

    (A) have done their best to avoid war with Great Britain
    (B) are too superstitious
    (C) are much more religious than their British counterparts
    (D) are destined to be a major force in world trade
    (E) have benefited from the grace of King George III

21. In the first paragraph, the author displays his

    (A) determination to break free of English rule at any price
    (B) belief that God will not allow an unjust power to succeed in war
    (C) toleration of all religious practices
    (D) decision to re-evaluate his religious beliefs
    (E) fear that British citizens have a stronger sense of morality than Americans do

22. The author cites the example of the tavern owner in lines 22–34 in order to

    (A) support the Whigs and show why they are a powerful political force
    (B) suggest that working-class citizens sometimes neglect their children
    (C) cite an example of how Tories are reluctant to fight
    (D) suggest that Tories tend to value their own welfare above the welfare of others
    (E) urge more Americans to speak out about political issues

GO ON TO THE NEXT PAGE

23. In line 34, the word "reflection" most nearly means

   (A) symmetry
   (B) reproduction
   (C) thought
   (D) mirror image
   (E) effect

24. According to the passage, a war waged for American independence

   (A) should be fought for religious reasons
   (B) is unwise
   (C) would upset the delicate balance of power in Europe
   (D) would increase trade with the rest of the world
   (E) is bound to happen, unless the British grant Americans their freedom

25. Which of the following statements best expresses the meaning of the metaphor used in the last sentence of the passage?

   (A) Breaking free from the mother country leaves the new republic vulnerable to aggression from other countries.
   (B) Arguments that remain unresolved will always develop into armed conflict.
   (C) America's greatest asset in its fight for independence is its abundant natural resources.
   (D) Americans may not always be free, but they will always desire freedom.
   (E) Before America embroils itself in a revolution, it must first quell its internal struggles.

STOP
**If you finish before time is called, you may check your work on this section only.
Do not turn to any other section in the test.**

Time—25 Minutes
20 Questions
(1–20)

In this section solve each problem, using any available space on the page for scratchwork. Then decide which is the best of the choices given and fill in the corresponding oval on the answer sheet.

Notes:
1. The use of a calculator is permitted. All numbers used are real numbers.
2. Figures that accompany problems in this test are intended to provide information useful in solving the problems. They are drawn as accurately as possible EXCEPT when it is stated in a specific problem that the figure is not drawn to scale. All figures lie in a plane unless otherwise indicated.

Reference Information

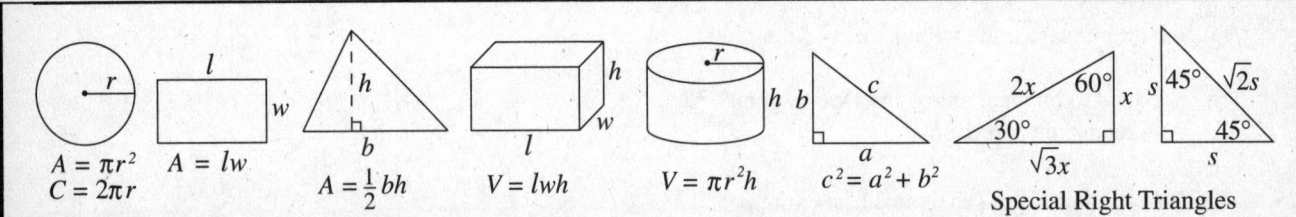

$A = \pi r^2$
$C = 2\pi r$

$A = lw$

$A = \frac{1}{2}bh$

$V = lwh$

$V = \pi r^2 h$

$c^2 = a^2 + b^2$

Special Right Triangles

The number of degrees of arc in a circle is 360.
The measure in degrees of a straight angle is 180.
The sum of the measures in degrees of the angles of a triangle is 180.

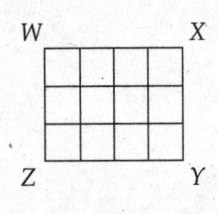

1. If each of the 12 small squares in the figure above has a side length of 2, what is the perimeter of rectangle WXYZ?

    (A) 28
    (B) 32
    (C) 36
    (D) 46
    (E) 56

2. If z is an even integer, which of the following must be an odd integer?

    (A) $3z$
    (B) $3z - 1$
    (C) $2z$
    (D) $2z - 2$
    (E) $z + 2$

3. The chart below shows the cost of producing 5 items and the cost of raw materials for each item. For which item do the raw materials represent the greatest fraction of the cost of production?

Item	Raw Materials	Cost of Production
A	$75	$10
B	$85	$12
C	$40	$8
D	$40	$7
E	$60	$8

    (A) Item A
    (B) Item B
    (C) Item C
    (D) Item D
    (E) Item E

GO ON TO THE NEXT PAGE

274 ◆ CRACKING THE PSAT/NMSQT

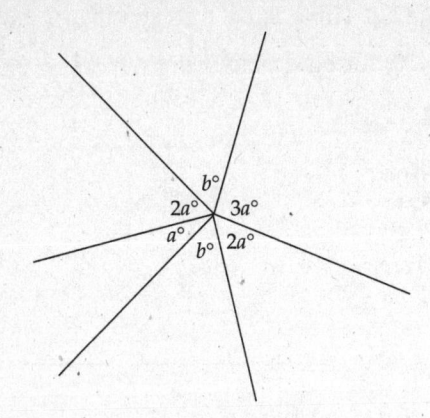

4. In the figure above, what is the value of 4a+b?

(A) 120
(B) 160
(C) 180
(D) 220
(E) 240

5. If $x = \dfrac{5n}{20}$, what is the value of n in terms of x?

(A) $\dfrac{x}{40}$

(B) $4x$

(C) $40x$

(D) $100x$

(E) $200x$

6. In the figure above, what is the value of x?

(A) 110
(B) 120
(C) 130
(D) 140
(E) 160

7. Eighty students went on a class trip. If there were 14 more boys than girls on the trip, how many girls went on the trip?

(A) 66
(B) 47
(C) 40
(D) 33
(E) 26

8. If the area of one face of a cube is 36, what is the volume of the cube?

(A) 18
(B) 36
(C) 64
(D) 72
(E) 216

GO ON TO THE NEXT PAGE

Bake Sale Results	
Item	Number Sold
Cupcakes	33
Cookies	68
Small cakes	w
Large cakes	z
Doughnuts	24

9. At a bake sale, a total of 260 items were sold, as shown in the table above. If four times as many small cakes as large cakes were sold, what is the value of z?

 (A) 22
 (B) 27
 (C) 32
 (D) 39
 (E) 135

10. For which of the following lists is the average (arithmetic mean) less than the median?

 (A) 1, 2, 6, 7, 8
 (B) 2, 4, 6, 8, 11
 (C) 4, 4, 6, 8, 8
 (D) 4, 5, 6, 7, 8
 (E) 4, 5, 6, 11, 12

11. During a sale, for every 3 shirts purchased at regular price, a customer can buy a fourth at 50% off. If the regular price for a shirt is $4.50, and a customer spent $31.50 on shirts, how many shirts did the customer purchase?

 (A) 5
 (B) 6
 (C) 7
 (D) 8
 (E) 9

12. If n is a positive integer greater than 2 and less than 10, for how many values of n is $\frac{n-1}{2}$ an integer?

 (A) None
 (B) One
 (C) Two
 (D) Three
 (E) Four

13. If 16 feet of a 96-foot-tall tree are below ground, what percent of the tree is above ground?

 (A) 16.6%
 (B) 20%
 (C) 25%
 (D) 33.3%
 (E) 83.3%

14. If $x - 6 = 3y$ and $x = 3 + 2y$, what is the value of y?

 (A) –3
 (B) –2
 (C) 0
 (D) 3
 (E) 6

15. What are the coordinates of the midpoint of the line segment with endpoints (6, –3) and (6, 9)?

 (A) (3, 3)
 (B) (3, 6)
 (C) (6, 1)
 (D) (6, 3)
 (E) (6, 6)

GO ON TO THE NEXT PAGE

16. The ratio of *a* to *b* is 4:7 and the ratio of *c* to *d* is 2:5. What is the ratio of *bc* to *ad*?

    (A) *a:bd*
    (B) *b:cd*
    (C) *b:ad*
    (D) *ad:c*
    (E) *cd:b*

17. A student took five tests. He scored an average (arithmetic mean) of 80 on the first three tests and an average of 90 on the other two. All of the following must be true EXCEPT:

    I. The student scored more than 85 on at least one test.
    II. The average (arithmetic mean) score for all five tests is less than 85.
    III. The student scored less than 80 on at least two tests.

    (A) I only
    (B) II only
    (C) III only
    (D) II and III
    (E) I and III

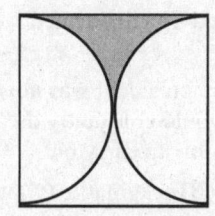

18. The figure above shows two semicircles inscribed in a square. If the square has a side of 10, what is the area of the shaded region?

    (A) $50 - 75\pi$
    (B) $50 - 25\pi$
    (C) $100 - 25\pi$
    (D) $\dfrac{100 - 25\pi}{2}$
    (E) $\dfrac{100 - 75\pi}{2}$

19. If *x* is a positive integer such that $\dfrac{x}{4}$ is an odd integer and $\dfrac{x}{3}$ is an even integer, which of the following statements must be true?

    I. $\dfrac{x}{4} - \dfrac{x}{3}$ is odd
    II. *x* is odd
    III. $\left(\dfrac{x}{3}\right)^2$ is odd

    (A) I only
    (B) II only
    (C) I and II
    (D) I and III
    (E) I, II and III

20. A circle and a triangle have equal areas. If the triangle has a base of 9 and an altitude of 8, what is the radius of the circle?

    (A) 6
    (B) 6π
    (C) $\dfrac{6}{\sqrt{\pi}}$
    (D) $\sqrt{72\pi}$
    (E) 72

STOP

**If you finish before time is called, you may check your work on this section only.
Do not turn to any other section in the test.**

Time—25 Minutes
25 Questions
(26–52)

For each question in this section, select the best answer from among the choices given and fill in the corresponding oval on the answer sheet.

Each sentence below has one or two blanks, each blank indicating that something has been omitted. Beneath the sentence are five words or sets of words labeled A through E. Choose the word or set of words that, when inserted in the sentence, best fits the meaning of the sentence as a whole.

Example:

Medieval kingdoms did not become constitutional republics overnight; on the contrary, the change was -------.

(A) unpopular (B) unexpected (C) advantageous

(D) sufficient (E) gradual

Ⓐ Ⓑ Ⓒ Ⓓ ●

---

26. Unlike her award-winning first book, Roberta's new volume can only be considered a ------- effort.

    (A) significant (B) mediocre (C) whimsical

    (D) feasible (E) laudable

27. Most animals respond to insignificant threats with excessive violence; in contrast, some remain ------- even when facing serious physical danger.

    (A) menacing (B) hostile (C) inane

    (D) jubilant (E) placid

28. Unfortunately, many of Aristotle's works are ------ to use, since they were ------- along with the ancient library at Alexandria.

    (A) unknown. .promoted
    (B) lost. .destroyed
    (C) meaningless. .investigated
    (D) important. .chastised
    (E) clear. .suppressed

29. Engineers attribute the building's ------- during the earthquake, which destroyed more rigid structures, to the surprising ------- of its steel girders.

    (A) obliteration. .strength
    (B) damage. .weakness
    (C) survival. .inadequacy
    (D) endurance. .suppleness
    (E) devastation. .inflexibility

30. Prior to the discovery of one intact ancient burial site in Central America, it had been thought that all of the Mayan tombs had been ------- by thieves.

    (A) levitated
    (B) exacerbated
    (C) inculpated
    (D) delayed
    (E) desecrated

31. Although the first viewers of *Waiting for Godot* jeered and called the play -------, later audiences came to recognize the ------- of the piece, and it soon became one of the classics of world theater.

    (A) abominable. .impenetrability
    (B) complicated. .fickleness
    (C) lenient. .unpleasantness
    (D) melancholy. .exultation
    (E) preposterous. .subtlety

32. In his later works, Langston Hughes' discussions of ethnic issues in America became increasingly -------, as he relied less on veiled criticism and more on direct confrontation.

    (A) concrete (B) coherent (C) forthright

    (D) confused (E) delineated

33. The company president was not a very ------- person; he would constantly dream up projects that were impossible to carry out.

    (A) radical (B) pragmatic (C) meticulous

    (D) suspenseful (E) inflammatory

GO ON TO THE NEXT PAGE

Each question below consists of a related pair of words or phrases, followed by five pairs of words or phrases labeled A through E. Select the pair that best expresses a relationship similar to that expressed in the original pair.

Example:

CRUMB : BREAD ::

(A) ounce : unit
(B) splinter : wood
(C) water : bucket
(D) twine : rope
(E) cream : butter

Ⓐ ● Ⓒ Ⓓ Ⓔ

34. CLASSROOM : TEACHER ::
    (A) flower : gardener
    (B) team : athlete
    (C) garage : car
    (D) hospital : surgeon
    (E) cashier : bookstore

35. ORAL : MOUTH ::
    (A) attainable : goal
    (B) relevant : idea
    (C) electric : wire
    (D) aquatic : water
    (E) manual : foot

36. RESOLUTE : DETERMINATION ::
    (A) pristine : grace
    (B) skeptical : doubt
    (C) tainted : honor
    (D) stringent : suggestion
    (E) wary : risk

37. SANCTUARY : WORSHIP ::
    (A) gymnasium : exercise
    (B) office : sales
    (C) lectern : debate
    (D) agenda : politician
    (E) television : performer

38. DIGRESS : SUBJECT ::
    (A) portray : ruse
    (B) speculate : gold
    (C) depict : character
    (D) monitor : health
    (E) stray : path

39. MAVERICK : INDIVIDUALISM ::
    (A) litigant : persecution
    (B) winner : competition
    (C) criminal : innocent
    (D) prevaricator : dishonesty
    (E) dullard : levity

40. ENIGMA : OBSCURE ::
    (A) mystery : criminal
    (B) contest : victorious
    (C) shield : protective
    (D) dilemma : invigorating
    (E) evidence : incriminating

GO ON TO THE NEXT PAGE

Questions 41–52 are based on the following passages.

The following passages both concern ecological conservation. Passage 1 discusses the Serengeti, one of the last remaining African nature preserves, while Passage 2 discusses a specific conservation study there.

Passage 1

There is no other plain in the world comparable to the Serengeti. Wild animals still graze in obscure corners of the African continent from Cape Town to
Line Chad, but as civilization moves in, the animals are
5 quickly crowded out; in Botswana, for example, the northwest corner was said up until 1973 to hold abundant game, but now the diamond industry is preparing to drill wells for its mines and the Okovanggo Basin, which sustained the game, may
10 be drained out. Every major civilization has eventually destroyed its wildlife, and civilization is fast overtaking Africa.

The Serengeti remains the great anachronism, its survival maintained through an odd, almost mystical
15 series of countervailing conditions that have thus far managed to tip a fragile balance slightly to the side of the animals: population increases vs. drought and famine; cattle proliferation vs. pestilence and disease; land pressure for cultivation vs. tourist
20 income; scientific research vs. the vagaries of nature.

The Serengeti's agonies are local and for the most part unrealized by the rest of the world; its importance as a cultural resource for the world
25 community, however, is unchallenged. Scientists see it as a sort of an ecological paradise regained, however briefly, and not only for its importance as the last gathering place for the rich diversity of African wildlife but as well for the light it may shed
30 on the larger question of man's survival.

"The Serengeti is basic to the concerns of conservation," says William Conway, director of the Bronx Zoo. "If animals can live there, so can man; if not, man cannot. It is the case of what is often
35 referred to as the canary simile—the miners in Wales took canaries into the pits to serve as an early-warning system; when the foul air killed the canaries, the miners knew it was time to get out. There are practical aspects to all this. The
40 production of the Salk vaccine required the destruction of six hundred thousand wild monkeys over a three-year period. Between this country and Japan, science is currently using them up at the rate of a hundred thousand a year." Peter Jackson,
45 director of information at the World Wildlife Fund, says, "All our domestic crops and animals have been bred from wild stock, and especially among plants it is the genetic resources available in the wild which have helped to produce new wild
50 yields." Conway asks, "Do we save animals for themselves or for ourselves? Will man set aside for tomorrow something he can use today? It hasn't happened yet. Does man truly want wildlife on Earth, and is he willing to make the sacrifices
55 necessary to keep it here?"

Passage 2

Of all his projects, John Owen's decision to establish a scientific observation in the midst of the Serengeti Plain was his most inspired. In 1961, the wildebeest appeared to be overgrazing the
60 grasslands of the Serengeti. Owen felt he ought to find out if this was so; and if it was, what should be done about it. Soon, in characteristic fashion, he virtually backed the new government into the establishment of an observatory station.

65 In order to answer Owen's early question of whether the wildebeest were overgrazing the Serengeti, the scientists first had to establish the relationship of the wildebeest to their food supply. In 1958, the Michael Grzimek Laboratory had
70 counted ninety-nine thousand wildebeest. In 1963, Lee and Martha Talbot counted two hundred and forty thousand. By 1969, there would be more than half a million. It appeared that, in fact, the wildebeest were not overgrazing the Serengeti; by
75 the mid-1960s some of the reason for this would become clear. There was a severe drought in 1960–

1961 that had since ended. However, although the grasses feeding the wildebeest within the park had become thick and healthy, the land surrounding the
80 Serengeti, which fed cattle, was overgrazed. Inexplicably, as the cattle outside the park were starving, the wildebeest inside were flourishing.

The fact that the wildebeest population was increasing is significant. More important, however,
85 is the fact that a principal regulating mechanism tended to keep their numbers below levels that would have damaged their habitat. In other words, even though the high rainfall throughout the 1960s produced more food for more animals, there were
90 never too many animals for the grass that was there. Thus, the wildebeest population was regulated by a symmetrical relationship between the wildebeests' birth and death rates, the number of animals adjusted by the death rate—starvation as a form of
95 control even in a time of abundance.

What had now become apparent to the scientists of the Research Institute was that the grasslands of the Serengeti formed a self-sustaining ecological system. Everything, they found, was interdependent
100 —fire, rain, soil, grass, the host of animals. Each living thing depended on the other, each flourished because of the other. The Serengeti, with its extraordinary residents, was at a stage, still undisturbed, of an evolutionary process that had
105 been going on for hundreds of thousands of years.

41. Passage 1 implies which one of the following about the northwest corner of Botswana?

    (A) All of its wildlife will be destroyed through increasing encroachment by civilization.
    (B) As of 1973, it was no longer home to as much wildlife as it had previously been.
    (C) Its problems are local concerns and have no effect on the world ecology.
    (D) The world must study its ecological destruction in order to prevent similar tragedies.
    (E) The Okovanggo Basin was drained to make room for diamond mines.

42. The author of Passage 1 believes that we should study the problems of the Serengeti plain because

    (A) many other regions of the world share similar concerns
    (B) of the disappearance of certain types of wildlife
    (C) the natural balance may be now tipping toward mankind
    (D) the results of this study may assist humanity in its quest for survival
    (E) of increasing development in the region

43. The author of Passage 1 quotes Conway (lines 31–44) in order to

    (A) point out the distinction between survival and conservation drawn in the previous paragraph
    (B) show why current conservation methods have failed to achieve the desired results
    (C) provide further support for the claim that conservation assists humans as well as animals
    (D) discuss conservation methods from earlier centuries
    (E) support the position that the Serengeti is no longer an interesting subject of study

44. The word "yields" (line 50) most nearly means

    (A) reservations
    (B) claims
    (C) types
    (D) traffic
    (E) difficulties

GO ON TO THE NEXT PAGE

45. The examples of the miners in Wales and the Salk vaccine (lines 35–42) provide support for which one of the following claims?

    (A) Animals may in some cases be able to help humans live longer and happier lives.
    (B) Wherever people can live, animals can live there also.
    (C) The natural competition between animals and humans in the wild is detrimental to humans.
    (D) Animals that cannot be tamed are of no use to humans.
    (E) Advances in medical science will be impossible without the continued use of animals for scientific experimentation.

46. The author of Passage 2 mentions that prior to John Owens

    (A) there had been no attempt made to study the Serengeti
    (B) the national government was reluctant to support any scientific research
    (C) there had been some investigation of the wildlife on the Serengeti
    (D) the Serengeti was a natural habitat virtually unknown to humans
    (E) other scientists had unsuccessfully attempted to enlist governmental support for their studies

47. The author discusses the three studies that counted the number of wildebeest (lines 68–72) in order to

    (A) show that many scientists were working on the same problem of wildebeest populations
    (B) support the claim that the Serengeti was not being overgrazed
    (C) discuss the effects of a severe drought on animal populations
    (D) demonstrate the importance of cattle in the Serengeti ecosystem
    (E) show the dramatic climactic changes that occurred during the 1960s

48. The phrase "principal regulating mechanism" in line 85 refers to

    (A) the natural limit placed on population growth by the food supply
    (B) the way in which the wildebeest were harmful to the environment
    (C) the difference between wildlife on the Serengeti and wildlife just outside the Serengeti
    (D) the effect of humanity's attempts to control disease in wildlife
    (E) the interaction of different types of wildlife in the Serengeti

49. According to the author of Passage 2, the primary conclusion of the Research Institute was that

    (A) the wildebeest was an isolated and unique case of wildlife population growth
    (B) humans were in danger of disturbing the ecological balance on the Serengeti
    (C) the Serengeti was a good example of a breakdown in a natural food chain
    (D) the Serengeti was a complex ecosystem with each member closely linked to the rest of the structure
    (E) the evolution of life on the Serengeti was coming to an end

GO ON TO THE NEXT PAGE

50. For which of the following claims made in Passage 1 does Passage 2 provide the strongest evidence?

(A) "Between this country and Japan, science is currently using them [wild monkeys] up at the rate of a hundred thousand a year." (lines 42–44)
(B) "Scientists see it as sort of an ecological paradise regained…for the light it may shed on the larger question of man's survival." (lines 25–30)
(C) "Every major civilization has eventually destroyed its wildlife, and civilization is fast overtaking Africa." (lines 10–12)
(D) "'All our domestic crops and animals have been bred from wild stock . . .'" (lines 46–47)
(E) "The Serengeti remains the great anachronism, its survival maintained through an odd, almost mystical series of countervailing conditions that have thus far managed to tip a fragile balance slightly to the side of the animals." (lines 13–17)

51. The author of Passage 1 would most likely argue that if the Serengeti continues to develop according to recent trends, it will probably

(A) eventually no longer be able to support wildlife
(B) remain relatively stable for the foreseeable future
(C) push back against the encroachment of civilization and regain lost territory
(D) rapidly evolve new species of plants and animals that are better adapted to coexisting with civilization
(E) be destroyed by researchers

52. Both authors would agree that the success of the Serengeti in maintaining its ecosystem is due in part to

(A) a variety of different counterbalancing elements, both natural and artificial
(B) humanity's lack of interest in the development of the plain
(C) conservation efforts focusing on maintaining the fragile ecosystem
(D) the fear of animals that keeps most people away from the Serengeti
(E) the success of certain species in fully utilizing the abundant natural resources

STOP
**If you finish before time is called, you may check your work on this section only.
Do not turn to any other section in the test.**

4 4 4 4 4 4 4

Time—25 Minutes
20 Questions
(21–40)

In this section, solve each problem using any available space on the page for scratchwork. Then decide which is the best of the choices given and fill in the corresponding oval on the answer sheet.

Notes:
1. The use of a calculator is permitted. All numbers used are real numbers.
2. Figures that accompany problems in this test are intended to provide information useful in solving the problems. They are drawn as accurately as possible EXCEPT when it is stated in a specific problem that the figure is not drawn to scale. All figures lie in a plane unless otherwise indicated.

Reference Information

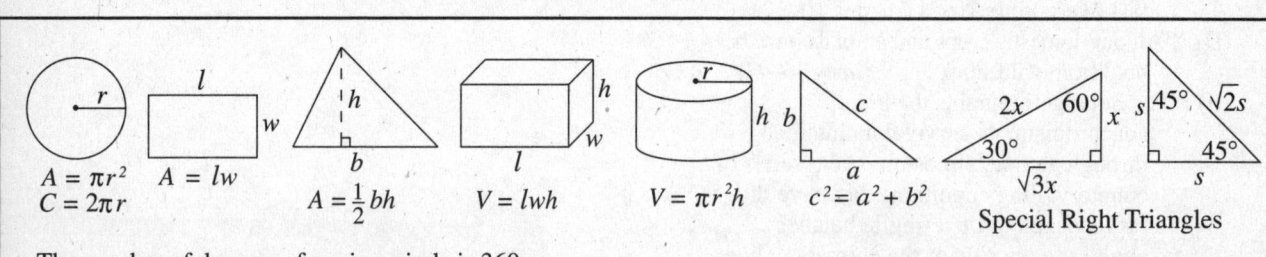

$A = \pi r^2$
$C = 2\pi r$

$A = lw$

$A = \frac{1}{2}bh$

$V = lwh$

$V = \pi r^2 h$

$c^2 = a^2 + b^2$

Special Right Triangles

The number of degrees of arc in a circle is 360.
The measure in degrees of a straight angle is 180.
The sum of the measures in degrees of the angles of a triangle is 180.

Directions for Quantitative Comparison Questions

Questions 21–32 each consist of two quantities in boxes, one in Column A and one in Column B. You are to compare the two quantities and on the answer sheet fill in oval

A if the quantity in Column A is greater;
B if the quantity in Column B is greater;
C if the two quantities are equal;
D if the relationship cannot be determined from the information given.

AN E RESPONSE WILL NOT BE SCORED.

Notes:
1. In some questions, information is given about one or both of the quantities to be compared. In such cases, the given information is centered above the two columns and is not boxed.
2. In a given question, a symbol that appears in both columns represents the same thing in Column A as it does in Column B.
3. Letters such as x, n, and k stand for real numbers.

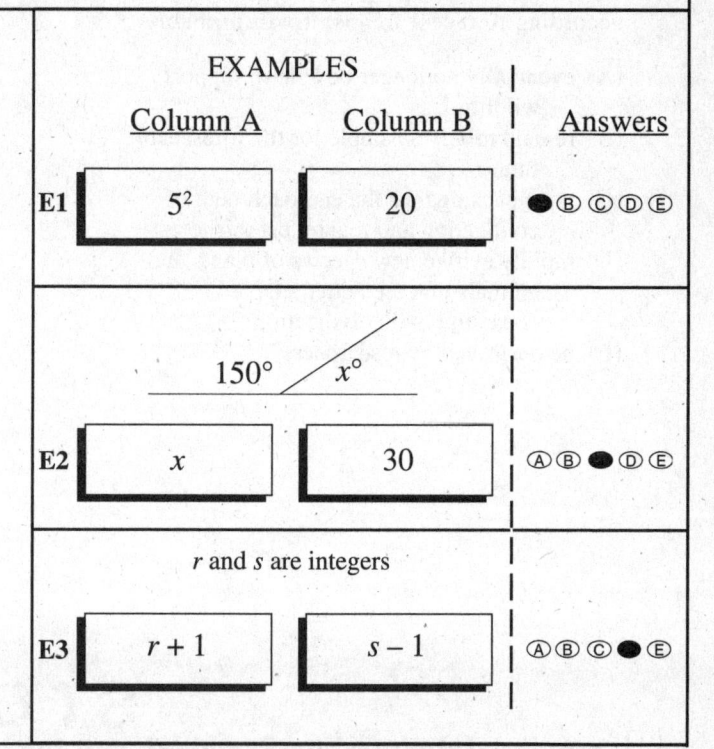

EXAMPLES

	Column A	Column B	Answers
E1	5^2	20	● B C D E
E2	x (with 150° and x°)	30	A B ● D E
E3	$r + 1$ (r and s are integers)	$s - 1$	A B C ● E

284 ◆ CRACKING THE PSAT/NMSQT

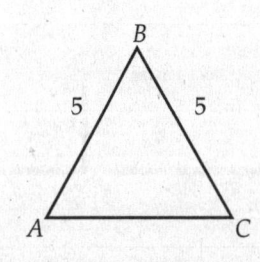

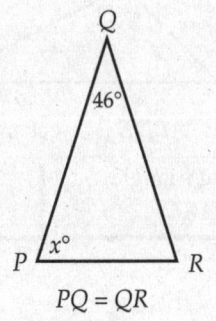

SUMMARY DIRECTIONS FOR QUANTITATIVE COMPARISON QUESTIONS

Answer: A if the quantity in Column A is greater;
B if the quantity in Column B is greater;
C if the two quantities are equal;
D if the relationship cannot be determined from the information given.

AN E RESPONSE WILL NOT BE SCORED.

	Column A	Column B
21.	\multicolumn{2}{c}{The cost of two pencils and one eraser is \$1.70.}
	The cost of one pencil	The cost of one eraser

	Column A	Column B
22.	\multicolumn{2}{c}{$\frac{2}{3}$ of a is 20.}
	$\frac{1}{6}$ of a	6

23.
Triangle with Q at top (46°), P at bottom-left with angle $x°$, R at bottom-right. $PQ = QR$.

Column A	Column B
x	65

24.

Column A	Column B
A rate of 180 pages per hour	A rate of 4 pages per minute

25. a, b, c, and d are positive integers.
$d - c = c - b = b - a$

Column A	Column B
$c - a$	$d - b$

26. Triangle with B at top, A at bottom-left, C at bottom-right; AB = 5, BC = 5.

Column A	Column B
Length of AC	5

27. $16 + a + a = 31 + a$

Column A	Column B
a	15

GO ON TO THE NEXT PAGE →

PRACTICE TEST 2 ◆ 285

4 4 4 4 4 4 4

SUMMARY DIRECTIONS FOR QUANTITATIVE COMPARISON QUESTIONS
Answer: A if the quantity in Column A is greater;
B if the quantity in Column B is greater;
C if the two quantities are equal;
D if the relationship cannot be determined from the information given.

AN E RESPONSE WILL NOT BE SCORED.

Column A	Column B		Column A	Column B

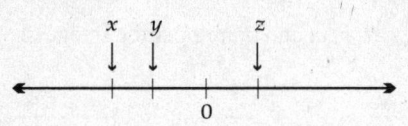

28. x, y, and z are points on the number line shown above.

xy	xz

29. | $\dfrac{6n}{5}$ | $\dfrac{5n}{6}$ |
|---|---|

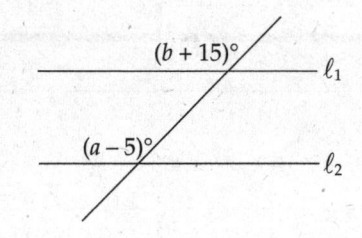

$(b+15)°$ — ℓ_1
$(a-5)°$ — ℓ_2
$\ell_1 \| \ell_2$

30. | a | b |
|---|---|

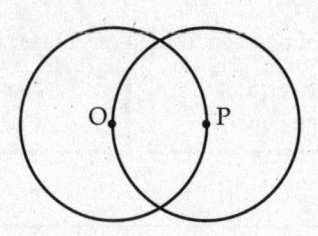

31. | area of circle with center O | area of circle with center P |
|---|---|

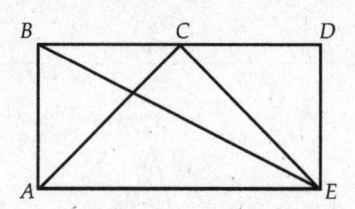

ABDE is a rectangle

32. | area of triangle *ABE* | area of triangle *ACE* |
|---|---|

GO ON TO THE NEXT PAGE →

286 ◆ CRACKING THE PSAT/NMSQT

4 4 4 4 4 4 4

Directions for Student-Produced Response Questions

Each of the remaining questions (33–40) requires you to solve the problem and enter your answer by marking the ovals in the special grid, as shown in the examples below.

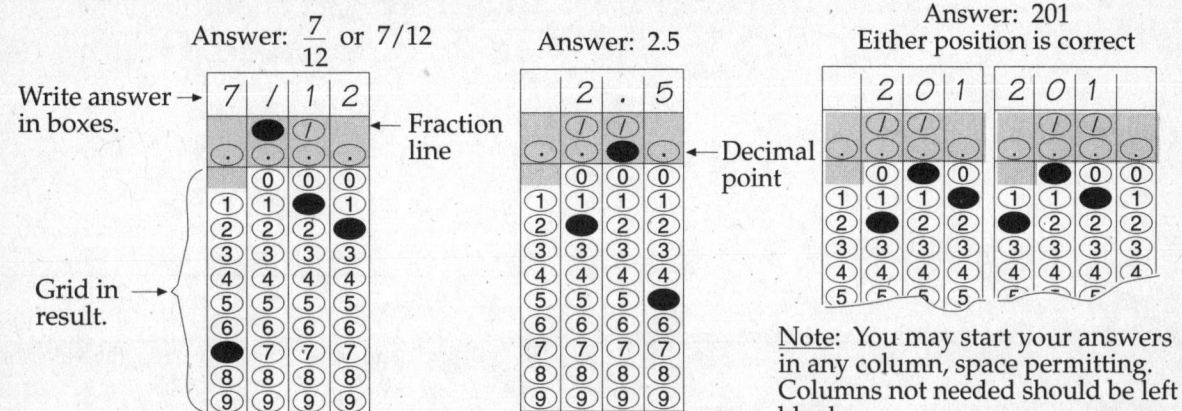

Answer: $\frac{7}{12}$ or 7/12

Answer: 2.5

Answer: 201
Either position is correct

Write answer in boxes.
Fraction line
Decimal point

Grid in result.

Note: You may start your answers in any column, space permitting. Columns not needed should be left blank.

- Mark no more than one oval in any column.
- Because the answer sheet will be machine-scored, **you will receive credit only if the ovals are filled in correctly.**
- Although not required, it is suggested that you write your answer in the boxes at the top of the columns to help you fill in the ovals accurately.
- Some problems may have more than one correct answer. In such cases, grid only one answer.
- No question has a negative answer.
- **Mixed numbers** such as $2\frac{1}{2}$ must be gridded as 2.5 or 5/2. (If `2 1 / 2` is gridded, it will be interpreted as $\frac{21}{2}$, not $2\frac{1}{2}$.)

- **Decimal Accuracy:** If you obtain a decimal answer, **enter the most accurate value the grid will accommodate.** For example, if you obtain an answer such as 0.6666..., you should record the result as .666 or .667. **Less accurate values such as .66 or .67 are not acceptable.**

Acceptable ways to grid $\frac{2}{3}$ = .6666...

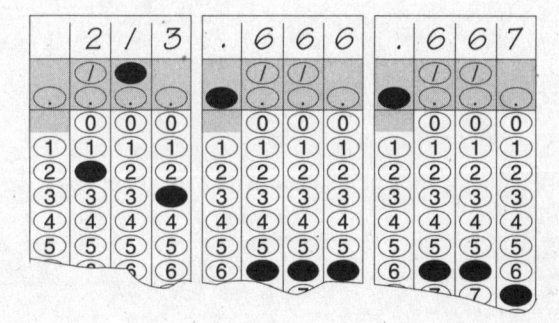

---

33. In the figure above, what is the value of $x + y$?

(Figure: lines ℓ_1 and ℓ_2 with $\ell_1 \parallel \ell_2$; angles $y°$ and $x°$ at top; angle 41° at bottom.)

34. The ratio of n to $6m$ is 3:12. What is the ratio of $2m$ to n? (Grid your answer as a fraction.)

GO ON TO THE NEXT PAGE

35. If $\frac{1}{2}a$, $\frac{1}{2}a$, and a are the degree measures of a triangle, what is the value of a?

36. What is the greatest of 4 consecutive integers whose sum is 414?

37. What is the area of a square with a diagonal of $3\sqrt{2}$?

38. If n is a prime number greater than 3, then $6n$ has exactly how many positive integer factors?

39. If $x + y = 5$ and $x^2 - y^2 = 16$, what is the value of $x - y$?

40. Two numbers have the property that their sum is equal to their product. If one of these numbers is 4, what is the other number?

STOP
If you finish before time is called, you may check your work on this section only.
Do not turn to any other section in the test.

NO TEST MATERIAL ON THIS PAGE.

5 ☐ 5 ☐ 5 ☐ 5 ☐ 5

Time—30 Minutes
39 Questions
(1–39)

For each question in this section, select the best answer from among the choices given and fill in the corresponding oval on the answer sheet.

Directions: The following sentences test your knowledge of grammar, usage, word choice, and idiom.
Some sentences are correct.
No sentence contains more than one error.

You will find that the error, if there is one, is underlined and lettered. Elements of the sentence that are not underlined will not be changed. In choosing answers, follow the requirements of standard written English.

If there is an error, select the <u>one underlined part</u> that must be changed to make the sentence correct and fill in the corresponding oval on your answer sheet.

If there is no error, fill in oval Ⓔ.

EXAMPLE:

<u>The other</u> delegates and <u>him</u> <u>immediately</u>
   A   B   C

accepted the resolution <u>drafted by</u> the
                                      D

neutral states. <u>No error</u>
                    E

SAMPLE ANSWER

Ⓐ ● Ⓒ Ⓓ Ⓔ

---

1. Leonardo da Vinci, <u>who painted</u> the *Mona Lisa*,
                          A

<u>was</u> not only a gifted artist <u>while</u> <u>he was</u> also a
 B   C   D

brilliant inventor. <u>No error</u>
                   E

2. The actors <u>were exhausted</u>, but each <u>was able</u> to
               A   B

remember <u>all</u> the complicated lines
          C

<u>on opening night</u>. <u>No error</u>
     D   E

3. Mary Anne was indebted <u>with</u> her mother <u>for</u> all
                           A   B

the hard work <u>her mother</u> <u>had done</u> in preparation
               C   D

for the party. <u>No error</u>
               E

4. One way <u>to determine</u> the accuracy of reference
            A

books <u>is</u> <u>to check</u> the credentials of
     B   C

its editorial board. <u>No error</u>
      D   E

5. The principal <u>was</u> <u>aggravated</u> by the
               A   B

<u>students' decision</u> to protest <u>during</u> Parents'
     C   D

Weekend. <u>No error</u>
         E

6. It <u>is</u> <u>more difficult</u> to learn to type
    A   B

<u>than</u> <u>mastering</u> a simple word processing
  C   D

program. <u>No error</u>
         E

GO ON TO THE NEXT PAGE ➡

7. The works of Stephen King <u>are</u> similar
                              A
   <u>to Peter Straub</u>, a fact that is not surprising <u>since</u>
   B   C
   the two men are friends and <u>have even collaborated</u>
                                D
   on two novels. <u>No error</u>
                   E

8. In flight, a flock of geese <u>encounters</u> <u>scarcely</u> no
                                A   B
   wind resistance <u>because</u> of the "v" formation <u>it</u>
                    C   D
   employs. <u>No error</u>
            E

9. <u>Of</u> the nominees <u>for</u> the Nobel Prize in literature
   A   B
   this year, <u>few</u> are <u>as qualified as</u> the English
              C   D
   novelist Anthony Powell. <u>No error</u>
                            E

10. Vital to any analysis <u>of the causes</u> of the Russian
                          A
    Revolution <u>are</u> an understanding <u>of the many</u>
               B   C
    alliances <u>between political parties</u> in the early
              D
    1900s. <u>No error</u>
           E

11. Many <u>of</u> the players <u>were</u> professionals <u>who</u>, in
         A   B   C
    prior years, <u>had received</u> gold medals. <u>No error</u>
                 D   E

12. <u>Placing</u> baking soda in a glass filled with vinegar
    A
    normally <u>result</u> <u>in</u> an interesting
             B   C
    chemical reaction. <u>No error</u>
    D   E

13. A <u>recent</u> conducted poll <u>shows</u> that people are
      A   B
    littering less frequently, a development
    <u>that reflects</u> a great change in the public's attitude
    C
    <u>toward</u> the environment. <u>No error</u>
    D   E

14. Neither <u>the giant alligator</u> <u>or</u> the tiny lizard
            A   B
    <u>is the cause</u> <u>of</u> Joey's nightmares. <u>No error</u>
    C   D   E

15. Marjorie, <u>the newest of</u> the two violinists who
              A
    <u>have</u> recently joined the symphony, <u>has</u> excellent
    B   C
    tone and a marvelous command <u>of</u> her instrument.
                                  D
    <u>No error</u>
    E

16. <u>The more</u> you read the <u>early</u> works of Michel
    A   B
    Tournier, <u>the more</u> they <u>begin</u> to provoke an
              C   D
    emotional reaction. <u>No error</u>
                        E

17. Although they are widely used, standardized test
            A
    scores are not a reliant indicator of a student's
          B   C   D
    academic potential. No error
                        E

18. His unusual style and his brilliant use of humor
    makes Marlowe a joy to read, even for students
      A   B   C
    who have never read him before. No error
              D   E

19. Since 1960, less than three graduates from our
               A   B
    school have won the Rhodes Scholarship.
           C   D
    No error
       E

Directions: In each of the following sentences, some part or all of the sentence is underlined. Below each sentence you will find five ways of phrasing the underlined part. Select the answer that produces the most effective sentence, one that is clear and exact, without awkwardness or ambiguity, and fill in the corresponding oval on your answer sheet. In choosing answers, follow the requirements of standard written English. Choose the answer that best expresses the meaning of the original sentence.

Answer (A) is always the same as the underlined part. Choose answer (A) if you think the original sentence needs no revision.

20. A large predatory snake, <u>the muscular body of a boa constrictor</u> can reach over 10 feet in length.

    (A) the muscular body of a boa constrictor
    (B) a boa constrictor whose muscular body
    (C) a boa constrictor's muscular body
    (D) the boa constrictor has a muscular body that
    (E) as well as having a muscular body, the boa constrictor

21. The audience's response was better than Martin could possibly have <u>expected, having received</u> a standing ovation and great cheers from the crowd.

    (A) expected, having received
    (B) expected; and so he was receiving
    (C) expected; he received
    (D) expected: including the reception of
    (E) expected, he was receiving

22. Watering your plant too often is as unhealthy <u>than if you do not water it</u> often enough.

    (A) than if you do not water it
    (B) as not watering it
    (C) as if one were not to water it
    (D) than not watering
    (E) as for not watering it

23. Not only did the ancient Egyptians know about the North Pole, <u>but they also knew its precise direction</u>.

    (A) but they also knew its precise direction
    (B) but they knew also its precise direction
    (C) also knowing its precise direction
    (D) also precisely knowing its direction
    (E) but knowing its precise direction as well

24. <u>The Luna space probes were the first to enter solar orbit and photograph the far side of the moon, in 1959 they were launched.</u>

    (A) The Luna space probes were the first to enter solar orbit and photograph the far side of the moon, in 1959 they were launched.
    (B) Launched in 1959, the Luna space probes were the first to enter solar orbit and photograph the far side of the moon.
    (C) In 1959, the first solar orbit and photograph of the far side of the moon was taking place when the Luna space probes were launched.
    (D) The launching of the Luna space probes was in 1959, the solar orbit was entered and the far side of the moon was photographed.
    (E) The first solar orbit was when the Luna space probes were launched in 1959, and the first photograph of the far side of the moon was taken as well.

25. Perhaps the best-known of all southern American writers, <u>William Faulkner's famous books include</u> *The Sound and the Fury* and *As I Lay Dying*.

    (A) William Faulkner's famous books include
    (B) William Faulkner's books are famous for including
    (C) William Faulkner has included among his famous books
    (D) William Faulkner is famous for such books as
    (E) William Faulkner is famous for including such books as

26. When the coach of the basketball team spoke, new uniforms for all the players were implied, but it was not promised by him.
    (A) new uniforms for all the players were implied, but it was not promised by him
    (B) new uniforms for all the players were implied, but he did not actually promise it
    (C) new uniforms for all the players were implied by him and not actually promised
    (D) he implied new uniforms for all the players, but they were not actually promised by him
    (E) he implied, but did not actually promise, that he would get new uniforms for all the players

27. When Michelle was younger, she was hired by a local furniture store to watch the store in the mornings as well as cleaning the windows.
    (A) as well as cleaning the windows
    (B) and she also cleaned the windows
    (C) as well as to clean the windows
    (D) the cleaning of windows also being done by her
    (E) together with cleaning the windows

28. Jason was nervous about the race he had to run, this nervousness gave him the energy to run even faster than he had expected.
    (A) this
    (B) furthermore
    (C) but this
    (D) for which
    (E) that

29. The earliest design for a helicopter drawn by Leonardo da Vinci, the Italian artist and inventor, more than four hundred years ago.
    (A) The earliest design for a helicopter drawn by Leonardo da Vinci
    (B) Among the earliest designs for a helicopter by Leonardo da Vinci
    (C) Leonardo da Vinci drew the earliest design for a helicopter
    (D) Leonardo da Vinci, creator of one of the earliest design for a helicopter
    (E) The earliest design for a helicopter was drawn by Leonardo da Vinci

30. After reading Mary Shelley's masterpiece *Frankenstein*, I couldn't hardly believe that she was only nineteen when she wrote it.
    (A) I couldn't hardly believe
    (B) I could hardly not believe
    (C) I could not hardly believe
    (D) I could hardly believe
    (E) I could hardly be believing

31. Ernest Hemingway is known not only for his clean, sparse style of writing, but also having an adventurous lifestyle.
    (A) but also having an adventurous lifestyle
    (B) but having an adventurous lifestyle
    (C) but also for his adventurous lifestyle
    (D) and he also had an adventurous lifestyle
    (E) an adventurous lifestyle was also his

32. Hydrogen, in combination with oxygen, forms the molecule we call water.
    (A) in combination with oxygen
    (B) in its combining with oxygen
    (C) in the combination of it and oxygen
    (D) having combined itself with oxygen
    (E) with oxygen in combination

33. Neither a broken leg nor an upset stomach has prevented Jason to play the flute in this year's concert.
    (A) has prevented Jason to play
    (B) have stopped Jason playing
    (C) have prevented Jason from playing
    (D) has prevented Jason from playing
    (E) have stopped Jason in his playing

GO ON TO THE NEXT PAGE

Directions: The following passage is an early draft of an essay. Some parts of the passage need to be rewritten.

Read the passage and answer the questions that follow. Some questions are about particular sentences or parts of the essay or the entire essay and ask you to consider organization and development. In making your decisions, follow the conventions of standard written English. After you have chosen your answer, fill in the corresponding oval on your answer sheet.

(1) I used to have an irrational fear of bees. (2) Anytime I heard a buzzing sound, my heart would start to beat faster and faster. (3) Sometimes breathing was hard.

(4) I've always loved working in my garden. (5) But once spring came around, all the bees came out. (6) I was terrified of going outside. (7) My garden began to wither away. (8) Finally, I decided to do something about it. (9) I called up my friend Anne. (10) Her uncle happens to be a beekeeper. (11) I wanted to ask if I could meet him. (12) Anne's uncle agreed to take me to his hives the next day. (13) From the second I woke up that day, I was petrified, but luckily, Anne's uncle was very understanding. (14) He suited me up in beekeeping gear so that I couldn't get stung, and then he showed me his bee hives.

(15) To my surprise, I found myself fascinated by them. (16) Anne's uncle described how the bees are organized in castes, how they act as pollinators, and how they make honey. (17) I was so interested by what he said that I went to the library that very night and researched bees for hours. (18) And now—now I can't keep away from bees. (19) Each morning, I have visited Anne's uncle, helping out with the hives, while in the afternoon, I devote my time to my garden surrounded by bees.

34. Which of the following is the best way to revise the underlined portions of sentences 2 and 3 (reproduced below) so that the two sentences are combined into one?

    Anytime I heard a buzzing sound, my heart would start to beat faster and <u>faster. Sometimes breathing was hard.</u>

    (A) faster, but sometimes breathing was hard
    (B) faster, and sometimes I would find it hard to breathe
    (C) faster, and sometimes harder to breathe
    (D) faster, so sometimes finding it hard to breathe
    (E) faster, while sometimes it was breathing that was hard

35. Which of the following sentences, if added after sentence 3, would best link the first paragraph with the rest of the essay?

    (A) It seems that I have had this fear of bees for an eternity.
    (B) There were even times that I couldn't move my body, so intense was my fear of bees.
    (C) Unfortunately, I couldn't ignore my fear of bees, because I have a garden.
    (D) Usually, gardening is a pleasurable experience.
    (E) I try not to be afraid of bees, but in my garden it's impossible.

36. Which of the following is the best way to revise and combine sentences 6 and 7 (reproduced below)?

    I was terrified of going outside. My garden began to wither away.

    (A) Being terrified of going outside, my garden began to wither away.
    (B) Though going outside terrified me, my garden began to wither away.
    (C) Since going outside did terrify me, it was then my garden began to wither away.
    (D) Going outside terrified me, and as a result, my garden began to wither away.
    (E) My garden, withering away, as I was terrified of going outside.

37. The phrase "to do something about it" in sentence 8 can best be made more specific by being rewritten as which of the following?

    (A) to make my garden grow again
    (B) to learn more about bees
    (C) to get in touch with a beekeeper
    (D) to combat my fear of bees
    (E) to reconsider my feelings

GO ON TO THE NEXT PAGE

38. To vary the pattern of short sentences in the second paragraph, which of the following would be the best way to combine sentences 10 and 11 (reproduced below)?

   Her uncle happens to be a beekeeper. I wanted to ask if I could meet him.

   (A) Her uncle happens to be a beekeeper, which made me ask if I could meet with him.
   (B) As her uncle is a beekeeper, a meeting with him I wanted to ask.
   (C) Her uncle being a beekeeper, I wanted to ask if my meeting him was possible.
   (D) I wanted to ask if I could meet, seeing that he happens to be a beekeeper, her uncle.
   (E) I wanted to ask if I could meet her uncle, who happens to be a beekeeper.

39. In the context of the third paragraph, which of the following is the best version of the underlined portion of sentence 19 (reproduced below)?

   Each morning, I have visited Anne's uncle helping out with the hives, while in the afternoon, I devote my time to my garden surrounded by bees.

   (A) (as it is now)
   (B) I visit Anne's uncle to help out
   (C) having visited Anne's uncle and helping out
   (D) visiting Anne's uncle to help out
   (E) visiting Anne's uncle has helped out

STOP
If you finish before time is called, you may check your work on this section only.
Do not turn to any other section in the test.

PRACTICE TEST 2 ANSWERS

Section 1	Section 2	Section 3	Section 4	Section 5	
1. B	1. A	26. B	21. D	1. C	31. C
2. E	2. B	27. E	22. B	2. E	32. A
3. A	3. A	28. B	23. A	3. A	33. D
4. B	4. C	29. D	24. B	4. D	34. B
5. C	5. B	30. E	25. C	5. B	35. C
6. E	6. A	31. E	26. D	6. D	36. D
7. B	7. D	32. C	27. C	7. B	37. D
8. D	8. E	33. B	28. A	8. B	38. E
9. B	9. B	34. D	29. D	9. E	39. B
10. B	10. A	35. D	30. A	10. B	
11. A	11. D	36. B	31. C	11. E	
12. E	12. E	37. A	32. C	12. B	
13. A	13. E	38. E	33. 139	13. A	
14. A	14. A	39. D	34. $\frac{4}{3}$	14. B	
15. D	15. D	40. C	35. 90	15. A	
16. B	16. B	41. B	36. 105	16. E	
17. A	17. C	42. D	37. 9	17. C	
18. D	18. D	43. C	38. 8	18. A	
19. C	19. D	44. C	39. $\frac{16}{5}$ or 3.2	19. A	
20. A	20. C	45. A		20. D	
21. B		46. C		21. C	
22. C		47. B		22. B	
23. C		48. A		23. A	
24. E		49. D	40. $\frac{4}{3}$ or 1.33	24. B	
25. D		50. E		25. D	
		51. B		26. E	
		52. A		27. C	
				28. C	
				29. E	
				30. D	

You will find a detailed explanation for each question beginning on page 302.

SCORING YOUR PRACTICE PSAT

VERBAL

After you have checked your answers against the answer key, you can calculate your score. For the two Verbal sections (Sections 1 and 3), add up the number of correct answers and the number of incorrect answers. Enter these numbers on the worksheet on the next page. Multiply the number of incorrect answers by .25 and subtract this result from the number of correct answers. Then round this to the nearest whole number to get your Verbal "raw score." Next, use the conversion table to convert your raw score to a scaled score.

MATH

Figuring your Math score is a bit trickier, because some of the questions have 5 answer choices (for these, the incorrect answer deduction is .25), some have 4 answer choices (for these, the incorrect answer deduction is .33), and some are Grid-Ins (which have no deduction for incorrect answers).

First, check your answers on Sections 2 and 4. For Section 2 and questions 21–32 of Section 4, put the number of correct answers and the number of incorrect answers into the worksheet on the next page. For questions 33–40 of Section 4, simply put in the number of correct answers. For Section 2, multiply the number of incorrect answers by .25 and subtract this total from the number of correct answers. For Section 4, multiply the number of incorrect answers by .33, and subtract this from the number of correct answers. For the Grid-In questions, simply put the number of correct answers into the box. Now, add up the totals for all three types of math questions to give you your total Math raw score. Then you can use the conversion table to find your scaled score.

WRITING SKILLS

The Writing Skills section should be scored just like the Verbal sections. Add up the number of correct answers and the number of incorrect answers from Section 5, and enter these numbers on the worksheet on the next page. Multiply the number of incorrect answers by .25 and subtract this result from the number of correct answers. Then round this to the nearest whole number. This is your Writing raw score. Next, use the conversion table to convert your raw scores to scaled scores.

WORKSHEET FOR CALCULATING YOUR SCORE

VERBAL

	Correct	Incorrect	
A. Sections 1 and 3	_____ − (.25 × _____) =		A
B. Total rounded Verbal raw score			B

MATHEMATICS

	Correct	Incorrect	
C. Section 2	_____ − (.25 × _____) =		C
D. Section 4 (Questions 21–32)	_____ − (.33 × _____) =		D
E. Section 4 (Questions 33–40)	_____ =		E
F. Total unrounded Math raw score (C + D + E)			F
G. Total rounded Math raw score			G

WRITING SKILLS

Section 5	_____ − (.25 × _____) =	
Total rounded Writing Skills raw score		

SCORE CONVERSION TABLE

Math Raw Score	Math Scaled Score	Verbal Raw Score	Verbal Scaled Score	Writing Skills Raw Score	Writing Skills Scaled Score
0	25	0	20	0	33
1	28	1	23	1	34
2	30	2	24	2	36
3	31	3	26	3	37
4	33	4	28	4	38
5	34	5	29	5	39
6	36	6	30	6	40
7	37	7	32	7	42
8	38	8	33	8	43
9	40	9	34	9	44
10	41	10	35	10	45
11	42	11	36	11	46
12	43	12	38	12	47
13	44	13	39	13	48
14	45	14	40	14	49
15	46	15	41	15	51
16	48	16	42	16	52
17	49	17	43	17	53
18	50	18	44	18	54
19	51	19	45	19	55
20	52	20	46	20	56
21	53	21	47	21	57
22	55	22	48	22	59
23	56	23	49	23	60
24	57	24	50	24	62
25	58	25	51	25	63
26	59	26	52	26	64
27	61	27	53	27	66
28	62	28	54	28	67
29	63	29	55	29	69
30	64	30	56	30	70
31	65	31	57	31	72
32	66	32	58	32	73
33	67	33	59	33	73
34	68	34	60	34	74
35	70	35	61	35	76
36	72	36	61	36	78
37	73	37	62	37	79
38	75	38	63	38	80
39	78	39	64	39	80
40	80	40	65		
		41	66		
		42	68		
		43	69		
		44	70		
		45	71		
		46	73		
		47	75		
		48	77		
		49	78		
		50	80		
		51	80		
		52	80		

16

Practice Test 2: Answers and Explanations

Section 1

1. **B** This sentence begins with the trigger word "though." This means that the meaning of the word in the blank will be the opposite of the meaning of the clue. Since the clue is "surprisingly quiet" we know that the meaning of the word in the blank should be a word that means something like "talkative." The closest choice available is B.

2. **E** Here's another great example of how putting your own word in the blank will help you out. The sentence starts positively by saying that a few critics liked Isabel's play. But the trigger word "although" tells you that the second part of the sentence will turn negative. What kind of thing would be necessary for a long run in the theaters? Not just being appreciated by a few critics—her play would need to be liked by a large number of people. So you probably picked a word like "broad" or "large" for the blank. Look down, and the word that comes closest is choice E.

3. **A** With a two-blank SC like this one, start with the blank that seems easier for you. In this case, let's try the second blank. We have the trigger word "despite" in this sentence, which tells us there will be a contrast between the "differences" that they had, and how they were able to act—even though they were very different, they were able to act together. This tells us that the meaning of the word in the second blank should be something like "mutual" or "shared." This allows us to eliminate B, D, and E. Now we can look at the first blank to help us decide between A and C. Since the word in the first blank needs to be a word like "different," A is a better choice than C.

4. **B** A good clue here is "couldn't see." So we need a word for the blank that means something like "dirty." The words are getting harder on this question, but you may well know that choices A, C, D, and E don't mean dirty. (If you don't know one of these words, of course, you shouldn't cross it off.) Cross off what you can, and take your best guess from the remaining choices. In this case, the answer is B.

5. **C** The clue in this sentence is "she checked every reference in her papers and always used the correct form." What kind of word would be good for this blank? Something like "serious," "careful," or "exacting." Since this is a hard question, it's going to have hard words. Cross off what you know can't be right, and then take your best guess from what's left. If you know these words, you can eliminate A, B, D, and E, and the answer is C. If you didn't know any of these words, be sure to write them down on flash cards and learn them!

6. **E** An hour is a measure of time. Is a kilogram a measure of scale? No, it's a measure of weight. Is length a measure of yardstick? No, a yardstick is used to measure length. Is a meter a measure of unit? No, a meter is a measure of distance. Is an index a measure of an encyclopedia? It might tell you where to find something in an encyclopedia, but an index doesn't really measure anything. Is a mile a measure of distance? Yes, so E is the answer.

7. **B** A vaccine prevents infection. Does a guard prevent prison? That doesn't make sense. Does a vault prevent theft? Sure. Does an army prevent war? Since an army wages war, this probably isn't a good defining sentence for the word "army." Does alcohol prevent intoxication? In fact, alcohol causes intoxication. Does an antiseptic prevent cleanliness? Exactly the opposite.

8. **D** Jubilation is a great deal of happiness. Is mine a great deal of force? No. Is unity a great deal of disagreement? Definitely not. Is decency a great deal of trickery? That's way off. Is agony a great deal of pain? Yes. Is hallway a great deal of light? No. So D is the best answer.

9. **B** Something garbled lacks clarity. Does something priceless lack value? Nope. Does something shallow lack depth? Absolutely. Does something displaced lack immigrant? That doesn't make much sense. Does something copied lack reproduction? Nope. Does something soft lack texture? No, soft is a sort of texture. So B is the answer.

10. **B** Capacious means having great volume. Does pale mean having a lot of color? Exactly the opposite. Does something precious have great value? Yes. Does something muffled lack detail? That doesn't make much sense. Does something servile lack bureaucracy? That's not the meaning of the word servile, which means slavish. Does something garish lack shape? Definitely not.

11. **A** This is a tough analogy: Remember, if you don't know some of the words in the answer choices, you have to leave those choices in (after all, they might be right) but you can eliminate any choice whose words you are sure have no relationship. In this case, if you know the words in choices C, D, and E, you can cross them out, since these word pairs have no good defining sentences. Even B doesn't really have a relationship if you are looking at it carefully. This leaves A as the answer. Emaciated means extremely thin. Likewise, audacious means very bold.

12. **E** From the blurb, we know that this passage is roughly about the conversion to the euro. Choices A and C don't mention the euro, so they are too general and can be eliminated. Choice B, in contrast, is too specific—accounting and cash-handling systems are only a detail mentioned in the first paragraph, and not the main idea. Likewise, choice D is discussed in the first paragraph, but not in the second. This makes E the best choice.

13. **A** For a Vocab-in-Context question such as this, you should put your finger over the word "sweeping," reread the sentence in context, and put your own word into the blank. A good clue here is the phrase "fundamentally change the nature of business in Europe." This means that the word we'd use to replace the word "sweeping" should be a word like "large" or "fundamental." The closest choice we have to this idea is choice A.

14. **A** Remember that even though a choice may be true, if it's not stated in the passage, it can't be the right answer. So the best way to find the answer to a question is to look back at the passage to find which choice can be supported based on what the passage says. The second paragraph states, "People may be reluctant to accept the euro for several reasons: an attachment to their national currency as a symbol of their homeland, the potential mistrust of a currency not controlled by their own national bank..." (lines 34–39). This means that people would trust a currency more if it were issued by their national bank, which is what choice A says.

15. **D** Here's another Vocab-in-Context question, so let's do it in the same way as before. Our clues to the word that we'd use to replace "boon" are the statements that people will "benefit from a wider choice of products and services" and " save billions of dollars annually." This means that we would use a word like "great" or "wonderful." The closest choice from the words we have is choice D.

16. **B** There are several choices here that represent things that the author might believe, but we have to find evidence that is stated in the passage to support our choice. For instance, the author might believe, but never actually says, that the introduction of the euro should be delayed. Therefore choice A just can't be right. The author does say, however, that after the introduction of the euro, "many businesses will find that they cannot compete in the new, more open, European market" (lines 19–21). This is paraphrased by choice B. Choice C is tempting, but be careful: The passage never actually discusses revenue and profitability, so this is not the best choice.

17. **A** The final paragraph states that experienced tourists will probably like the euro because they will no longer have to change money, but at the same time will also feel a bit sad at the loss of the different currencies. This mixed feeling is best described by choice A. Choices B, C, D, and E are much too strong, and can be eliminated.

18. **D** This question will take longer than most because it is an EXCEPT question, so you may want to save it for last. To solve it, we need to find which four items are discussed, and eliminate them. The author does discuss the need for business to change their accounting systems, consumer resistance, the cost of new bills and coins, and the increased competition. The need to adapt bank cards, however, is not mentioned in the passage.

19. **C** Choice A is a little too emotional for a passage as factual as this one is, so choice A can be eliminated. Choices B and E can also be eliminated for this reason. If the author were indifferent, the passage wouldn't have been written, so choice D can be crossed off. We're left with choice C as our answer.

20. **A** The first sentence of the passage states the author's belief that Americans "have so earnestly and repeatedly sought to avoid the calamities of war by every decent method… ." That is another way of saying that they have tried to avoid a war, which is what choice A says.

21. **B** Remember that the answer to every reading question on the PSAT will be based on what is actually said in the passage. In the first paragraph, the author says, "Neither have I so much of the infidel in me as to suppose that He has relinquished the government of the world and given us up to the care of devils, and as I do not I cannot see on what grounds the king of Britain can look up to heaven for help against us…" (lines 7–12). Put in our own words, this says that the British will not be helped by any higher power against the Americans. Choice B is a paraphrase of this idea.

22. **C** Let's look back at the passage around the lines cited and see what is said at that point. The opening sentence of the third paragraph says that the tavern owner exemplified the "principles that are held by the Tories." Just prior to this, the author says that Tories are cowards, so the example cited must be an example of why Tories are cowards. This is a good example of how, if you know what point the example is supposed to support, you can know what the example says even before reading its details.

23. **C** Here we have a Vocab-in-Context question, so let's cover the word with our finger and put our own word in its place. In this case, we would probably use a word like "idea" or "notion." The closest choice from among the choices we have is choice C.

24. **E** In the final lines of the passage, the author states "I am confident that America will never be happy until she gets clear of foreign dominion. Wars without ceasing will break out until that period arrives" (lines 40–43). Now we need to look at the answer choices to find a paraphrase of this line. Nothing is said about religion, the balance of trade, or the balance of power in Europe, so choices A, C, and D can be eliminated. Choice E looks like a paraphrase of this line, which makes it the best answer.

25. **D** Just prior to the last line, the passage says that "America will never be happy until she gets clear of foreign dominion." This tells us that the metaphor is specifically about American independence. This will allow us to eliminate choices A and B, since they are not specifically about American independence. Since the metaphor isn't really about natural resources, choice C can also be eliminated. Finally, no internal struggles are mentioned in this paragraph, so choice E can also be crossed off.

SECTION 2

1. **A** We can see that the perimeter of this rectangle is made up of 14 segments—four sides each on top and bottom, and three each on the left and right sides. Each of these segments has length 2, so the whole perimeter will be 14 times 2, or 28.

2. **B** Let's try plugging in a number for z to solve this problem. What if we try making $z = 2$? (Remember that we have to obey the rule in the question, which says that z must be an even integer.) If $z = 2$, then choice A becomes 6, choice B becomes 5, choice C becomes 4, choice D becomes 2, and choice E becomes 4. Since the question asks which of the following must be an odd integer, we can eliminate any of the choices that are not odd integers. This means we get to eliminate A, C, D, and E. This leaves us only with choice B, which must be our answer.

3. **A**   To solve this the long way, we would need to set up a fraction for each item of the cost of the raw materials over the cost of production, and then see which is the greatest fraction. But let's save some time by guesstimating. We can see that items C and D are the lowest—their raw materials are approximately half of the cost of production, whereas the others are all much more than half, so we can eliminate C and D. Now we can make fractions from the rest: Which is largest, $\frac{75}{100}$, $\frac{85}{120}$, or $\frac{60}{85}$? Put these into your calculator and you'll find that A is the largest at 0.75.

4. **C**   For a question like this, pay close attention to what you're being asked to solve for. It's a little funny to be asked to solve for $4a + b$. This means that we probably don't have to figure out the values of a or b; we only need to figure out something that looks like $4a + b$. If we look at the figure, we see that there are a bunch of a's and b's that make 360 degrees. In fact, let's count them: There are a total of 8 a's and 2 b's that make up the 360 degrees. This means we can write an equation: $8a + 2b = 360$. Now if we divide every term by 2, we get: $4a + b = 180$.

5. **B**   This question has the words "in terms of" in it, so we know this is a good Plugging-In problem. Let's try plugging in a nice easy number for n. If we make $n = 2$, then we can solve so that x must be equal to $\frac{1}{2}$. The question then asks for the value of n. According to the numbers we picked, $n = 2$. So let's write that number down and circle it. Now whichever answer choice says 2 (remembering that $x = \frac{1}{2}$) will be our answer. Choice A is equal to $\frac{\frac{1}{2}}{40}$, which does not equal 2. Choice B is equal to $4 \times \frac{1}{2}$, which *does* equal 2. Check the other choices to be sure; you'll find that only B gives us the answer of 2.

6. **A**   For this problem, we have two parallel lines and a line that crosses them. This always creates two sets of angles that have the same measure. In this case, we know that x will be equal to the sum of 20 degrees plus the right angle, which measures 90, so we know that x will be equal to 110 degrees.

7. **D** This is a classic example of Plugging In The Answer choices. While it's possible to set up an equation to solve this one, it's almost always much safer to simply try plugging in the answers until you find the one that works. Let's start with choice C. If there are 40 girls on the trip, and 14 more boys than girls, then there will be 54 boys on the trip. 40 girls + 54 boys = 94 total students, which is too many—the problem says that we have a total of 80. So C can't be right, and since it gives us a total number of students that's too large, we should try for a smaller number of girls (choices D or E). How about choice D? If there are 33 girls on the trip, and 14 more boys than girls, then we will have 47 boys. 47 boys + 33 girls = 80 students, which is the number we were supposed to have. This means that D is the answer.

8. **E** This question is testing whether you understand how to calculate the volume of a cube. Remember that the volume of any object is equal to the base times the height times the depth. Since each of these is the same on a cube, we can just take any one side and cube it (or multiply it by itself, and then by itself again) to get the volume. But first we need to figure out the length of the sides. Since the area is 36, and the area is equal to one side squared, we know that each side must measure 6. Therefore the volume of the cube will be $6 \times 6 \times 6$, or 216.

9. **B** Let's start by figuring out what w and z together need to add up to. We know that there were a total of 260 items sold. The cupcakes, cookies, and doughnuts make up a total of 33 + 68 + 24 = 125 of those items. That means that w and z must make up the other 135. So we know that $w + z = 135$. We also know that there are four times as many small cakes as large ones, which means that $w = 4z$. Now it's possible to solve algebraically, but that's probably not the smartest approach—a smarter one would be to try to plug in the answer choices. Let's try it: If we start with choice C, and assume that $z = 32$, then w would have to be four times this, or 112. But then 32 + 112 equals something bigger then 135. So choice C can't be right, and we need a smaller number. Let's try choice B. If $z = 27$, then w will be four times 27, or 108. Does 108 + 27 = 135? Yes, so B is the answer.

10. **A** For this problem, you'll have to remember the meaning of "median," which is the middle number in any group of numbers. In this case, you'll notice that the median of each group of numbers is 6. So the question is: Which group has an average which is less than 6? Of course, one way to solve this is to find the average of each group using your calculator. With a little test-taking logic, though, we can narrow down the choices. Choices C and D have numbers that are evenly spaced around the middle number (6) so you can probably tell at a glance that their average will both be 6. Choices B and E have numbers to the right of 6 that are farther from 6 than the numbers on the left, so their averages will be greater than 6. Verify your work by finding the average of the numbers under choice A—it's the only one with an average less than 6.

11. **D** This is another great question for Plugging In The Answer choices. Let's start with choice C. If a customer buys seven shirts, then the total bill will be

shirt 1	4.50
shirt 2	4.50
shirt 3	4.50
shirt 4 (50% off)	2.25
shirt 5	4.50
shirt 6	4.50
shirt 7	4.50
Total:	29.25

This is a bit smaller than the $31.50 that we know the customer spent, so choice C can be eliminated and we should try a larger number. How about choice D? For 8 shirts, the total would be

shirt 1	4.50
shirt 2	4.50
shirt 3	4.50
shirt 4 (50% off)	2.25
shirt 5	4.50
shirt 6	4.50
shirt 7	4.50
shirt 8 (50% off)	2.25
Total:	31.50

So D is the answer.

12. **E** The easiest way to solve this problem is simply to list the possible values for *n*, and see which of them satisfy the rule that $\frac{n-1}{2}$ is an integer. We know that *n* must be greater than 2 and less than 10, so that leaves the numbers 3, 4, 5, 6, 7, 8, and 9.

    Now let's try each of these: If we put each of these numbers in for *n* in the expression $\frac{n-1}{2}$, the numbers 3, 5, 7, and 9 give us integers. So there is a total of four values for *n* that satisfy the rule.

13. **E** To figure out what percent of the tree is above ground, we need to see what fraction of the 96-foot tree is below ground—that is, what fractional part 16 is of 96. $\frac{16}{96} = \frac{1}{6}$, which is the same as 16.67%. Therefore, the fraction of the tree above ground would be 83.33%.

14. **A** Probably the easiest way to solve this problem is to rewrite the first equation $x - 6 = 3y$ as $x = 3y + 6$. Now we have two equations, $x = 3y + 6$ and $x = 3 + 2y$, and we can set them equal to each other, as $3y + 6 = 3 + 2y$. Now we can solve for *y*, and get $y = -3$.

15. **D** If it helps you, draw a quick sketch of these points to help visualize this problem—though there's no need to do so. If the line segment is defined by points (6, –3) and (6, 9), we know that the *x*-coordinate (6) doesn't change. The line therefore goes from –3 to 9 on the *y*-axis. This is a distance of 12 points, so halfway will be 6 points from each end. This places the midpoint at 3 on the *y*-axis. So the final coordinates of the midpoint will be (6, 3).

16. **B** If the ratio of *a* to *b* is 4:7 and the ratio of *c* to *d* is 2:5 then we can simply plug in the numbers 4 for *a*, 7 for *b*, 2 for *c* and 5 for *d*. This makes the ratio of *bc* to *ad* equal to (7)(2) to (4)(5), which is a ratio of 14 to 20 (or 7 to 10). Now we just need to see which choice says this by plugging these same numbers into the answer choices. This shows us that choice B is the answer.

17. **C** If the student scored an average of 90 on two of the tests, then we know that at least one of those tests must have had a score of 90 or better. This shows us that roman numeral I must be true. Likewise, if the average of 3 tests was 80 and the average of 2 tests was 90, then we can find the average of all 5 tests: Using our average pie we know that the sum of the 3 tests must be 3 times 80, or 240, while the sum of the scores on the 2 tests must be 2 times 90, or 180. This makes the sum total of all five tests equal to 240 + 180, or 420. Divide this by 5 to get the average, which is 84. So roman numeral II must also be true. However, number III does not have to be true—for instance, the scores could actually have been 80, 80, 80, 90, and 90, whereby no single test would have a score lower than 80. Now, be careful! The question asks: all of the following must be true EXCEPT. So we need to pick the choice or choices that do NOT have to be true, which is roman numeral III only.

18. **D** First, let's figure out the area of the square. Since the square has a side of 10, its total area will be 100. Now let's remove the area of the circle to get the size of the remaining area (which includes the shaded region, and the identically shaped area just below it). Since these are each semicircles, together they will make one complete circle, with a radius of 5. (We know the radius is 5 because it's half of one side of the square.) This means that the area of the circle will be 25π. So once we remove the area of the circle, what is left is $100 - 25\pi$. Now the shaded region is only half of this, so we need to divide by two, and the area of the shaded region will be $\dfrac{100 - 25\pi}{2}$.

19. **D** This is a difficult problem, but a smart approach will allow us to avoid doing a great deal of the work. We know from the question that no matter what the value of x, $\dfrac{x}{4}$ is an odd integer and $\dfrac{x}{3}$ is an even integer. This means that for roman numeral I, $\dfrac{x}{4} - \dfrac{x}{3}$ will always be an odd integer, because an odd integer minus an even integer will always be odd. (You can see this from a few examples: $3 - 4 = -1$, and $7 - 4 = 3$.) This means that roman numeral I will always be true. Roman numeral III will also be easy to do: We know that $\dfrac{x}{3}$ is an even integer, and an even integer times itself will always be even. This means that roman numeral III will also always be true. The only choice that has both I and III in it is choice D.

PRACTICE TEST 2: ANSWERS AND EXPLANATIONS ◆ 311

20. **C** Let's start by finding the area of the triangle. We know that the triangle has a base of 9 and a height of 8, so its area will be $\frac{1}{2} \times 9 \times 8$, or 36. Now, we know that the triangle and the circle have equal areas, so the circle must also have area 36. To solve for the radius of the circle, remember the formula for the area of a circle, which is $a = \pi r^2$. We know the area is 36, so we know that $36 = \pi r^2$.

To solve for the radius r we first need to divide each side by π, which gives us $\frac{36}{\pi} = r^2$.

Now we take the square root of each side

$$\sqrt{\frac{36}{\pi}} = r, \text{ so}$$

$$\frac{6}{\sqrt{\pi}} = r$$

SECTION 3

26. **B** The clue in this sentence is "award-winning" and the trigger is "unlike." So we know that her second book must not have been as outstanding as her first. This means that the word in the blank should be a word like "not outstanding." The closest choice to this idea is B.

27. **E** There is a good trigger in this sentence, "in contrast," which tells us that the word in the blank is going to be the opposite of what we are given in the clue. The clue here is "respond with excessive violence." So the word in the blank will be a word that means the opposite of excessive violence—a word like "peace" or "quiet" would work fantastically. Now check your answer choices.

28. **B** For this problem, we have the trigger word "since," which tells us that the first blank and the second blank must have similar meanings—either both are positive words, or both are negative words. Moreover, the sentence begins with the word "unfortunately," which gives us a good hint that these words have to be negative—words like "unreadable" and "ruined." This allows us to eliminate choices A, C, D, and E.

29. **D** Let's start with the first blank. We know that the earthquake destroyed other structures, so the word in the first blank must mean a word like "survival." This will eliminate A, B, and E. Now to decide between C and D, we should look at the second blank. The second blank explains why the building survived the earthquake, so the second blank should be a word that means "strength" or "sturdiness." Choice C then definitely can't work, so D is the answer.

30. **E** This sentence uses a curious trigger, which is the contrast between before and after. The sentence says that before a certain discovery, people thought one thing about the Mayan tombs. Since this discovery was of a site that was "intact" it must have been thought that all of the sites were not intact. This means that the word in the blank should be a word like "not intact" or "damaged" or "destroyed." The choice that comes closest to this in meaning is E.

31. **E** Remember that on a two-blank question, you should do one blank at a time. You can do them in whichever order you want, starting with the blank that seems easier for you. In this case, let's try the first blank. We know that the audience "jeered" and called the play -------; the combination of "jeered" and the trigger word "and" means that the word in the first blank should be a negative word, like "lousy." This will eliminate choices B, C, and D, since these aren't negative words. Now we've got choices A and E left. For the second blank, notice the trigger word "although" at the beginning of the sentence. This means that the second blank is going to be a positive word, in contrast to the negative words in the first phrase. So for the second blank we would put in a word like "great." (Remember that your words don't need to be very exact—just the general idea will do.) This will eliminate choice A, and leave E as the best answer.

32. **C** The clue in this sentence is "relied less on veiled criticism and more on direct confrontation." This means that the word in the blank should be a word that means "direct." The word that comes closest to this idea is C.

33. **B** In this question we've got a semicolon, which is a punctuation trigger that tells us that the phrase after the semicolon describes the word in the blank. So we need to find a word that means "would constantly dream up projects that were impossible to carry out." This means that the president was not a very "practical" or "sensible" person. Now we can look down and try to find the word that comes closest in meaning to this idea. If there are words here you don't know, you should leave them in, but if you cross off the ones you know are wrong, you can increase your chance at a correct guess. The word that means "practical" or "sensible" is choice B.

34. **D** This stem pair is probably easier to work with backward. A teacher works in a classroom. Does a gardener work in a flower? A gardener works with, but not in, flowers. Does an athlete work in a team? Well, not in the sense of "inside of," so we can eliminate this one. Does a car work in a garage? Nope. Does a surgeon work in a hospital? Yes. Does a bookstore work in a cashier? Definitely not.

35. **D** Oral means having to do with the mouth. Does attainable mean having to do with goals? Well, some goals are attainable and some aren't, but "attainable" doesn't mean "having to do with goals." Does relevant mean having to do with ideas? Not particularly. Does electric mean having to do with wires? No; some wires might be electric and others might not be. Does aquatic mean having to do with water? Absolutely. Does manual mean having to do with the foot? In fact, it means having to do with the hands.

36. **B** Someone resolute exhibits determination. Does someone pristine exhibit grace? Sometimes, but that's not the meaning of the word "pristine." Does someone skeptical exhibit doubt? Yes, that's exactly what "skeptical" means. Does someone tainted exhibit honor? Definitely not. Does someone stringent exhibit suggestion? That doesn't make any sense. Does someone wary exhibit risk? No, a wary person fears or avoids risk.

37. **A** A sanctuary is a place for worship. Is a gymnasium a place for exercise? Yes. Is an office a place for sales? Yes, or at least sometimes. So we can leave it in for now. Is a lectern a place for a debate? A debate *might* take place at a lectern, but so can a lot of other things; we can eliminate this choice. Is an agenda a place for a politician? No, so eliminate D. Is television a place for a performer? Sort of, but television is not really a "place," nor is it primarily for performers. This choice probably isn't as strong as A or B. Now let's look more closely at A and B. Choice B probably isn't as strong as choice A, since an office is not primarily a place for sales. It's a place for all kinds of business, whether or not sales are involved. It's okay to leave in choices that seem like they might fit; after you've crossed off what you know is wrong, then you can come back and look more closely at choices that seem possible.

38. **E** To digress means to veer away from the subject. Likewise, to stray means to veer away from a path. But if you had a hard time making a sentence for this pair, you can still cross off some choices by working backward: Choices A and D have no defining relationship; after you cross these off, you can (and should!) at least take an intelligent guess.

39. **D** This is a hard analogy, so we should expect it to use hard words. If you're not sure of the meaning of most of these words, but have a sense of them, you can probably use Side of the Fence. If all you know is that "maverick" and "individualism" are on the same side of the fence, you will be able to eliminate choices that are on opposite sides of the fence, such as C and E. You can then guess from among the remaining choices. If you do know the words, you could make the sentence, "Individualism is a characteristic of a maverick." Does this work for choices A, B, or D? Persecution really isn't a property of a litigant, so we can eliminate A. Likewise, competition isn't a property of a winner (though it might be something in which a winner plays a role). Dishonesty is a property of a prevaricator, so the best answer is D. However, you should expect to get these hard questions through POE.

40. **C** Here's another tough one. If you're not sure how to make a sentence here, at least cross off what you can by working backward. Choices A and D have no defining relationship, so we can eliminate them. If you do know the words, you can make a sentence like, "An enigma has the property of being obscure." Likewise, a shield has the property of being protective.

41. **B** We can use the lead words "northwest corner of Botswana" to help us find the place in the passage where the answer to this question will be found. Botswana is only mentioned in the first paragraph of Passage 1, so let's go back to that part of the passage and see what is said. It states that "the northwest corner was said up until 1973 to hold abundant game, but... ." This tells us that now, it does not hold such abundant game. Now let's look for a choice that paraphrases this idea. The choice that states that Botswana does not hold such abundant game is choice B.

42. **D** Remember that for every reading question on the PSAT, there will be evidence in the passage that makes one choice better than the others—your job is to find that evidence. For this question, a logical place to look would be in the third and fourth paragraphs, where the author discusses the scientists who study the Serengeti. At the end of the third paragraph in lines 29–30 the author says that scientists study it "for the light it may shed on the larger question of man's survival." This makes D the best choice.

43. **C** The point of the fourth paragraph is to illustrate how animals benefit humans, and therefore why conservation is a good idea. In this context, the author cites Conway, who says, "The Serengeti is basic to the concerns of conservation. If animals can live there, so can man." This means that Conway connects the idea of the survival of the Serengeti to human concerns—that conservation also benefits humans. Now let's look for a choice that paraphrases this idea, and choice C does exactly that.

44. **C** For a Vocab-in-Context question like this one, we should cover the word in question, reread it in context, and put our own word into the blank. In this case, the author is discussing plant and animal varieties that have evolved from the wild; a good word for this blank would be "new plant and animal species." The closest choice to this idea is C.

45. **A** If we go back to the fourth paragraph of Passage 1, where the Welsh miners and Salk are mentioned, and figure out the point of the paragraph, this will tell us what the point of the examples is. The second sentence says, "If animals can live there, so can man; if not, man cannot." What follows, then, will be examples of how animals are relevant to human survival. This makes A the best choice. While choice B seems to say something close to what the passage says, it is extreme in wording and therefore much stronger than what the passage says. The passage only says that where animals can't live humans can't live either, and not that wherever animals can live, humans can also live. Choices D and E are also quite extremely worded, and for that reason should be avoided.

46. **C** If we look back to the first and second paragraphs of Passage 2, we find the following facts: Owen started his study after 1961; in 1958, the Grzimek Laboratory had done an earlier count of the wildebeest. This best supports choice C. We can also eliminate choices A and D, as they are extreme; and there's no evidence that would establish whether B or E are true or not. Therefore C is the best choice.

47. **B** To figure out the meaning of the studies, we need to look at the first paragraph of Passage 2. There it states that "the wildebeest appeared to be overgrazing." It was to answer this question that the studies were undertaken, with the result showing that, "It appeared that, in fact, the wildebeest were not overgrazing…" (lines 72–74). This is paraphrased by choice B.

48. **A** Let's go back to line 85 and read this phrase in context. The idea of a "principal regulating mechanism" is summarized a few lines later, in lines 91–95, by calling it "a symmetrical relationship between the wildebeests' birth and death rates…starvation as a form of control even in a time of abundance." This means that something about the food supply was controlling the population of wildebeest. Now we need to find which choice roughly paraphrases this idea—choice A.

49. **D** We can use the lead words "Research Institute" to help find the answer to this question: The institute's conclusion is given in the final paragraph of Passage 2, which states that the "Serengeti formed a self-sustaining ecological system. Everything…was interdependent…Each living thing depended on the other…" (lines 98–101). This best supports choice D.

50. **E** This is a tough question, and you may want to save it for last. If you try it, assume that you'll work it by POE. Passage 2 says nothing about using up wild monkeys for science, so choice A can be eliminated. Likewise, it says nothing about the encroachment of civilization or the breeding of domestic plants and animals, so C and D can also be eliminated. Choice B is a possibility, but Passage 2 provides much stronger support for E, since the passage discusses in detail the counterbalancing conditions that allow the wildebeest to grow while controlling their population.

51. **B** In the first two paragraphs of Passage 1, the author states that while in many places civilization is destroying wildlife, that the Serengeti is an exception whose survival is being maintained by "conditions that have thus far managed to tip a fragile balance slightly to the side of the animals…" (lines 15–17). So if this trend continues, the Serengeti will continue to survive in this careful balance, neither being destroyed by civilization nor pushing back civilization. This best supports choice B.

52. **A** In Passage 1, the second paragraph states that the Serengeti is maintained by "conditions that have thus far managed to tip a fragile balance slightly to the side of the animals…" (lines 15–17). Likewise, the author of Passage 2 claims that the balance of the wildebeest population is maintained by a variety of conditions, all of which are interdependent. This supports choice A. We also know that B and D are incorrect, since neither passage says that humans are afraid or disinterested, and Passage 1 doesn't discuss a specific species, so choice E also can't be right. Finally, choice C can be eliminated since conservation efforts are only discussed in Passage 1.

Section 4

21. **D** While we know the cost of two pencils and one eraser, we don't have any way of figuring out how much each item costs alone. It could be that each pencil costs 70 cents and the eraser costs 30 cents, or that each pencil costs 35 cents and the eraser costs one dollar.

22. **B** If $\frac{2}{3}$ of a is 20, then we can translate this as $\frac{2}{3} \times a = 20$ and solve, ending up with $a = 30$. This means that column A will be equal to 5. So column B is larger.

23. **A** Since we know that $PQ = QR$, we know that angle P and angle R must have the same measure. Since we know that angle Q is equal to 46 degrees, we know that together, angles P and R must measure $180 - 46$, or 134 degrees. Angle P and angle R must each therefore measure 67 degrees, making column A larger than column B.

24. **B** To see how these columns compare, we need to see both rates in pages per minute or in pages per hour. Let's convert column B: There are 60 minutes in 1 hour, so to convert a rate of 4 pages per minute into a rate of some number of pages per hour, we just need to multiply each factor by 60, and we see that 4 pages per minute is the same as 240 pages per hour. This means that column B is larger than column A.

25. **C** Since we've got variables in this problem, let's plug in. The tricky part will be finding numbers that obey the rule that $d - c = c - b = b - a$. To make it easier, let's start with just two of these numbers, and let's try plugging in some easy values. Let's make $d = 1$ and $c = 2$. This means that $d - c = -1$. (Even though the result is negative, the values for d and c themselves are still positive, so we are obeying all the rules in the problem.) So if $c = 2$, and we know that $c - b$ must also equal -1, then we'll have to make $b = 3$. Further, if $b = 3$ and we know that $b - a$ must also equal -1, then we'll have to make $a = 4$. So now we have $d = 1, c = 2, b = 3$, and $a = 4$.

Now we compare column A and column B. Column A asks for $c - a$, which, with our numbers, reads $2 - 4$, or -2. Column B asks for $d - b$, which, with our numbers, reads $1 - 3$, which is also -2. This means that the two columns are equal. If you wish, try plugging in again with different numbers; you'll find that in every case (as long as you obey the rules in the question) the two columns turn out to be equal.

26. **D** Just because the picture looks like an equilateral triangle, doesn't mean that it is. The third side might be a bit larger or a bit smaller than 5. Remember: On Quant Comp, you need to see whether the figure could be drawn differently—if you can make one column either greater or smaller than the other, then the actual answer is D.

27. **C** This problem may look messy, but if you take it one step at a time, it shouldn't be too bad. Start by writing this as a normal equation:
$$16 + 2a = 31 + a$$

Now let's put all the a's on one side, by subtracting an a off each side:
$$16 + a = 31$$

Finally, put all the numbers on the right side of the equation by subtracting 16 from each side:
$$a = 15$$

Therefore, the two columns are equal.

28. **A** We don't know what the exact values of x, y, and z are, but we don't have to know. All we need to know is that x and y are both negative numbers, so the product xy will be positive; since x is negative and z is positive, the product xz will be negative. This means that column A must be larger.

29. **D** We've got variables in this problem, so we should plug in. Let's start with an easy number and plug in 2 for n. In this case, column A becomes $\frac{12}{5}$ and column B becomes $\frac{10}{6}$. In this case, column A is larger than column B, so we can eliminate choices B and C. Now let's plug in a weird number and see if we can find a case where column A is *not* larger. How about $n = 0$? In this case, both column A and column B become 0. Since we've found a case where column A is not larger than column B, we can cross off choice A and our answer must be D.

30. **A** Since this figure shows two parallel lines and a line that crosses them, we know that the angles labeled $(b + 15)$ and $(a - 5)$ must be equal. So we can write the equation:

$$b + 15 = a - 5$$

By adding 5 to each side, we get

$$b + 20 = a$$

This means that a must be larger than b.

31. **C** It may look like we don't have enough information to solve this problem, but we actually do. Since each circle passes through the center of the other circle, these two circles must have the same size. (You can tell, because the line OP is a radius of each circle. Since the circles have the same radius, they must have the same area.)

32. **C** While we don't know the actual base and height of the two triangles, we know that they have the same base and the same height—for each triangle, the base is the length of AE, and the height is the distance from A to B. So the two triangles must have the same area.

33. **139** We don't actually have to know the individual values of x and y to solve this problem. We know that we have two parallel lines in this diagram, so we know that the angle opposite the angle measuring 41 degrees must also measure 41 degrees.

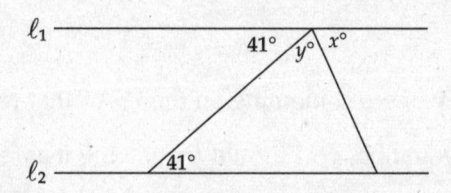

Therefore, we have an angle of 41 degrees plus the angles marked x and y on the same line—which tells us that their sum must be 180. So we know that $41 + x + y = 180$, and that $x + y$ therefore must equal 139.

34. $\dfrac{4}{3}$ If the ratio of n to $6m$ is 3:12, we can simply plug in numbers that would work for this ratio: Let's plug in 3 for n and 2 for m. This makes it true that the ratio of n to $6m$ is 3:12. Now the question asks, what is the ratio of $2m$ to n? Using our numbers for m and n, this becomes a ratio of 2(2) to 3, or 4:3, which we grid as the fraction $\dfrac{4}{3}$.

35. **90** We know that the angles in a triangle always add up to 180, so we know that $\frac{1}{2}a + \frac{1}{2}a + a = 180$. Now we can solve for a. If we add $\frac{1}{2}a + \frac{1}{2}a + a$, we get $2a$, so we know that $2a = 180$ and that $a = 90$.

36. **105** The best way to try to find 4 consecutive integers whose sum is 414 is to start by finding the average: Each number is somewhere in the neighborhood of 103. So let's just start trying these numbers: 103 + 104 + 105 + 106 equals 418, which is too large. So let's try 102 + 103 + 104 + 105. That makes 414, so these are our four consecutive integers. The question asks for the greatest of them, so the answer is 105.

37. **9** Remember that the ratio of the sides of an isosceles right triangle (which is the same as half of a square) is $x:x:x\sqrt{2}$. So to get a diagonal of $3\sqrt{2}$, the sides of the triangle (and therefore of the square) must be equal to 3. If the sides of the square are equal to 3, then its area will be equal to 3 times 3, or 9.

38. **8** Let's try Plugging In on this problem. We need to choose a value for n that is a prime number greater then 3, so let's try using 5. The question then reads: How many factors of 30 are there? The factors of 30 are 1 and 30, 2 and 15, 3 and 10, 5 and 6, for a total of 8 factors. For whichever values of n you try, you'll always get the same answer.

39. **$\frac{16}{5}$, or 3.2** Whenever you see something on the PSAT that resembles a quadratic equation, you should try solving it as if it were a quadratic equation. We know that $x^2 - y^2 = 16$, and since $x^2 - y^2$ can be written as $(x + y)(x - y)$, we know that $(x + y)(x - y) = 16$. The question also tells us that $(x + y) = 5$, so we know that $5(x - y) = 16$. The question then asks us for $(x - y)$, which we can now solve for: $\frac{16}{5}$, or 3.2.

40. $\frac{4}{3}$, If the sum of 4 and some number (we can call it x) is equal to
   or 1.33   the product of 4 and that number, we can write the equation
   $4 + x = 4x$. Now we can solve for x:

$$4 + x = 4x$$

by subtracting x from each side we get:

$$4 = 3x$$

$$\text{so, } \frac{4}{3} = x$$

This makes our answer $\frac{4}{3}$ or 1.33.

Section 5

1. **C** The correct idiom is *not only...but also*. This sentence uses *not only* followed by *while*.

2. **E** There is no error in this sentence. Don't forget that about one-fifth of the sentences have no error in them!

3. **A** The correct idiom is "indebted *to*."

4. **D** This is a great example of a pronoun error. Since the sentence discusses reference books (which is plural) we need to keep using the plural—*their* editorial *boards*.

5. **B** This is a question of diction, or word choice. The word "aggravated" means to make a situation or problem worse. To describe someone's annoyance, use the word "irritated."

6. **D** Whenever a comparison is made, make sure that the items compared are in parallel form. The sentence tries to compare "to learn to type" with "mastering." These two phrases are not in parallel form; writing them correctly would require changing "mastering" to "to master."

7. **B** At issue in this question is another matter of parallel construction. The sentence starts by discussing the *works* of Stephen King; this should be compared to the *works* of Peter Straub, and not directly to Straub himself. The sentence should read, "The works of Stephen King are similar to the works of Peter Straub... ."

8. **B** *Scarcely no* is a double negative, which is not considered proper in standard written English.

9. **E** There is no error in this sentence.

10. **B** The subject of this sentence is *an understanding* which is singular. Therefore the verb *are* (which is plural) is incorrect. Be sure not to be misled by the plural noun (*causes*) in the sentence—it's not the subject.

11. **E** There is no error in this sentence.

12. **B** The subject in this sentence is the placing of baking soda in a glass, which acts as a singular subject because it's a single action. Therefore the verb should be the singular form *results*.

13. **A** Remember that adjectives modify nouns and pronouns, and adverbs modify everything else (verbs, adjectives, and other adverbs). Since the word *recent* modifies another adjective (the word *conducted*), it should be the adverb *recently*.

14. **B** Whenever you see *neither* make sure it's accompanied by *nor*.

15. **A** Don't forget: If you're comparing three or more things, you can use the *–est* form of a comparative, but if you're comparing only two things, you should use the *–er* form. The sentence should read *the newer of the two*.

16. **E** There is no error in this sentence.

17. **C** This is another case of diction, or word choice. A person can be *reliant* on someone or something, but evidence is considered to be *reliable*.

18. **A** The subject in this sentence is *his unusual style and his brilliant use of humor*, which is plural. Therefore the subject should be followed by plural verb form *make*.

19. **A** Remember to use *fewer* for things that are countable (like dogs, pens, tables) and *less* for things that aren't (like rice, water, and happiness.) Since graduates are countable individuals, the appropriate word is *fewer* instead of *less*.

20. **D** The sentence as written has a problem, because the opening phrase *a large predatory snake* is followed immediately by *the muscular body*, which makes it sounds as if the muscular body is a large predatory snake. The words *a large predatory snake* should modify *the boa constrictor*. Only B and D place *boa constrictor* in the correct spot, and B makes an incomplete sentence, so D is the best answer.

21. **C** Be very careful of verbs that end in *–ing* on the PSAT. They often indicate awkward constructions that should be avoided. "Having received" in this case is a good example of this type of problem. Choices B and D are wordy, and choice E simply splices two sentences together with a comma.

22. **B** Since we're beginning a comparison with "as," we need to finish with another "as" (for example, "as big as a house") and not the word "than." This eliminates A and D. The word "for" in choice E doesn't make any sense. Between B and C, choice B is shorter and therefore the PSAT answer.

23. **A** Since the other choices introduce mistakes (C, D, and E introduce an *–ing* construction, and choice B misplaces the word "also"), the best choice is the sentence as written, which is choice A.

24. **B** Choice A splices two sentences together with a comma, and is a passive construction, which we want to avoid. Choice C appears to say that the first solar orbit was taking place in 1959, which isn't right. Choice D awkwardly adds "the solar orbit was entered" without specifying what entered it. Finally, choice E is wordier than it needs to be.

25. **D** The sentence as written contains a problem at the beginning—the sentence starts with *the best known of all southern American writers* and continues by discussing not Faulkner, but *William Faulkner's books*. But it's not his books that should be described by the phrase *the best known of all southern American writers*. Therefore the underlined portion must start with "William Faulkner" and not "William Faulkner's books." This will eliminate A and B. Choices C and E don't make sense, so D is the best answer.

26. **E** Saying "it was not implied by him" is a passive voice construction that could be put into the active voice as "he did not imply it." All of choices A, B, C, and D have this passive construction, so E is the best answer.

27. **C** Whenever you have verbs in a list, they should all be in parallel tense and form. In this case, we know that Michelle was hired *to watch* the store, so we need to use the verb form *to clean*. Only choice C does this.

28. **C** The sentence as written is missing a conjunction, so we can eliminate A. Choices D and E also don't fit the role of conjunction, so they can also be crossed off. Further, we need a conjunction that shows a contrast—on the one hand, Jason was nervous, but he still performed well. Choice B doesn't express a contrast, so the answer must be C.

29. **E** As it is written, the sentence is missing a verb. This allows us to eliminate A. Choices B and D don't have a verb either, so they can't be right. Choice C has a verb, but it won't fit with the rest of the sentence, since "the Italian artist and inventor" would then describe Leonardo's helicopter instead of Leonardo. This leaves us with E.

30. **D** *Couldn't hardly* is a double negative, which we know can't be right. Likewise, choices B and C are also double negatives, since they include "not" along with "hardly." Finally, *be believing* isn't correct, so we're left with D.

31. **C** Since we have a list of two things that Hemingway was known for, we have to make sure that those items are in parallel form. We know he was known "for his...writing" so we need to follow this with "for his adventurous lifestyle." The only choice that does this is C.

32. **A** There is no error in the sentence as written, and each of B, C, D, and E are wordy or awkward.

33. **D** When you use "neither...nor" with singular things such as "a broken leg" and "an upset stomach," the subject is considered singular. Therefore we need to use "has" and not "have." This will eliminate choices B, C, and E. Also, the correct idiom is "prevent *from*," which eliminates choice A.

34. **B** Let's take a look at each of our answer choices. They all begin the same (with the word "faster") so we need to find where they start to differ among themselves. Just after the comma we see our first difference: Some use a change-direction word such as "but" or "while" and others a same-direction word such as "and" or "so." Since the idea of difficulty with breathing goes along with a rapidly beating heart, we know we don't want a change-direction word, so we can eliminate choices A and E. Choice C is missing a verb, and choice D has the wrong verb tense, so we can also cross them off.

35. **C** This question asks us to link what happens in the first paragraph, where we find out that the author is afraid of bees, to what happens in the next paragraph, which starts with a discussion of the author's garden. This means we need to find a choice that talks both about the fear of bees and the author's garden. Only choices C and E do this, so we can cross off A, B, and D. Now we're down to C and E. Which is better? If we read further into the second paragraph, we see that the author decides to do something about her fear of bees. This means that a good transitional sentence will explain that her garden gives her a reason to want to change and get over her fear of bees. This is what choice C does.

36. **D** Combining these two sentences requires some kind of connecting word or phrase. The first question to ask ourselves is: What sort of connecting word do we need? Do these sentences have contrasting ideas? No, so we can eliminate B. We can also eliminate A for its awkward use of "being." In fact, these sentences have a cause and effect relationship—the first sentence is what causes the situation in the second sentence. So we need a word like "because" or "so" or "since." The only choices that express a causal relation are C and D. Between these two choices, C has the awkward use of "did" in the first clause, so D is the better choice.

37. **D** In this case, the word "it" in sentence 8 is vague, so we should figure out what the word "it" is referring to and make it more specific. The beginning of the paragraph tells us that the author's love of gardening makes it a problem for her to be afraid of bees; in the rest of the paragraph she takes steps to deal with this fear. So we know that it is the fear of bees that she wants to do something about. The choice that makes this clear is D.

38. **E** The best way to approach this question is by POE. Let's start with the worst choices. Choice B is a mess at the end, when it says "a meeting with him I wanted to ask." This doesn't make any sense, so we can eliminate B. Choice C should be eliminated for using the word "being"—it's not impossible to use it correctly, but it's almost always used incorrectly on the PSAT. Choice D is awkward because it places the phrase "her uncle" all the way at the end, when it really belongs next to the word "meet." Between choices A and E, both of which are grammatically acceptable, choice E is shorter and clearer.

39. **B** Since the verb tenses are what change in the answer choices, we can be fairly sure that this question is going to ask us about a verb tense problem. The verb tense of the verb "devote" in the second half of the sentence is the ordinary present tense. Therefore we want the verb "to visit" to also be in the ordinary present tense form "visit."

The Princeton Review

YOUR NAME: _____
(Print)   Last   First   M.I.

SIGNATURE: _____ DATE: ___/___/___

HOME ADDRESS: _____
(Print)   Number and Street

_____
City   State   Zip Code

PHONE NO.: _____
(Print)

Start with number 1 for each new section. If a section has fewer questions than answer spaces, leave the extra answer spaces blank.

SECTION 1

1 A B C D E	11 A B C D E	21 A B C D E	31 A B C D E
2 A B C D E	12 A B C D E	22 A B C D E	32 A B C D E
3 A B C D E	13 A B C D E	23 A B C D E	33 A B C D E
4 A B C D E	14 A B C D E	24 A B C D E	34 A B C D E
5 A B C D E	15 A B C D E	25 A B C D E	35 A B C D E
6 A B C D E	16 A B C D E	26 A B C D E	36 A B C D E
7 A B C D E	17 A B C D E	27 A B C D E	37 A B C D E
8 A B C D E	18 A B C D E	28 A B C D E	38 A B C D E
9 A B C D E	19 A B C D E	29 A B C D E	39 A B C D E
10 A B C D E	20 A B C D E	30 A B C D E	40 A B C D E

SECTION 2

1 A B C D E	11 A B C D E	21 A B C D E	31 A B C D E
2 A B C D E	12 A B C D E	22 A B C D E	32 A B C D E
3 A B C D E	13 A B C D E	23 A B C D E	33 A B C D E
4 A B C D E	14 A B C D E	24 A B C D E	34 A B C D E
5 A B C D E	15 A B C D E	25 A B C D E	35 A B C D E
6 A B C D E	16 A B C D E	26 A B C D E	36 A B C D E
7 A B C D E	17 A B C D E	27 A B C D E	37 A B C D E
8 A B C D E	18 A B C D E	28 A B C D E	38 A B C D E
9 A B C D E	19 A B C D E	29 A B C D E	39 A B C D E
10 A B C D E	20 A B C D E	30 A B C D E	40 A B C D E

SECTION 3

26 A B C D E	37 A B C D E	47 A B C D E
27 A B C D E	38 A B C D E	48 A B C D E
29 A B C D E	39 A B C D E	49 A B C D E
30 A B C D E	40 A B C D E	50 A B C D E
31 A B C D E	41 A B C D E	51 A B C D E
32 A B C D E	42 A B C D E	52 A B C D E
33 A B C D E	43 A B C D E	53 A B C D E
34 A B C D E	44 A B C D E	54 A B C D E
35 A B C D E	45 A B C D E	55 A B C D E
36 A B C D E	46 A B C D E	56 A B C D E

DO NOT MARK IN THIS AREA

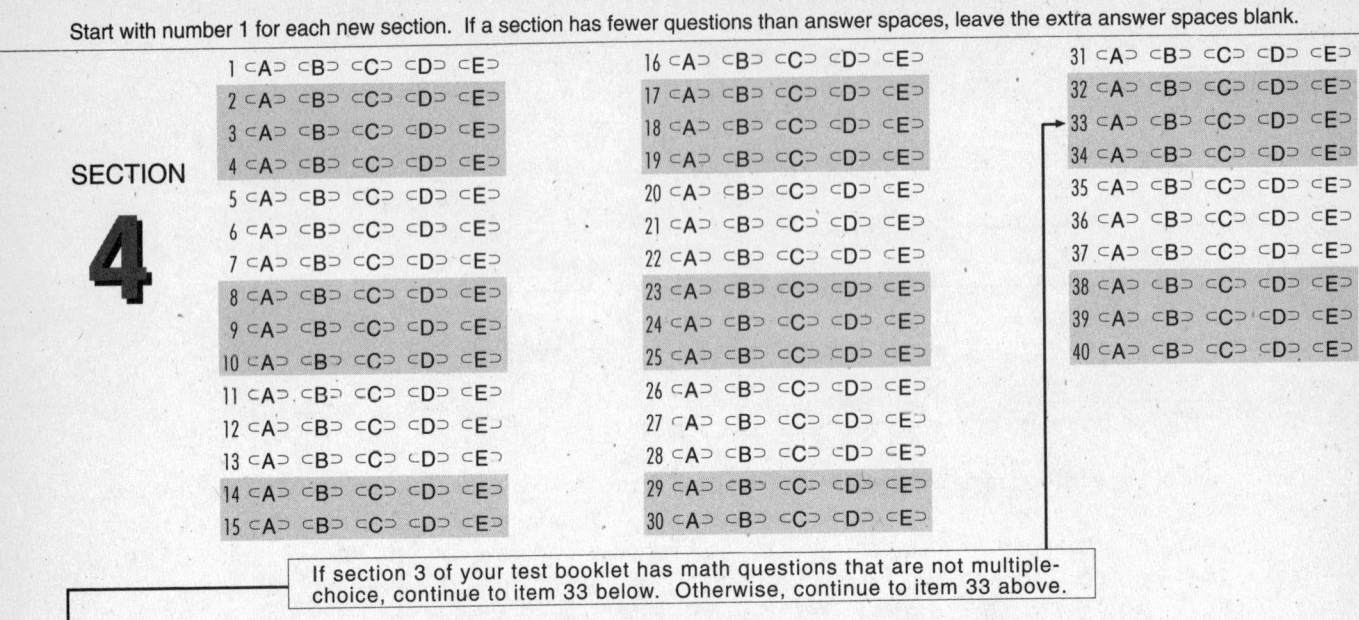

Use a No. 2 pencil only. Be sure each mark is dark and completely fills the intended oval. Completely erase any errors or stray marks.

Start with number 1 for each new section. If a section has fewer questions than answer spaces, leave the extra answer spaces blank.

SECTION 4

1. A B C D E
2. A B C D E
3. A B C D E
4. A B C D E
5. A B C D E
6. A B C D E
7. A B C D E
8. A B C D E
9. A B C D E
10. A B C D E
11. A B C D E
12. A B C D E
13. A B C D E
14. A B C D E
15. A B C D E

16. A B C D E
17. A B C D E
18. A B C D E
19. A B C D E
20. A B C D E
21. A B C D E
22. A B C D E
23. A B C D E
24. A B C D E
25. A B C D E
26. A B C D E
27. A B C D E
28. A B C D E
29. A B C D E
30. A B C D E

31. A B C D E
32. A B C D E
33. A B C D E
34. A B C D E
35. A B C D E
36. A B C D E
37. A B C D E
38. A B C D E
39. A B C D E
40. A B C D E

If section 3 of your test booklet has math questions that are not multiple-choice, continue to item 33 below. Otherwise, continue to item 33 above.

ONLY ANSWERS ENTERED IN THE OVALS IN EACH GRID AREA WILL BE SCORED.
YOU WILL NOT RECEIVE CREDIT FOR ANYTHING WRITTEN IN THE BOXES ABOVE THE OVALS.

BE SURE TO ERASE ANY ERRORS OR STRAY MARKS COMPLETELY.

PLEASE PRINT YOUR INITIALS

First   Middle   Last

Use a No. 2 pencil only. Be sure each mark is dark and completely fills the intended oval. Completely erase any errors or stray marks.

Start with number 1 for each new section. If a section has fewer questions than answer spaces, leave the extra answer spaces blank.

SECTION 5

1 A B C D E	11 A B C D E	21 A B C D E	31 A B C D E
2 A B C D E	12 A B C D E	22 A B C D E	32 A B C D E
3 A B C D E	13 A B C D E	23 A B C D E	33 A B C D E
4 A B C D E	14 A B C D E	24 A B C D E	34 A B C D E
5 A B C D E	15 A B C D E	25 A B C D E	35 A B C D E
6 A B C D E	16 A B C D E	26 A B C D E	36 A B C D E
7 A B C D E	17 A B C D E	27 A B C D E	37 A B C D E
8 A B C D E	18 A B C D E	28 A B C D E	38 A B C D E
9 A B C D E	19 A B C D E	29 A B C D E	39 A B C D E
10 A B C D E	20 A B C D E	30 A B C D E	40 A B C D E

The Princeton Review

YOUR NAME: _____
(Print) Last / First / M.I.

SIGNATURE: _____ **DATE:** __/__/__

HOME ADDRESS: _____
(Print) Number and Street

_____
City / State / Zip Code

PHONE NO.: _____
(Print)

Start with number 1 for each new section. If a section has fewer questions than answer spaces, leave the extra answer spaces blank.

SECTION 1

1. A B C D E
2. A B C D E
3. A B C D E
4. A B C D E
5. A B C D E
6. A B C D E
7. A B C D E
8. A B C D E
9. A B C D E
10. A B C D E
11. A B C D E
12. A B C D E
13. A B C D E
14. A B C D E
15. A B C D E
16. A B C D E
17. A B C D E
18. A B C D E
19. A B C D E
20. A B C D E
21. A B C D E
22. A B C D E
23. A B C D E
24. A B C D E
25. A B C D E
26. A B C D E
27. A B C D E
28. A B C D E
29. A B C D E
30. A B C D E
31. A B C D E
32. A B C D E
33. A B C D E
34. A B C D E
35. A B C D E
36. A B C D E
37. A B C D E
38. A B C D E
39. A B C D E
40. A B C D E

SECTION 2

1. A B C D E
2. A B C D E
3. A B C D E
4. A B C D E
5. A B C D E
6. A B C D E
7. A B C D E
8. A B C D E
9. A B C D E
10. A B C D E
11. A B C D E
12. A B C D E
13. A B C D E
14. A B C D E
15. A B C D E
16. A B C D E
17. A B C D E
18. A B C D E
19. A B C D E
20. A B C D E
21. A B C D E
22. A B C D E
23. A B C D E
24. A B C D E
25. A B C D E
26. A B C D E
27. A B C D E
28. A B C D E
29. A B C D E
30. A B C D E
31. A B C D E
32. A B C D E
33. A B C D E
34. A B C D E
35. A B C D E
36. A B C D E
37. A B C D E
38. A B C D E
39. A B C D E
40. A B C D E

SECTION 3

26. A B C D E
27. A B C D E
28. A B C D E
29. A B C D E
30. A B C D E
31. A B C D E
32. A B C D E
33. A B C D E
34. A B C D E
35. A B C D E
36. A B C D E
37. A B C D E
38. A B C D E
39. A B C D E
40. A B C D E
41. A B C D E
42. A B C D E
43. A B C D E
44. A B C D E
45. A B C D E
46. A B C D E
47. A B C D E
48. A B C D E
49. A B C D E
50. A B C D E
51. A B C D E
52. A B C D E
53. A B C D E
54. A B C D E
55. A B C D E
56. A B C D E

DO NOT MARK IN THIS AREA

Use a No. 2 pencil only. Be sure each mark is dark and completely fills the intended oval. Completely erase any errors or stray marks.

Start with number 1 for each new section. If a section has fewer questions than answer spaces, leave the extra answer spaces blank.

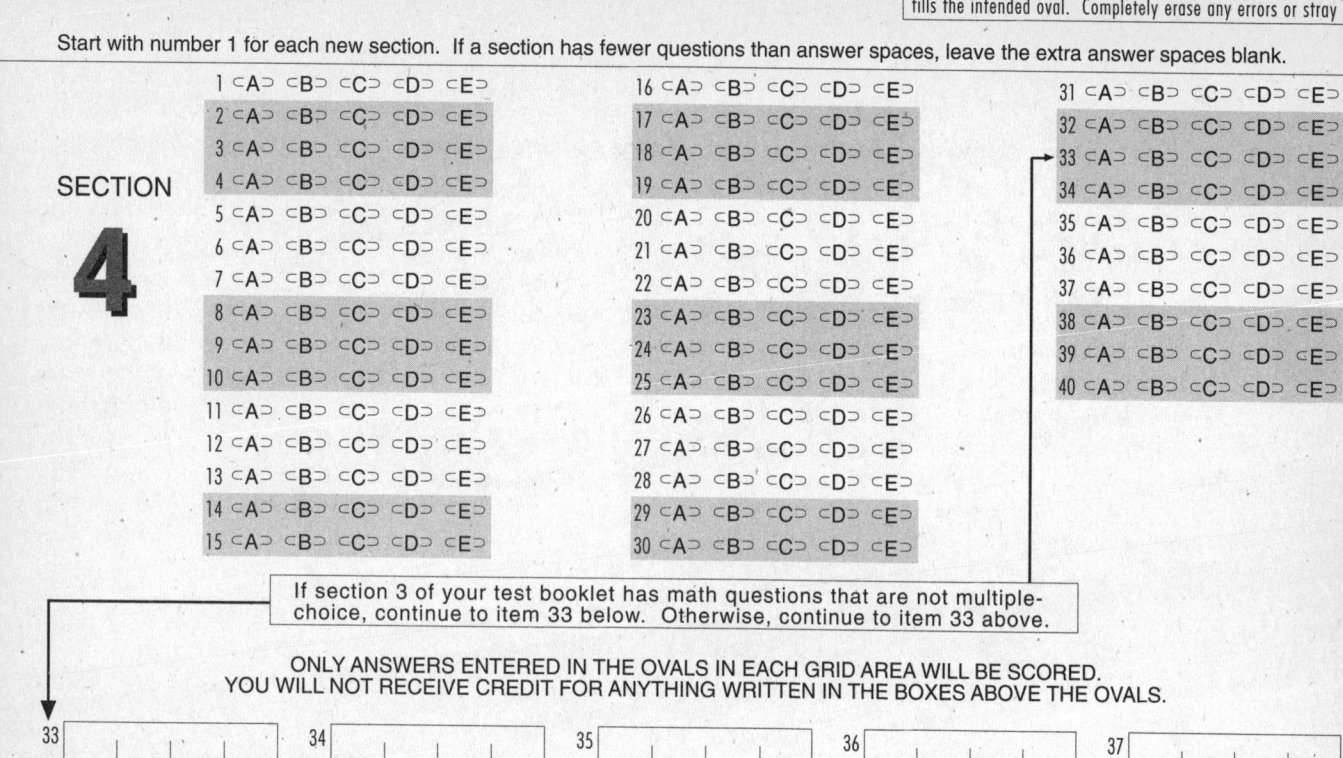

SECTION 4

1. A B C D E
2. A B C D E
3. A B C D E
4. A B C D E
5. A B C D E
6. A B C D E
7. A B C D E
8. A B C D E
9. A B C D E
10. A B C D E
11. A B C D E
12. A B C D E
13. A B C D E
14. A B C D E
15. A B C D E

16. A B C D E
17. A B C D E
18. A B C D E
19. A B C D E
20. A B C D E
21. A B C D E
22. A B C D E
23. A B C D E
24. A B C D E
25. A B C D E
26. A B C D E
27. A B C D E
28. A B C D E
29. A B C D E
30. A B C D E

31. A B C D E
32. A B C D E
33. A B C D E
34. A B C D E
35. A B C D E
36. A B C D E
37. A B C D E
38. A B C D E
39. A B C D E
40. A B C D E

If section 3 of your test booklet has math questions that are not multiple-choice, continue to item 33 below. Otherwise, continue to item 33 above.

ONLY ANSWERS ENTERED IN THE OVALS IN EACH GRID AREA WILL BE SCORED.
YOU WILL NOT RECEIVE CREDIT FOR ANYTHING WRITTEN IN THE BOXES ABOVE THE OVALS.

[Grid-in answer boxes numbered 33, 34, 35, 36, 37, 38, 39, 40 with digits 0-9 and fraction/decimal markers]

BE SURE TO ERASE ANY ERRORS OR STRAY MARKS COMPLETELY.

PLEASE PRINT YOUR INITIALS

First Middle Last

Use a No. 2 pencil only. Be sure each mark is dark and completely fills the intended oval. Completely erase any errors or stray marks.

Start with number 1 for each new section. If a section has fewer questions than answer spaces, leave the extra answer spaces blank.

SECTION 5

1 A B C D E	11 A B C D E	21 A B C D E	31 A B C D E
2 A B C D E	12 A B C D E	22 A B C D E	32 A B C D E
3 A B C D E	13 A B C D E	23 A B C D E	33 A B C D E
4 A B C D E	14 A B C D E	24 A B C D E	34 A B C D E
5 A B C D E	15 A B C D E	25 A B C D E	35 A B C D E
6 A B C D E	16 A B C D E	26 A B C D E	36 A B C D E
7 A B C D E	17 A B C D E	27 A B C D E	37 A B C D E
8 A B C D E	18 A B C D E	28 A B C D E	38 A B C D E
9 A B C D E	19 A B C D E	29 A B C D E	39 A B C D E
10 A B C D E	20 A B C D E	30 A B C D E	40 A B C D E

NOTES

NOTES

NOTES

NOTES

The Princeton Review
Better Scores. Better Schools.

Get Your Best Score.

Like what you've seen so far? Try a Princeton Review classroom course, online course, or private tutoring program for comprehensive test preparation.

Save $50 right now!
Just mention this book when you call to enroll in a classroom course, online course, or tutoring program.

Not valid for previously enrolled students, *ExpressOnline*, or tutoring programs of less than ten hours. Cannot be combined with other offers. Expires 9/30/2004.

800-2Review | PrincetonReview.com

The Princeton Review
Better Scores. Better Schools.

Test Prep Anytime, Anywhere.

With a **Princeton Review Online Course**, you'll have access to all of our proven techniques and strategies through engaging, interactive lessons over the Internet. We offer three online course options to meet your needs. **Call us for details!**

The Princeton Review is not affiliated with Princeton University.

888-500-PREP | PrincetonReview.com

The Princeton Review
Better Scores. Better Schools.

The Ultimate in Personalized Attention.

With a Princeton Review **1-2-1 Private Tutoring Program**, you'll get focused instruction with one of our top-rated instructors at times and locations most convenient for you. Plus, you'll have access to our online lessons and resources.

800-2Review | **PrincetonReview.com**

The Princeton Review is not affiliated with Princeton University.

The Princeton Review

Find the Right School

**BEST 345 COLLEGES
2004 EDITION**
0-375-76337-6 • $21.95

**COMPLETE BOOK OF COLLEGES
2004 EDITION**
0-375-76330-9 • $24.95

**COMPLETE BOOK OF
DISTANCE LEARNING SCHOOLS**
0-375-76204-3 • $21.00

AMERICA'S ELITE COLLEGES
The Smart Buyer's Guide to the Ivy League and Other Top Schools
0-375-76206-X • $15.95

Get in

**CRACKING THE SAT
2004 EDITION**
0-375-76331-7 • $19.00

**CRACKING THE SAT
WITH SAMPLE TESTS ON CD-ROM
2004 EDITION**
0-375-76330-9 • $30.95

**MATH WORKOUT FOR THE SAT
2ND EDITION**
0-375-76177-2 • $14.95

**VERBAL WORKOUT FOR THE SAT
2ND EDITION**
0-375-76176-4 • $14.95

**CRACKING THE ACT
2003 EDITION**
0-375-76317-1 • $19.00

**CRACKING THE ACT WITH
SAMPLE TESTS ON CD-ROM
2003 EDITION**
0-375-76318-X • $29.95

**CRASH COURSE FOR THE ACT
2ND EDITION**
The Last-Minute Guide to Scoring High
0-375-75364-3 • $9.95

**CRASH COURSE FOR THE SAT
2ND EDITION**
The Last-Minute Guide to Scoring High
0-375-75361-9 • $9.95

Get Help Paying for it

DOLLARS & SENSE FOR COLLEGE STUDENTS
How Not to Run Out of Money by Midterms
0-375-75206-4 • $10.95

**PAYING FOR COLLEGE WITHOUT GOING BROKE
2004 EDITION**
0-375-76350-3 • $20.00

**THE SCHOLARSHIP ADVISOR
5TH EDITION**
0-375-76210-8 • $26.00

Make the Grade with Study Guides for the AP and SAT II Exams

AP Exams

CRACKING THE AP BIOLOGY
2002-2003 EDITION
0-375-76221-3 • $18.00

CRACKING THE AP CALCULUS AB & BC
2002-2003 EDITION
0-375-76222-1 • $19.00

CRACKING THE AP CHEMISTRY
2002-2003 EDITION
0-375-76223-X • $18.00

CRACKING THE AP ECONOMICS (MACRO & MICRO)
2002-2003 EDITION
0-375-76224-8 • $18.00

CRACKING THE AP ENGLISH LITERATURE
2002-2003 EDITION
0-375-76225-6 • $18.00

CRACKING THE AP EUROPEAN HISTORY
2002-2003 EDITION
0-375-76226-4 • $18.00

CRACKING THE AP PHYSICS
2002-2003 EDITION
0-375-76227-2 • $19.00

CRACKING THE AP PSYCHOLOGY
2002-2003 EDITION
0-375-76228-0 • $18.00

CRACKING THE AP SPANISH
2002-2003 EDITION
0-375-76229-9 • $18.00

CRACKING THE AP STATISTICS
2002-2003 EDITION
0-375-76232-9 • $18.00

CRACKING THE AP U.S. GOVERNMENT AND POLITICS
2002-2003 EDITION
0-375-76230-2 • $18.00

CRACKING THE AP U.S. HISTORY
2002-2003 EDITION
0-375-76231-0 • $18.00

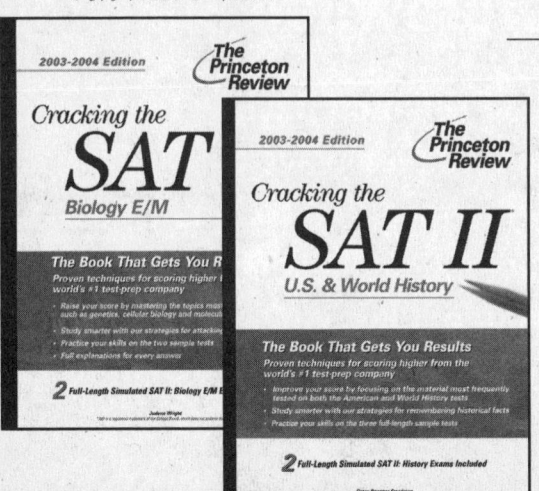

SAT II Exams

CRACKING THE SAT II: BIOLOGY
2003-2004 EDITION
0-375-76294-9 • $18.00

CRACKING THE SAT II: CHEMISTRY
2003-2004 EDITION
0-375-76296-5 • $17.00

CRACKING THE SAT II: FRENCH
2003-2004 EDITION
0-375-76295-7 • $17.00

CRACKING THE SAT II: WRITING & LITERATURE
2003-2004 EDITION
0-375-76301-5 • $17.00

CRACKING THE SAT II: MATH
2003-2004 EDITION
0-375-76298-1 • $18.00

CRACKING THE SAT II: PHYSICS
2003-2004 EDITION
0-375-76299-X • $18.00

CRACKING THE SAT II: SPANISH
2003-2004 EDITION
0-375-76300-7 • $17.00

CRACKING THE SAT II: U.S. & WORLD HISTORY
2003-2004 EDITION
0-375-76297-3 • $18.00

The Princeton Review

Available at Bookstores Everywhere.
www.PrincetonReview.com

The Princeton Review
Better Scores. Better Schools.

Don't waste time in an overcrowded classroom.

With a **Princeton Review Classroom Course**, you'll always get small classes for personal attention, enthusiastic instructors, and a **score improvement guarantee**. Plus, you'll have access to our online lessons and resources.

SAT   ACT   SAT II   PSAT

800-2Review | PrincetonReview.com

The Princeton Review is not affiliated with Princeton University.